PRAISE FOR RESIDENT PUNK

"Legs McNeil revisits his hard-knock adolescence and run-ins with Lou Reed, the Ramones, and Talking Heads with a finely honed sense of mischief. Essential reading for anyone who came along too late for CBGB—or arrived on time but can't quite recall what happened."

—Graydon Carter, former editor of *Vanity Fair* and cofounder of *Air Mail* and *Spy*

"Having read this propulsive, gasp-inducing mosh pit of memories, I'm not 100% sure that 100% of Legs lived to tell this tale. But what's left of him has written a knockout book."

—Patton Oswalt, actor and comedian

"Legs is a true original and he was THERE, baby. Personally, I can never get enough of this . . ."

—John Taylor, musician and author of *In the Pleasure Groove: Love, Death, and Duran Duran*

"Legs McNeil has made a profession out of inviting mockery. Few have been able to resist accepting, but among his admirers have been Sinead O'Connor, Norman Mailer, and a sexually disadvantaged elderly rich woman in the vicinity of Cheshire, Connecticut. I did love finding out about his childhood. Eddie Haskell (look him up) was a kindred soul. Obsequious ineptitude, with a suburban-swamp dash of surly, as survival tactic and comedy engine. The Legs is still standing. You have to salute him. Viva Legs!"

—Richard Hell, rock star and poet

"Legs tells a story I remember well;
through a haze of heroin and coke-soaked lenses told in utterances that stink of puke and stale beer,
when Times Square was a real red-light district temple to vice and depravity and the Bowery had real 'dive-bars.'
The music was as raw, violent, and dangerous as the streets.
Literature came out of pulp paperbacks.
Politics came out of *Screw Magazine*.
And art came out of underground comix and fanzines.
It was a time when we were all innocent before our fall from paradise."

—Joe Coleman, artist

"Legs McNeil has always been the coolest guy in the room. He's also a brilliant writer. *Resident Punk* is a heartfelt, hilarious, hell-bent journey through a downtown NYC that's been lost forever. A fantastic memoir."

—Elizabeth Hand, award-winning author of *A Haunting on the Hill*

"The sordid story of a dissolute youth."

—Roberta Bayley, photographer who shot the Ramones' first album

"I have known Legs for half a century. Always thought he was a keeper. This funny, wise, autumnal yet still dukes-up autobiography proves it. Punk roots here!"

—Mark Jacobson, author of *The Lampshade: A Holocaust Detective Story from Buchenwald to New Orleans*

"I'm not fucking kidding, it's great. Funny, evocative; makes me yearn to have been there, even though that scene was never my thing. I kind of obsess about books about New York history. This belongs on a shelf with those. The way his writing captures his speaking voice is amazing. Especially with things like, 'Fuck you, asshole!!'"

—Curtis "Booger" Armstrong, actor

RESIDENT PUNK

ALSO BY LEGS MCNEIL

Please Kill Me: The Uncensored Oral History of Punk (with Gillian McCain)

The Other Hollywood: The Uncensored Oral History of the Porn Film Industry (with Jennifer Osborne and Peter Pavia)

Dear Nobody: The True Story of Mary Rose (with Gillian McCain)

FILM:

Pusherman: Frank Lucas & The True Story of American Gangster

Linda Lovelace's Loose Lips, The Last Interview

ALSO BY CRISPIN KOTT

Rock and Roll Explorer Guide to New York City (with Mike Katz)

Rock and Roll Explorer Guide to San Francisco and the Bay Area (with Mike Katz)

RESIDENT PUNK

HOW I SMOKED, DRANK, AND STUMBLED MY WAY THROUGH THE '70S PUNK SCENE (AND BEYOND)

LEGS McNEIL WITH CRISPIN KOTT

BENBELLA

BenBella Books, Inc.
Dallas, TX

BenBella Books, Inc.
8080 N. Central Expressway
Suite 1700
Dallas, TX 75206
benbellabooks.com
Send feedback to feedback@benbellabooks.com

BenBella is a federally registered trademark.

Printed in the United States of America
10 9 8 7 6 5 4 3 2 1

Library of Congress Control Number: 2026013897
ISBN 9781637749463 (hardcover)
ISBN 9781637749470 (electronic)

Editing by Rick Chillot
Copyediting by Scott Calamar
Proofreading by Mary White
Text design and composition by Aaron Edmiston
Cover design by Devin Watson
Front cover photo © Chris Stein
Back cover photo by Unsplash / avechenri
Printed by Lake Book Manufacturing

To my gorgeous wife, Alexis Arakelian,
and my generous friend, Gary Kott

CONTENTS

FOREWORD

BY CHRIS STEIN

Legs tells me we met fifty odd years ago in 1975. I remember stuff more successfully if I've taken a picture of said stuff, so I'll go with his suggestion.

I do remember around that time (which was a best of/worst of period) that we, the various inhabitants of this idyllic hellscape that had as its vague center a beat-up shitty bar on the Bowery, began seeing flyers glued up in the area announcing "PUNK IS COMING." The reaction, as I recall, was many constituents proclaiming this to be the worst band name of all time.

It soon became apparent that *PUNK* was in fact the name of what was intended to be a local periodical, and the name was quickly forgiven. Somewhere around here we met John Holmstrom and Legs McNeil (there was another guy, Ged Dunn, who I was less familiar with), who were working on the "magazine."

These two presented as an incarnation of an old 1959 TV show, *Dobie Gillis*. This is a stretch as an analogy, since the younger members of the audience here probably won't get the reference, but it just takes a minute to research. Basically the show was about a clever but somewhat straight-laced dude whose best buddy was a maniacal beatnik named Maynard G.

Krebs. While Dobie did whatever he did, went to school, whatever, Maynard decried the work ethic of normies and only wanted to party and play bongos. Had the show appeared in a later era, he would have undoubtedly been getting high as a motherfucker too.

The relationship between the bands and the *PUNK* magazine guys went on for the formative years of the CBGB milieu. Pictures were always being taken. I even contributed some drawings and weirdness. The fumetti (look it up) issues were memorable group affairs that had epic mega casts of the locals. Andy W even showed up in one.

Throughout, Legs was a buddy. He, together with Debbie and myself, were drunkenly approaching CB's one afternoon when he announced he would leap over a parking meter that was almost directly in front of the club. Legs rose majestically into the air, successfully clearing the meter only to fall on his head. His head meeting the concrete produced such a loud bang that people within the bar came running out to check on him. He shook it off and we continued on, presumably inside to see whatever was going on.

I was of course always a fan of *Please Kill Me*, though I also have thought that the mayhem and violence of the time was more far and few between, that is, not so concentrated. But the book and stories stand the test of time.

I treasure those days, and in spite of the difficulties, as things progress it becomes more and more apparent what's missing (or maybe oversaturated) from our modern culture. I can't go into lessons from the past; that's up to Legs here.

Anyway, the last few times I ran into him, Legs reminded me of late-stage Lee Marvin.

I'm glad Legs is still reporting.

Chris Stein
New York City, 2026

Legs McNeil thought of the word punk . . . 'cause it kind of described what he is . . . where he was . . . he was eighteen or nineteen when we started it. Legs at the time was really a punk. Every time we would go into a bar . . . he would get thrown out . . . he'd get drunk all the time . . . he didn't own anything of his own . . . he still just sleeps over at people's houses . . . he's directionless . . . you know, he's your archetypal punk.

—John Holmstrom, Punk Art catalogue,
Washington Project for the Arts,
Washington, DC, 1978

ONE

Me and my parents on the Bowery. (I believe I'm drunker than them.)

Photo by Chris Stein

CBGB's was a hellhole of a Bowery bar, like the place where you went for your last drink before slitting your wrists upstairs at the Palace Hotel. The entrance to CBGB was right next door to a stairway that led to the bum crash pad upstairs. The bums would steal each other's shoes and get thrown out of the windows when they were caught.

One time Dee Dee Ramone told me it was a "two-bum night." An ambulance truck was pulling out from the curb in front of CB, onto Bowery, without its lights or sirens blaring, as if to emphasize, *"Why bother? Dead is dead!"*

Dee Dee had an evil smirk as he explained that two bums had been thrown out of the windows of the Palace Hotel, and I believe he was writing a song about it in his head, called "Two-Bum Night," as he always enjoyed a sick sense of humor.

But who didn't? New York City was in ruins, as two or three burned-out tenement buildings littered every block on the Lower East Side. They'd been torched by the landlords to collect the insurance money since the rent money wasn't paying the bills. It was the end of "White Flight," the term that referenced white people's escape to the suburbs, leaving the city to minorities, bums, drunks, mobsters, hustlers, junkies, whores, and outcasts like me.

The torched tenements were immediately occupied by the dope dealers, who lowered baskets or empty paint cans on ropes from the top floor to collect the cash from the waiting junkies downstairs. Cash was always collected first, before they lowered cellophane packets of either heroin or cocaine down to the lines of customers. New York City really was like living in a film noir ultra nightmare, and it reminded me of a giant war-torn city whose soul screamed, ***"YES!"***

How we found CBGB is a long, weird story that starts in Cheshire, Connecticut, my least favorite place. It's where John Holmstrom, Ged Dunn, and I grew up. I don't know what John and Ged were like as kids, but I spent all my time going to the swamp three times a day to catch turtles and snakes to add to my collection for my turtle pen—a giant sandbox with a pool in the middle, that I built in my backyard.

My mom used to hose me off on the back stoop since I'd be covered in the thick black mud from catching snapping turtles waist-deep in the pits of oozing black silt, where the snapping turtles hid. They were my favorites since they were reptiles most reminiscent of dinosaurs with their powerful beak-like jaws and pronounced ridged carapace (upper shell) and long, menacing claws. I could actually see the dinosaurs in the *Chelydra serpentine*, the common snapping turtle, the coolest thing to collect in Connecticut for free, since we were the brokest family in town. I thought I'd become a herpetologist, a guy who studied reptiles, and dreamed of curing cancer with snake venom or toad toxins, but my math skills were so lousy that I flunked biology.

But my obsession with reptiles earned me the nickname "Swamp Rat," later shortened to "Rat," when I got to high school. Yeah, just what everyone wants to be called, like some Ratso Rizzo character . . .

I always hated when I read biographies from the grammar school library, books like *Francis Marion, the Swamp Fox of the American Revolution* or *Clara Barton, Brave Nurse,* about the American self-taught Civil War nurse who founded the Red Cross—there were *always* those obligatory first chapters on their childhoods. I'd think, *Fuck this, get to the good stuff,* instead of reading how they had to walk ten miles in the snow to school or had to eat tree bark during the frigid winters.

So I'm not going to bore the reader. I'll make this quick. My father, Edward Joseph McNeil, died of cancer three months after I was born. The lawyer told my mom, Ellen McNeil, she'd never be able to keep our tract house after my dad's death, so she dug in and went for any type of job. It was 1956, when women were denied their own checking accounts or credit cards. She finally went back to work at the United Illuminating Company, the local power corporation, where she first met my father.

Apparently my mother didn't want to get married, but my father won her heart by giving her rides from New Haven to see her mother, Bridgette Clossick, who had committed herself to the state mental institution in Middletown, Connecticut. The nuthouse was officially known as Connecticut

Valley Hospital and historically known as the Connecticut General Hospital for the Insane, perhaps the scariest place on the planet.

When I'd ask my mom, "Why are there bars on the windows?" she'd say, "This is where they put old people." Right then I vowed never to grow old.

And the reason my grandmother, Bridgette Clossick, committed herself was because her husband, William Clossick, Sr., had blown his brains out in the chicken coop with a shotgun, and she just gave up. She was diagnosed with being agoraphobic, which literally means "fear of the marketplace." She had a fear of leaving her farmhouse in North Haven, Connecticut.

I don't blame her.

The reason for my grandfather's suicide remains a mystery to this day, along with any other information about my family on both the McNeil and Clossick sides. Except that my maternal grandfather fought in the Battle of the Argonne Forest during World War I, was wounded by mustard gas, and lost an eye and a lung. That's how he became an American citizen.

Apparently Bridgette and William didn't have a very happy marriage, and my grandmother hated Connecticut.

But not as much as I did.

The first inkling that living in Connecticut was not going to be very pleasant was when I went to the first day of first grade, and my teacher, Mrs. Coward, took the roll call and asked for a "Roderick."

All of us kids were laughing at such a goofy name until she asked for a "Roderick McNeil," and I rushed to her desk and told Mrs. Coward my name was Eddie McNeil. She said, no, I was "Roderick" McNeil and pointed to the name in the red hand-lettered attendance ledger. I begged her to call me "Eddie."

When I got home from school I approached my mom, who was washing dishes at the kitchen sink, and asked her why she didn't tell me my real name was Roderick, and how had I gotten such a stupid name? Mom replied, nonplussed, "I have no idea, ask your father when you get to Heaven."

Which left me wondering, what else didn't she tell me? Turns out there was a lot.

The next clue to the unpleasantness of my life was my regular six-month trip to the "measuring doctor," which I looked forward to because that doctor never gave me a shot. Since I was so skinny, whenever the regular doctor injected me with a needle, I was in agony for weeks afterwards.

The measuring doctor's office was in the basement of the hospital, the place where the walls of brightly painted cinder blocks transformed into crooked red bricks. Hanging from the ceiling in the hallway were assorted prosthetics: plastic arms and legs of various shapes and sizes to act as replacements for amputated limbs. Another early indication of the horrors of life.

It turns out I was born with my right leg two inches longer than the left and was forced to wear a two-inch lift on my left shoe that made me look like I was wearing a Herman Munster boot. Fuck that, I just wanted to be normal, like everyone else.

To make matters worse, I was told I would need "corrective surgery" when I stopped growing. It also turns out I'm severely dyslexic. My junior high school guidance counselor told my mother it was the most extreme case of dyslexia the Cheshire school system had ever seen, and that there was no cure for it. Thanks a lot.

When I was fifteen and sixteen, I had my "corrective" surgery to shorten my right femur by two inches, and I spent a summer in a body cast and couldn't walk for almost six months. Basically they cut off my right leg, removed two inches of my right femur, and slid a metal rod down my right hip to the knee and used garbage bag twisty ties to hold the femur to the metal rod, until the bone fused together. That took a year.

I was fucked; I couldn't walk, nor even spell, nor add, nor subtract, nor multiply, nor divide. I still can't. But I could escape through the magic of books, Budweiser, and Marlboros, hoping I could find a place where other fuckups like me belonged.

TWO

My best friend in school was Tom Hearn, another fatherless fuckup who hated high school as much as I did. Luckily Tommy had his license and a car, a green Chevy Nova, and he'd pick me up when I'd be trying to sleep off my daily hangover.

Tom would call at 9 AM and say, "Eddie, where are you? Don't you realize what time it is? You're gonna miss Mr. Blake's mass media class! Take a shower and I'll pick you up in ten minutes!"

I'd jump in the shower and run out the door half-dressed and hop in his car, and Tommy would just grin and ask me, "So what do you want to do now?"

I'd say, "What time is it? Mr. Blake's mass media class doesn't start until twelve thirty?"

He'd say, "Eight thirty."

I'd say, *"You fucking asshole!"*

He'd just laugh, as Tom also had a younger sister, Margaret, who took high school very seriously, so he had to get her to school on time. So he'd drop her off at school at eight fifteen and then call me because he'd be so bored and couldn't face another day of learning stuff he had no use for.

Once inside the Nova, Tom would put the car in gear and we'd go to Morton's Pharmacy, where I'd order a vanilla Coke and a Ring Ding for breakfast and smoke half a pack of cigarettes. Then we'd go to Tommy's house at 11:30 AM because his TV got channel 5 from New York City, which broadcast reruns of *Green Acres*, our favorite show.

Tommy's mother worked as Cheshire's "visiting nurse," so she was seldom home during the day. My TV only got channels 8, 3, and the UHF channel 30—with the shittiest kids shows on television—a 90-year-old Ranger Andy playing banjo, singing "You'll find it in the Bible." Talk about a deprived childhood!

The reason I could get away with this is because my mom had to be at work at the U. I. Company at nine o'clock, which meant she had to leave the house at eight thirty, and if I could just tolerate my mom banging on the door from eight to eight thirty, I had it made.

Fortunately my older sister, Lauren, who later became an esteemed epidemiologist for the State of Connecticut, had gotten married in 1972 and moved out. So I moved into her bedroom, which had a lock on the bedroom door.

My older brother, Craig McNeil, moved to Colorado, also in 1972, to become a professional photographer and a hot dog skier. Both my brother and sister had been planning their escapes from our house for years. Thanks, guys, what about me? I think they were both happy to be away from their embarrassing little brother.

The reason everyone was in such a hurry to leave was because of my mother's boyfriend, "Carl the Janitor," literally our grammar school janitor, who had gotten fired for drinking on the job. Carl was about a hundred years older than my mom, who was a good-looking woman, and who I'd ask during our infrequent pensive moments together: "Mom, why don't you marry someone rich?"

She'd give me a nasty look and say, "Who wants to marry a woman with three kids? Besides, I loved your father very much . . ."

"Yeah, but he's gone," I'd say. "He left you."

She'd tear up, I'd apologize, and that would be the end of our two minutes of mother-son time. My sister used to beg my mother to ask Carl to just stay away one night a week, but my mother couldn't do it.

Carl got off work at 3 PM and immediately went to our house, where he parked himself at the same spot at the kitchen table and drank cups of Taster's Choice instant coffee, one after another, and sat there stirring it between gulps. The sound of the spoon clanging against the ceramic cup still haunts me to this day. The only words he ever spoke to me were "Cross!" when he was my grammar school crossing guard, and, when he was sitting at our kitchen table: "Did you do your homework?" I'd tell him I didn't have any and disappear into the basement where I'd dream of getting out of that house or burning it to the ground.

Mom would get home around five thirty depending on traffic, and she'd immediately ask, "Ed, can you get me a beer?" And I'd run back to the basement where Carl the Janitor kept the other fridge stocked with an endless supply of Budweiser; I'd pour my mother's beer into a glass and finish the bottom of the can myself. The best time of the day, when I'd feel that warm glow in my abdomen, and the alcohol would wash over my brain, and I'd feel this rare sensation, normality.

Tommy Hearn saved my life on many nights because I used to run away from home whenever I could. I'd be drunk, stumbling along the roadside, trying to hitchhike to anywhere from where I was, and Tommy would pass me by, pull his car over to the side of the road, and just open the passenger door and wait patiently for me to notice he was there.

I'd stagger into the car and steal one of Tommy's cigarettes, and we'd spend the night driving around—as Chuck Berry said, "*With no particular place to go . . .*"

Tommy's family was exactly like mine, except I didn't have a younger sister. My father didn't live long enough. Tom had an older sister, Claudia, the oldest in the family, like my older sister, Lauren. Except that Claudia

Me in our living room. (The carpet is a green shag rug, no kidding!)

Photo by Tom Hearn

was perhaps the funniest older sister one could ever hope for. Lauren was as serious as they come, always working on some disease project to get her public health degree, which led her to store mountains of petri dishes of gonorrhea in our upstairs refrigerator.

Tommy would walk into our made-in-a-week tract house and open the refrigerator door and say, *"So Lauren, got any good gonococci percolating in here? Mmmm hmmm! Is it soup yet?"*

Tommy also had a good-looking older brother, Patrick Hearn, who got all the girls, just like my brother, Craig, did. My brother looked exactly like my father, and my mother loved walking into church with Craig on her arm, especially after JFK was assassinated, and her status as widow was elevated to that of Jackie Kennedy's.

While I didn't realize it at the time, the assassination of John Fitzgerald Kennedy was the beginning of the end of the American Empire, and the beginning of the USA being transformed from the "good guys" into the "bad guys."

I called my brother "Grunt" because apparently he was inarticulate. But, boy, could he work! He was always paving the driveway or putting new shingles on the roof—squatting up there, shirtless and bathed in sweat, and I'd think, "What the *fuck* are you *doing*?"

I couldn't even hit a nail with a hammer. Still can't.

Grunt was my mother's favorite, while she was jealous of my sister for marrying a handsome marketing director. Mom just blamed everything on me, and it *was* usually my fault; I couldn't even open a box of cereal without spilling half of it all over the floor. I still can't.

The older I got, the more of a mess and the weirder I became. I was a full-fledged chain-smoking, crude, undisciplined, horny, long-haired, teenage alcoholic—a bitter failed hippie 'cause no matter how many anti-war demonstrations I went to, I never got laid. I was also a constant truant and perpetual runaway, since my home life was one continuous argument. My vocabulary was limited to "Fuck you," or "That sucks," or "I'll pay you back tomorrow," or "Cool." But rarely was anything cool in Connecticut.

I had to face that whatever future was in store for me, I'd have to make it for myself, ignoring all the rules and regulations that had been drilled into me, to invent a new way to be and a new way to learn.

I didn't know exactly what this new way of learning would look like, but I knew from the magic of books that others before me had felt like I did, especially Fyodor Dostoevsky when in his story, *Notes from Underground,* he wrote:

> *I remember there was a period in my life when I tried with all my might to become a hero. I longed to achieve something lofty, something sublime. And do you know what I did? One day I decided to challenge a certain*

officer. The whole point was that he never saw me, and simply moved me out of the way, like a fly. Not rudely, no—very politely—but he moved me, and I remained humiliated.

For years I brooded over it. I analyzed it. I even tried to meet him again, to place myself in his path. I carefully studied his routes and habits. Finally, I decided to bump into him.

I even had a new coat made for the occasion. I wanted to be as respectable as he was. For weeks I rehearsed—walking straight ahead without stepping aside. It was harder than you'd think! I trembled each time he approached, and I always moved aside at the last moment. But eventually, I did it. I didn't yield. We bumped shoulders.

And do you know what happened? Nothing. He didn't even notice me. He simply went on walking, as if nothing had happened.

That nothingness resounded inside me, and for as much as I read, I realized I did not possess the vocabulary to express all my humiliations.

No, there had to be more than this, there had to be some joy out there. There had to be a party somewhere, with others who knew what I knew. The only problem was: How to get an invitation to the party?

THREE

As fate would have it, Tom Hearn's older sister, Claudia, had dated a guy named John Holmstrom. He had a theater group called The Apocalypse Players that performed plays written by members of Theater of the Absurd, a 1950s existential movement that expressed what happens when human existence lacks meaning or purpose and communication breaks down.

Yeah, now this was something I could really get behind!

Tommy and I had a scam going putting on rock concerts at St. Bridget's Catholic Church, benefits for such charities as the March of Dimes, where I would skim money off the top in order to buy cigarettes and beer for a couple of weeks. Not only was I a drunk but a thief as well.

Tommy was the one who suggested I contact John Holmstrom and get The Apocalypse Players to perform at our next charity event. Tommy always thought my ideas were ridiculous but went along with them anyway because there was nothing better to do.

Tom called Holmstrom and John was brilliant, as well as being an extreme contrarian, meaning a person who opposes or rejects popular opinion. He was someone who always argued the unpopular or unknown position, which did not win him any friends.

I loved watching John argue his point, especially in this time when the Vietnam War was raging, Watergate was just starting to surface, and we finally saw Richard Nixon for the lying asshole he'd prove to be.

And the California hippie sound of folk-rock dominating the pop charts didn't help matters much either. The only good thing to come out in pop music were Stevie Wonder's *Innervisions* and Alice Cooper's *Love It to Death*. The only new music I heard was from Top 40 radio and from friends' record collections. Friends like Lee and Mandy Cowls, who fed me, gave me cigarettes, bought me beers sometimes, and let me sleep it off in their neighbor's playhouse.

Hanging out with Holmstrom was like a college education in itself, as he possessed arcane knowledge on everything that was cool or hysterically funny, from Harvey Kurtzman being the original founder of *Mad* magazine—as opposed to William Gaines, who took full credit—to Eugène Ionesco, the absurdist playwright who penned *The Bald Soprano*, fighting with existential philosopher Jean-Paul Sartre, the guy who wrote the play *No Exit*, over the authoritarianism of communism and fascism.

Oh those wacky French philosophers, who knew what they'd argue about next?

Holmstrom opened my eyes to so many new thoughts and ideas, and for some reason he liked me. Or at least tolerated me.

And Holmstrom found my weekly antics—running away from home, weaseling beer and cigarettes out of every mark I could find, and run-ins with the cops—hysterically funny.

So much so, that he realized I'd evolved into a low-level operator who could get a few things accomplished. Or rather, try to get a few things accomplished. So he offered me the job managing The Apocalypse Players.

I couldn't even manage my newspaper route! I'd wake up with my daily hangover and see the stacks of twine-bound newspapers piled high in the driveway, and realize how much work delivering them was gonna be, and I'd dump the stacks into the swamp.

In printing class, I printed up hundreds of business cards that read "The Apocalypse Players," and underneath it, "Manager: Eddie McNeil," with my home phone number.

But I spelled "Apocalypse" wrong, so all the business cards had to be tossed out. And I even flunked that class, among all the others I never bothered to show up for.

When Tommy and I would show up at high school, we were frequently suspended for skipping class or some other minor infraction. And those were the best of times, because we could return to school and play in the hallways—staring through the classroom doorways at all the dweebs working on their algebra problems. One time Tommy grabbed a long, flat janitor's cart, the kind that held two trash barrels, and I climbed into one of the barrels and used the broom as a machine gun.

Tommy pushed the cart so it was flying down the miles of hallways as I mowed down imaginary Nazis feeling like Vic Morrow in *Combat!* Unfortunately, the bell rang, the classes emptied into the hallways, and suddenly we were dodging and weaving through the crowds until we found a near-empty hallway near the library. We took a hard right turn and ran over Principal Mischler and knocked him to the floor. We were going that fast.

We were stunned, Mr. Mischler was stunned, until he saw me and Tommy, realized he'd just suspended us, got to his feet, and shouted, ***"YOU TWO! GET OUT!"*** We tried to apologize profusely, but he just screamed, ***"JUST GET OUT!"***

So we went back to Morton's Pharmacy and smoked more cigarettes with the Lady Bus Drivers, a gang of butch ladies who drove Cheshire's snotty brats back and forth to school.

The Lady Bus Drivers hung out at Morton's in between their morning and afternoon shifts, drinking coffee and smoking Tiparillos, those long, thin cigars that were shaped like cigarettes, with a classic white plastic tip "for your smoking pleasure." Those are words you never hear anymore.

They loved when Tommy and I came in so they could hear our latest stories of getting suspended from school, playing armored janitor's cart, and mowing down the principal. They loved that story most of all.

I got the theater group a few gigs at the coffeehouse that Tommy and I had taken over in the basement of Humiston School, a building that had been converted into the board of education. The coffeehouse was an alternative hangout to the Harmon Leonard, Jr. Youth Center, which was founded by a local veterinarian when his son blew himself up with a homemade hand grenade.

That's what kind of town it was, too many rich kids with too much frustration on their hands.

Right around the start of high school I got my first girlfriend, Irene Caracas. We lasted a few weeks, standard teenage romance length. She broke up with me and broke my heart just to date a handsome jock. It happened at Cliff's Pizza, where gangs of kids hung out on Friday nights. I can still remember staring into a half-eaten slice topped with pepperoni wondering what I'd done wrong.

That night, Irene was killed by a car when she ran across the street towards a phone booth; it was a rainy night and she slipped and was hit by Mr. Simisky, a chemistry teacher at Cheshire High. I didn't see it happen, but I remember this Hawaiian guy everyone called "Pineapple," who worked as a handyman at the youth center, standing in the middle of the street with buckets of water trying to wash away all the blood mingling with the rain puddles on the black pavement.

I was completely fucked up over Irene's death, even more so when I realized I was more obsessed with her being killed than I ever was with her when she was alive. It was the first time I faced my own mortality.

I was crying when I got home, and all my mother said was, "*You're too young to be going out with girls.*"

The moment she said it, something switched on in me. I knew I was getting out. I was going to New York and nothing was going to stop me. Up until then I was still trying to be a good kid, still trying to fit in, and failing miserably, but I was doing my version of trying.

Now there was nothing there for me. There never really was.

The youth center fast became a giant ping-pong table that was regularly patrolled by the cops. You couldn't drink or smoke weed there, so a bunch of older hippies started the Bag End coffeehouse in the basement of Humiston School. "Bag End" was a ridiculous name one of the older kids came up with, because they were a fan of J. R. R. Tolkien's *The Hobbit* and *The Lord of the Rings,* books I never bothered to read. And I assure you, *will* never bother to read.

Even though I hated J. R. R. Tolkien, I loved fairy tales and mythology. Best of all was the book *The Battle of the Frogs and the Mice,* based on the Homeric fable by George Martin, with the coolest illustrations by Fred Gwynne—yes, *that* Fred Gwynne, who played Herman Munster on *The Munsters*!

How great is that! *The Battle of the Frogs and the Mice* showcased frogs and mice dressed like Roman soldiers massacring each other. They were very, very cool drawings of frogs impaling mice on Roman spears, or mice slicing frogs' arms off, all while adorned in Roman swords, shields, and helmets. Illustrations at their finest, and all drawn by the incredible Herman Munster!

One of my favorite questions to ask people is, "What saved your life more, books or music?"

Most people answer music, and they seem to think I will, too, but books saved me more than anything. In a good book, I'd lose myself forever, or at least until I was able to leave the Connecticut doldrums. I promised myself that if I was to ever get to do something as cool as write a book, it had to be as cool as *The Battle of the Frogs and the Mice.*

If I ever wrote a book, I'd think, it would be a book *you had to read,* as opposed to a book you *wanted* to read. A necessity, not a distraction.

Not that I didn't love distractions as much as the next guy. I'd sit at the lunch counter for an hour at Morton's Pharmacy and order a seltzer water, 'cause it was free, and devour *Mad* magazine cover to cover. I'd put my fingers in my ears to cut out the sound and immerse myself in the world of *Mad*. One of the best features was the back cover fold-ins, where you folded the back cover together and came up with an entirely new image. Like folding over the Land O'Lakes Indian maiden so her knees became her tits. A childhood rite of passage.

The also-amazing thing about Morton's Pharmacy was that it had a fabulous rack of paperback books, right behind the lunch counter, so you just had to swivel on your stool and see the hundreds of cheap books, ranging from *The Killing of Sharon Tate* by Lawrence Schiller to *The Mod Squad Five: Julie Blows Link!* (I loved Cheez Whiz along with my Ionesco.)

Even more attractive about these pulps: they were so easy to steal. I'd just place a paperback under my arm and walk out with my hand in my jacket pocket, my armpit firmly clutching the book. Shoplifting was so much easier then.

In the center of Cheshire, behind the public library, was the Farm Shop Plaza, which possessed the Amity Pharmacy, as well as the local Marshalls, where John Holmstrom worked as a stock boy right out of high school. Holmstrom always wore a proper suit jacket from Goodwill over a T-shirt, bell-bottom jeans, and inexpensive flat sneakers.

Holmstrom got a cheap apartment in the center of town and gave me a copy of the key so I could listen to all his cool records. John had excellent taste in music, and he had all the old Chuck Berry records that included "Maybellene," "Johnny B. Goode," and "No Particular Place to Go," as well as all the original Lenny Bruce albums; the ones where Lenny was having picnics in graveyards, titled *The Sick Humor of Lenny Bruce*!

Tommy and I did a lot of our drinking in cemeteries and were quite aware of the sick humor of the modern world. Like when the cops busted us with our quarts of Bud, and they were about to slap on the handcuffs and take us in. But the cop would make the mistake of scolding us with *"Does your father know you're out here drinking beer?"*

We'd stare at our feet, kicking rocks, all maudlin, and mumble, "My father's dead . . ." Our ace in the hole!

Our "Dead Fathers" routine became our Get-Out-of-Jail-Free card, as the cop was usually embarrassed and always just made us pour out the beer and let us go with a warning. Yeah, we worked that one to death. I mean, we both figured not having a father had to count for something, right?

Besides, most kids we knew hated their fathers, so maybe we were the fortunate ones?

John Holmstrom never talked about his parents. It wasn't until years later he told me that his father was in the POW camp that *The Great Escape* starring Steve McQueen was based on. "Only they wouldn't let him go through the tunnel 'cause he couldn't speak German," Holmstrom told me, and I thought, *Jesus, World War II really fucked up a lot of our parents.*

I think John's father became a bad drunk; that's all I knew about Holmstrom's family.

John Holmstrom was a brilliant artist and the best teacher I ever had, because he'd always translate complex concepts into terms that I could relate to. He had the rare ability to articulate why something was cool—which is actually a very difficult concept, when you think about it.

He was the first person I ever met who was taking every art form and trying to create something new by distorting the configuration and parameters of whatever structure he was working with.

Like the beautiful portrait of Christ on his mantelpiece over his non-working fireplace in his apartment. It kinda looked like a normal holy picture, but the closer you got to the portrait, the more the thick, chunky globs of paint became evident, reminiscent of something Vincent van Gogh might've painted. The portrait of Christ really got to me and made me think, *This guy's really got something going on here . . .*

I loved this "corruption of the medium idea" that Holmstrom had going, and it worked with my dyslexia. As a matter of fact, I can still write backwards perfectly. Except for my misspellings.

Even better about John was that he was working at Marshalls in order to save up money to go to the School of Visual Arts in New York City, the Land of Oz.

He was getting out!

The last public performance of The Apocalypse Players was one which, I think, I had something to do with setting up. Or maybe it was Ged Dunn, who was the president of the student council. It was held in the new multimillion-dollar auditorium inside Cheshire High School, and it was an utter disaster.

The first indication that it was going to be a nightmare was that all the actors in the group were a bunch of straight, intellectual, arty, rich kids. They only joined The Apocalypse Players to check off the box on their college entrance applications emphasizing their eclectic tastes for a more varied extracurricular activity.

And they hated me, and couldn't imagine why Holmstrom was hanging out with such a loser. I can't help it if they didn't share my sense of humor. John, to his credit, would just shrug them off.

The second thing that went wrong was that the lighting director never showed up—or maybe was never hired by me. So at the last minute, John asked me, "You know how to do lights?"

I thought, "Fuck you, I know how to turn on a light switch," but I had no clue that there's an art to conducting the lights at a theatrical performance. Thus I was dispatched to the lighting booth upstairs in the back of the auditorium. The lighting board was a state-of-the-art professional console with tons of knobs and buttons and faders.

I didn't have a clue.

Every time I should have gone to a fade out at the end of a scene, I went to a total blackout, so the audience would think the play was over.

The play was eventually stopped by Cheshire Police Sgt. O'Leary, who stood before the audience and announced, ***"THIS ISN'T A PERFORMANCE, IT'S SYSTEMATIC DESTRUCTION OF PRIVATE PROPERTY!"***

What prompted the end of The Apocalypse Players was that the actor playing Groucho Marx threw a pie at another actor, missed him, and it plopped on the curtain. It wasn't even a real pie but a tin of shaving cream.

No big deal, but Holmstrom was thrilled by being shut down by police. He acted like it was the greatest thing that ever happened to him. I'd never seen him so happy, and I thought, *What balls this guy has!*

The rest of the cast were appalled and couldn't wait to disappear. They acted like it was my fault since the lighting cues were so confusing. Sgt. O'Leary probably just got fed up with the amateurish production and found an excuse to shut us down, so I might've contributed to the end.

Holmstrom left for New York City shortly after that to attend the School of Visual Arts.

I was just left with hanging around with Tommy, getting drunk, and doing a fuck load of nothing but going to the library and rereading *My Autobiography* by Charlie Chaplin.

In a 2023 review on the online writing magazine Writing.ie, book critic Milena Tseneva explained how she discovered this masterpiece:

> *It became a little strange to me how the book was there all the time, among my grandmother's other books, without noticing it before. Finding it once again convinced me that there is some mysterious magic around all the books in this world and some books always find you when it's time to read them.*

I felt the same way, the book found me.

In his review of *My Autobiography* in *The New Yorker*, Steve Futterman wrote:

> *(Chaplin) masterfully narrates a youth of Dickensian dimensions, including abject poverty, a drunken, absent father, a loving mother literally going mad, life on the streets, even a stay in the workhouse. It's horrible and wrenching, and Chaplin goes to the races with it all, turning tragedy into gripping drama.*

Jesus! I'd had it pretty fucking easy compared to this guy! I mean, *a fucking workhouse?*

And Chaplin never presented himself as a victim. He just kept going. *My Autobiography* inspired my soul. To do what? I didn't know.

That's when I got a letter from Holmstrom betting me one hundred dollars that he was going to become a millionaire before me. I was shocked that he'd ever suspect that I'd ever become a millionaire.

Holmstrom somehow felt threatened by me . . . *by me? **Me?***

The only threat I ever posed was to myself.

And then came the "corrective surgery . . ."

But more on that later.

When I recovered from the surgery on my leg and could walk again, Tommy and I started thinking more of our nonfutures. There was a photographer named Larry Kerson who contacted a new youth counselor named John Mauceri about forming a group of kids who wanted to make movies. But film and processing cost money, and even though I was working after school in a disposable hypodermic needle factory cleaning the grinding machines, filmmaking was still an expensive hobby.

Especially since I'd always overfill the grinding machines so I could hang out in the factory john, smoking cigarettes and reading. Of course the water would flood the factory floor, and the foreman would shout: ***"McNeil!!!"***

I would have fired my ass. I guess it was the dead-father deal, or the fact that he pitied fuckups like me, but he was a nice guy and kept giving me breaks.

The solution to our film and processing money appeared out of nowhere. Suddenly a local dry cleaner was converted into a film store and processing lab. The new Carbor Photo had a dry cleaner's sign outside that screamed: ***"STREAK-IN FOR FREE FILM!"***

Since I'd already spent my film budget on beer and cigarettes, it seemed like the only way out.

"Streaking" was a '70s fad. Like Pet Rocks, which were actual rocks packaged in custom cardboard boxes, complete with ventilation holes and straw bedding, imitating a pet carrier. Don't blame me, it was the 1970s, when a book like *I'm OK–You're OK* was on *The New York Times* Best Seller list for two years and sold over fifteen million copies.

Trust me, you weren't okay.

The world had slowly turned beige and cuddly. Folk-rock had won over garage bands.

And "streaking," the fad of running naked through a public place, became a humorous prank. Since I'd already blown my budget, that sign in the window was a sign from God.

"You're not gonna do this, are you?" Tommy asked.

"I don't have any choice."

I asked him to buy me a tallboy of Budweiser for courage and arranged to have him pull the car as close to the Carbor Photo door as possible, and I ran inside while Tommy yelled to me, ***"Remember it's Tri-X film, TRI-X!"***

"The sign said to streak-in for free film," I told the shocked guy behind the counter.

He was just staring at my balls.

"Can you get it?" I asked, squirming a bit too urgently.

He went to his stock room and came back with a package of Tri-X.

"Two," I demanded, and he went back and got me another pack.

I jumped back in the Nova and we sped off.

The next day in the *New Haven Register*, in the front-page "Today's Bright Spot" box reserved for a humorous quip on the day, was a paragraph on the film store's sign and my anonymous response.

Carl the Janitor read it out loud at the kitchen table, and he and my mom laughed about *"What some people will do . . ."*

I remained stone-faced and got my mother another beer.

Tommy and I got so into filmmaking that we started skipping class to shoot in New Haven. Not that we needed any excuse. We did this so often that we were going to wind up each a credit short of graduation. Mr. Blake, the head of the Cheshire High School English Department, took pity on us and said we could make up the credit with "Independent Study in Mass Media." That sounded like a lot of work until he pulled out a crisp fifty-dollar bill for each of us and told us to go shoot a movie.

I immediately spent my windfall on cigarettes and beer and made an animation of President Nixon turning into a pig. Tommy made a spectacular comedy titled *Bob's Locker Party*.

Shot entirely at Cheshire High, *Bob's Locker Party* was a short film about a troublemaking student who turns his locker into a beer-soaked den of iniquity. In a clever twist, Tommy used stop-motion, shooting a frame at a time. The locker could fit an entire person inside, but this technique made it seem infinite. The halls and classrooms were shot in black and white, while the outside world and "Bob's Locker" were shot in color.

"Bob" was played by our late friend Bob Nethery, and the film featured me, as well as many of our classmates; even Principal Robert Mischler and a bunch of teachers made an appearance. It was a sensation, at least in Cheshire High.

One day John Holmstrom called me from New York City and told me he was doing a comic strip called *Joe* for *Bananas,* a Scholastic magazine publication for junior high or middle schoolers, and he asked me if I wanted to help write some of the *Joe* strips.

Joe was a Holmstrom original, and he got the job thanks to Harvey Kurtzman, one of the founders of *Mad* magazine, and the creator and longtime writer and artist of *Little Annie Fanny,* a comic strip about a naïve buxom blonde who wound up naked by the end of all 107 of her stories in *Playboy.* Kurtzman was Holmstrom's mentor at the School of Visual Arts, and he could really kick open a lot of doors for young comic creators.

Every bit of *Joe* was created by Holmstrom until he hit a creative wall. And that's when he called me in Cheshire, because who better to tell a *Joe* story than a real-life Joe?

Besides, I was already coming up with my own sordid tales in a creative writing class in high school. I'd come up with the ideas, and Holmstrom would do the art and lettering, just like he would later in *PUNK.* He told me he was paid $300 per strip for *Joe,* and we'd split that fifty-fifty. Cigarettes were fifty cents a pack, and a quart of beer was a buck fifty, so every *Joe* script was a good month.

The only problem was that I wasn't much of a writer, except for the occasional story I wrote for my creative writing class about trying to escape working at the disposable hypodermic needle factory. The other kids in class thought they were funny, but the perky blonde teacher hated them. She'd assigned us haikus: Japanese poems of seventeen syllables, structured in three lines of five, seven, and five syllables. This wasn't creative writing but a stupid math problem!

The perky blonde teacher was an asshole, who delighted in reminding us that she knew a screenwriter who wrote for the hit TV show *M*A*S*H,* perhaps the most self-righteous show in the history of television. Whatta fucking tool!

Needless to say, I flunked my creative writing class, along with algebra, and I was informed that I wouldn't be graduating from high school. Tommy also flunked algebra, but he was forced to go to summer school to get his diploma. There was no way I was going to summer school! I was getting out! Even with my shitty grades, I'd been accepted at the School of Visual Arts to study filmmaking and planned on moving in with Holmstrom at his apartment on East 24th Street.

I saw moving to New York City as the kind of adventure I hadn't had since I was thirteen years old. I started that summer of 1969 playing with Matchbox cars in Cheshire, Connecticut, and finished it a juvenile delinquent dope dealer in Mazatlán, Mexico.

My mom had severe COPD, the kind that leaves you gasping for air, and she decided Arizona's dry heat might help. So when Carl the Janitor whisked my mother away to Arizona for the summer, Uncle Bill entered the picture and whisked me and my older brother, Craig, to North Truro, a popular local surfing spot way up on Massachusetts's "winklepicker tip." Craig had this obsession with surfing, yammering on about a mythical wave in San Blas, Mexico, between Mazatlán and Guadalajara that he'd read about in *Surfer* magazine. Surfing was alright, but Mexico had a really nice ring to it.

Uncle Bill wasn't what responsible adults would call a model chaperone. He'd just dropped us in the dunes at North Truro, telling us, "Sleep on the beach and don't get caught by the cops" as he drove away. We ended up partying with some hippies around a bonfire, helping ourselves to their bottles of wine. I got smashed, slept on the beach, and as Uncle Bill had instructed, didn't get caught by the cops.

I wasn't into pot; my nervous system was so shot from alcohol that whenever I smoked it, I always got too paranoid. But I chain-smoked cigarettes like a fiend. At thirteen, I already had the lungs of an ashtray and the liver of a Richard Burton.

When he wasn't on his surfboard, Craig wouldn't shut the fuck up about San Blas, Mexico. "The perfect wave isn't in *Massachusetts*, Eddie; it's three thousand miles away in *San Blas*!"

"Okay, Grunt, okay!"

I'd laugh, taking another slug off another bottle of cheap wine and dreaming of copping a feel of one of the loose hippie chicks we were hanging around. But somehow, Craig manifested this Mexican fantasy into reality, and the next thing I knew, we were going.

Of course, there was a catch: We had to make a pit stop to pick up Uncle Bill's car at a Christian health camp in rural Arkansas. Uncle Bill was tight with fringe types—white supremacist, Bible-thumping old hippies eating organic slop, and a handful of paranoid communal kooks building concrete arks "for the Lord."

Uncle Bill was nuts, by the way. Certifiably nuts. Diagnosed paranoid-schizophrenic. After my grandparents checked out, Uncle Bill became my mother's guardian. For a while he lived in our basement, sleeping on an old army cot next to the furnace. Sometimes we'd be sitting at the dinner table and we'd hear a plane overhead, and my mother would tell us to run outside and see if it was Uncle Bill; he was a licensed pilot. The plane would fly over our house and dip its wings to say hello. Uncle Bill was always pulling pranks like that. We thought he was a riot, and he really was. But he was also nuts.

So, off we went, riding a series of Trailways buses from New Haven, Connecticut, to a desolate corner of Arkansas, to get Uncle Bill's car. We were inhaling diesel fumes and cigar smoke for a sweaty, endless week only to arrive at this "Christian Health Camp."

If you've ever actually heard about a cult, from Synanon to Heaven's Gate, it's because they had panache. There was something flashy about those cult leaders that drew countless hopeless dupes to their doorsteps. The promise of redemption, or life after death. Or no-holes-barred carnal fuckfests.

The "cult" we went to in Arkansas was nothing more than four sanctimonious assholes—five if you count a baby—living in mud shacks. No electricity, no running water. And there were snakes—literal poisonous snakes. Water moccasins, copperheads. The kind I'd rarely ever see back home in Cheshire. And the cult blamed me for the infestation; they said *I* invited the snakes. And honestly? I thought maybe they were right. Like, *Yeah, I called the snakes. What of it? Just wait till I tell 'em to crawl into your sleeping bag in the middle of the night, fuckface!*

The food? Garbage. Hippie vegetarian shit that tasted like the inside of a wet cardboard box. I survived on contraband potato chips, warm cans of Coke, and the generosity of this backwoods guy, Bubba, who slipped me homemade wine and rolled my cigarettes because I was too clumsy to do it myself. Coca-Cola and potato chips were like heaven to me, but the health camp cult *hated* the stuff. I'd think, *I'm thirteen years old and you're gonna preach against Coca-Cola and potato chips and make me eat this fucking shit that tastes like mud? Fuck you, asshole! This is why the snakes came!*

One thing my mother insisted was that Uncle Bill take us to church every Sunday. And though he was a Seventh-day Adventist or something, hated the Catholic Church, and believed the Sabbath was on Saturday, Uncle Bill did what my mother asked every Sunday that summer.

At this rural Catholic church in Arkansas, a devout family invited us to lunch and we just ate everything they put in front of us, peanut butter and jelly sandwich after peanut butter and jelly sandwich. Piles of them, like something out of a Dr. Seuss book.

The family had a horse, and my brother thought he'd be a cowboy, and he jumped on the saddle and was immediately thrown. That's the kind of unruly kids we were. We were just maniacs.

After a week in that Arkansan hellhole, we said adios to the snakes and hit the road: Buttfuck, Arkansas, to South Padre Island, Texas. Back then, Padre was no spring-break puke-a-rama. Just sand, surf, and lingering wreckage from Hurricane Beulah, which had flattened its coast nearly two years earlier. Nestled in the cradle of the Gulf of Mexico, South Padre Island was a magnet for waves, drawing them—and surfers—in with irresistible force. Especially during hurricane season when tropical storms barreling in off the Atlantic Ocean wriggled and pummeled their way across Florida and blasted the western Gulf Coast.

The waves that summer were gnarly—huge, filthy, and deadly. Especially when Hurricane Celia wiped out Port Aransas up the coast of South Padre Island, and a battered surfboard washed up on the shore. Its rider didn't.

But Craig was fearless, paddling out like the undertow wasn't trying to drag him screaming to hell. I stayed onshore, mesmerized. He was a beast out there, leaning into curls like they were his bitch. I stood and watched my brother surf these lethal waves, and he was so damn good that eventually I stopped worrying. For him, South Padre Island was a natural progression.

At home he was always checking the weather report, and he'd say, "A hurricane is coming, the surf is gonna be great!" and we'd head to the beach in Rhode Island, or Newport, or Narragansett.

But even back home, I didn't really much care about surfing, anyway. The people on the beach, the *scene*—that was my trip. Always was.

When I was a kid, since I didn't have a father, fathers of my friends would take me along to baseball games. Nobody had ever explained baseball to me, so I didn't understand what was happening on the field, or why it was so fucking boring. Besides, I never cared who won or lost.

Instead, I'd wander into the stadium bars, with everyone smoking cigarettes and cigars and drinking beer. I was fascinated by the scene, the impenetrable tribal jive. And I'm sure anyone's dad who ever took me to Yankee Stadium realized it. *Fuck the baseball game. This is my game.*

And the same happened with surfing. I admired my brother and was blown away by his tenacity, but what I really got off on were the people on the shore.

Back in North Truro, Uncle Bill was mostly absent from our lives. He'd drop us off and disappear, maybe seeking out more weirdo cultists, who knows? But he'd give us each a dollar a day for lunch, which would get us a tuna fish sandwich and a glass of milk or a Coke. Not a bad per diem in 1969. It was the first time in my life anyone had ever given me money, and it came from a stash my mother had scraped together so we could have an adventure while she was in Arizona.

I knew I was a spare part on this trip. If Craig hadn't taken me along, my mother never would have approved my brother's summer surfing scheme.

My mom loved Grunt because he looked exactly like my father. She even loaned him five grand to buy a fiberglass Saab Sonett two-seater sports car that resembled a Jaguar. Cherry. It was a gorgeous car that he only let me drive once: I hit a pothole and he screamed at me as he took over the wheel. But Grunt paid my mom back every cent of that loan. He and I couldn't have been more different if we tried.

This idea that we are not born into the families that we belong to, that you could adopt your own family, was percolating in my brain. Which is probably why I'd eventually get so attached to so many people I worked with; I loved that connection.

Later on, my exploits would lead me to form new families with good friends who got me, and I didn't have to explain to them who or what I was.

I was awed by my brother's surfing ability. I saw him inside of the curl. I watched him wait for a swell of big waves, and when he spied the right one he paddled gracefully and *caught it!* Craig really was a pro, but even better was his absolute passion for riding the waves.

It was like swamping for me. Passion is passion. One of the greatest gifts bestowed on us. I didn't have to become a surfing fanatic to get it; I understood Grunt's joy, and that's all I needed to see. Good for him! He'd found his thing, God bless him! And I'd be left to find my thing, whatever that might be.

We were on South Padre Island for around three weeks, meeting up each night in a motel, then going our separate ways the next morning, me and my brother to the beach, Uncle Bill to hang with Benjamin Roden, founder of the Branch Davidians. We didn't plan on being there that long, but we kept trying and failing to cross the border into Mexico.

We didn't have passports, and none of us spoke Spanish, so it took us weeks of trying to figure out that the border guards wanted "*dinero para cerveza*"—money for beer. Shit. If it was that fucking easy, why was it so hard for us to figure it out?

In Mexico Uncle Bill, Grunt, and I had an apartment right on the beach in Mazatlán. We'd say maybe a couple of words to each other now and then: "What are you doing today?" "Nuthin' . . ."

But I didn't really care. I was having adventures in a bigger world than I'd ever seen in Cheshire. All I did back home was visit the swamp three times a day. Here, while my brother surfed, and Uncle Bill did whatever the schizophrenic Born-Again Christians of the world did, I'd explore the city.

Somehow, I wound up hanging around with a pack of local shoeshine boys; they were scruffy and smoked cigarettes and drank beer, and despite my not speaking any Spanish, these were my people, and they welcomed me into the fold.

And Canadian tourists being Canadian tourists, they'd ask us if we could score them some pot.

"Hey, kids, can you get us some pot?" And I'd turn to the shoeshine boys and mime smoking a joint, and we'd all bust out laughing. And then I'd put on a serious face and turn back at the Canadian tourists and say, "Yeah, sure." And they'd give us a bunch of money, and for two dollars we could get a shopping bag full of weed, give the rubes a pinch of that, and since none of us got high on our own supply, the rest was profit. You can't cool down with a joint! *Cerveza fria, por favor!*

Leonardo was my best friend in Mazatlán. He was this good-looking shoeshine boy and delivery boy for his eight brothers' carpentry business. Leonardo was the guy I was with when we'd run by the whorehouse and shout, *"Puta! Puta! Puta!"* and giggle madly around the corner. Let me remind you that we were only thirteen years old.

Of course we were making enough money selling pot to Canadian tourists that we could've marched right into the bordello and had our pick of the lot. But, c'mon, we were just kids! Naïve, and barely able to talk to girls.

Leonardo would have to work half a day, and then he and I and the rest of the shoeshine gang would gather at this outdoor café on the beach with banana leaves for a roof and a great jukebox. The owner would slice up a couple dozen oysters, then chop the top off a big green coconut, stick a straw in it, and that would be lunch.

Since the exchange rate was one American dollar to twelve pesos and change, I was walking around with wads of cash. While I was waiting for Leonardo to finish work, I'd check out the local bar scene, and I even got up the nerve to approach the bar, pulled out the wad of cash—and the bartenders always served me. Me, a thirteen-year-old kid!

God I loved Mexico! Everything was so corrupt!

Then I made the mistake of ordering a shot of tequila and I wet my pants on the way home. And Mexican cigarettes were shit, and American ones were hard to come by. But we managed to secure a connection somehow.

One night we had to drive deep into the jungle to pick up two shopping bags filled with pot that had just been cultivated. We gave the guy, who looked exactly like Danny Trejo, our five dollars and he just glared as he passed the bags to us. I was scared shitless, but Leonardo was cool, he shot him his enchanting smile, and we climbed back into the VW bus and drove back to the city.

I just wanted to get rid of the weed, since the apartment I shared with Uncle Bill and Grunt was across the street from a police station. We didn't go back to the apartment but to a luxury condo right off the beach.

The condo belonged to the Canadians and it had an elevator, something Leonardo had never experienced before. He quickly became obsessed with riding the elevator up and down the four floors and giggling madly, as I went in to deliver the pot and get paid our forty or fifty dollars. Our markup wasn't that high if you think about the penalties for a thirteen-year-old gringo dealing pot in Mexico in 1969. It was as dumb as it was thrilling.

I don't know where Uncle Bill was during all this; probably out fixing the car, since we'd been in a three-car collision in the heights of the Sierra Madres, kind of a continuation of the USA's Rocky Mountains. That was on the way to Mazatlán.

I was sitting in the passenger seat next to Uncle Bill, who was driving.

"I think there's a car parked in the road up there," I said as I grabbed the dashboard.

"No problem, no problem," Uncle Bill mumbled, not taking his foot off the gas. CRASH!

After about two hours, with Uncle Bill working under the hood, as the sun was coming up, I suddenly noticed that there were people, Indigenous Mexicans—those people with the perfectly chiseled cheek bones and that exquisite skin and thick black hair—surrounding us.

Where they came from, I didn't have a clue. We were high up in the Sierra Madres, on a very vertical slope, and we hadn't seen any signs of civilization for hours, and suddenly we're surrounded by twenty or thirty people.

Uncle Bill got the car going well enough to drive us to a curbside mountain café, and Craig and I had breakfast while Uncle Bill climbed back under the hood.

It actually wasn't a café but someone's house that was failing to become a café, but the breakfast was delicious, scrambled eggs with some delicious Mexican shit mixed in.

This place was much more relaxed than the States.

Hanging out with Leonardo, I was beginning to hate gringos too.

It was exhilarating to be wandering around this Mexican city of 116,000 people and watching how the city worked. Craig surfed the consistent four-to-six-foot waves from sunup to sundown, as I continued exploring the culture. Then one day Craig wiped out on his board and washed up on a bed of sea urchins, the porcupines of the sea. *Fuck!* He was in a hospital, or clinic, and Uncle Bill went and healed him.

I think it was while he was recovering from his run-in with the sea urchins that we finally made it to San Blas. I'm not sure exactly when, but I know that some time that summer we went to check out the beaches of San Blas, and I wasn't impressed. Neither was my brother.

The dream was over. Talk about the power of myth. "The Perfect Wave."

You could see how it was possible for the wave to break on this island, and you could ride the right side in for almost a mile, but that would have to be a really good day.

Here the surf was flat, so why give up consistent five-foot waves in Mazatlán?

Besides, there weren't any bars visible in San Blas, so why bother?

But I was impressed that my older brother would follow his dream to its conclusion, having surfed every day he could walk, once we got to the seashore.

As suddenly as we'd arrived, we had to leave, with Uncle Bill driving us back across the Texas border, where we caught connecting flights back to New York City.

Though I did one heroic thing before I left Mazatlán: I gave Leonardo the remaining profits from our summer drug dealing, about two hundred bucks, and helped him escape out of Mexico. Leonardo loved the idea of the United States so much that he talked me into arranging for an American hippie couple we'd made friends with to create a false bottom in the back of their VW bug and smuggle him across the border. I pray he made it.

Now I could add human trafficker to my list of transgressions.

FOUR

That trip to Mexico was the most exciting thing I'd ever done in my life, until years later when I moved to Manhattan and got the same sort of thrill. Holmstrom was living on the top floor of a three-story walk-up right around the corner from the School of Visual Arts, and he let me crash there after I left Cheshire. It was as close to the School of Visual Arts as I'd ever get; I was accepted by the school, but since I didn't have a high school diploma, I figured, *Why bother?* But you know, it was a good thing I didn't go to college because it would have been a waste of money. I'd have just stayed drunk until they threw me out.

Anyway, writers don't go to school; they abhor academia. They live and write, like Jack Kerouac, who dropped out of Columbia University and almost immediately hooked up with Allen Ginsberg, Neal Cassady, and other Beats.

Once I started writing *Joe*, I kept coming up with other ideas, like a story about a guy who bleeds to death in a hospital waiting room because the nurse won't let him see a doctor until he answers a bunch of questions, which I thought was hilarious. Not exactly *Joe* material, but I didn't ever try to submit them anywhere because who would even publish them? Had I known about *Saturday Night Live* I might have tried to sell them there. Even now I think they were good enough to be turned into a comedy show sketch.

After a few months working and living *Joe*, I suddenly found myself having to go work and live somewhere else. The School of Visual Arts bought the building where Holmstrom lived and offered him a few thousand bucks to move out. I wasn't on the lease so I wasn't offered anything. "There's the door. Good luck . . ."

Instead of writing about guys bleeding out in hospitals or coming up with teen-friendly *Joe* stories, I was spending my days looking for a job and a place to live. Which in New York City, or anywhere really, isn't too much fun. But almost anywhere else in the world, that search doesn't end in a closet at a hippie film commune in a sixth-floor walk-up on the corner of 14th Street and Second Avenue. Right next to a methadone clinic. Junkies were always passed out in the doorways, so there was no way to get in the front door. It seemed like the entire city was strung out on dope.

"Total Impact," the name of the hippie film commune, was the creation of David Secter. He was a young filmmaker who was still a student at the University of Toronto in the mid-'60s when he wrote and directed *Winter Kept Us Warm*, an autobiographical romantic drama with coded gay subtext. It was the first English-language Canadian film ever screened at Cannes.

I was walking down Second Avenue and saw a guy holding a 16 mm Arriflex, and I knew enough about film cameras to realize they were making a movie. So I asked if I could have a job and was told to go inside and find David Secter. They didn't pay cash, only room and board, and since I had neither at that time it seemed like a pretty good deal.

Plus I found a side gig carrying groceries up the stairs for these two little old ladies who'd emigrated from somewhere in the Eastern Bloc, maybe the Ukraine. They were very nice, but they paid in nonfilter Chesterfields, which burned so badly I imagined my lungs turning to ash with every puff. But beggars can't be choosers.

My bedroom was an actual windowless closet on the sixth floor of Total Impact, just large enough for a twin mattress and a few shelves. It wasn't what I'd call homey, but it was home for close to a year. And I didn't spend every night in there anyway.

For around six or seven weeks I was . . . "dating" isn't the word, no . . . I was fucking an absolutely gorgeous Black woman who was part of the Total Impact co-op. And she had a bedroom, too, with windows. I'd knock on her door after dinner and wind up sleeping over. Her skin was so dark and mine so white, and I'd put our arms together and wonder at the contrast.

My suburban racism drained out of me with every orgasm.

Total Impact was an anything-goes hippie commune where sex was a constant. But we didn't exactly show off whatever it was we were doing in that bedroom. Maybe she was embarrassed to be seen fooling around with a suburban flunky, living in a closet.

Eventually she left Total Impact and became a Jehovah's Witness, and I can't remember if I was surprised. I'd once asked her about her life before Total Impact, and she told me she'd been married with children somewhere in the suburbs. One day she decided she couldn't hack that life anymore and wound up in a shitty film co-op in a shitty building on shitty East 14th Street.

Even after that admission I felt she generally had it together and thought it was only a matter of time before she wound up returning to her family in the suburbs. Instead, like so many hippies before her, she jumped from one cult to another.

I wasn't ready to leave Total Impact, not yet. I had no illusions that we were creating art, and though I never moved out of the closet while I was there, I did move up in the ranks.

The first time I met Ron Jeremy, he blew himself. Literally.

I didn't actually "meet" him, like shaking hands or comparing cocks or saying hello. But I did see him casually perform auto-fellatio in a room full of strangers at Total Impact.

Ron, dressed in a polyester open shirt, with a short Jew-fro and black cop mustache, was there to audition for a porn film Total Impact was making to try to finance *Getting Together*, which, like *Winter Kept Us Warm*, was basically a David Secter biopic, this one about a Madison Avenue copywriter who drops out of society after taking LSD and starts a film commune in Manhattan's East Village. This might've been an original idea in 1965, but in 1974, it was rancid.

The porno was called *Blow Dry*, as in, "*Shampoo Teases, Blow Dry Pleases!*"

Yeah, one of the first X-rated films that was based on a popular film of the day. This one was a rip-off of *Shampoo*, and Ron was trying to launch his pornographic film career, hoping to get a part. Though the room was full of Total Impact hangers-on, me included, Ron was mostly auditioning for Joey Asaro, an Italian producer from Brooklyn with a Fu Manchu mustache and goatee, who leaned back in his chair and asked, "Got any special talents?"

"Other than having a big dick?" Ron grinned.

"Yeah," Joey nodded, absently petting his beard.

"I can blow myself," Ron answered.

"No kidding?" Joey smiled, leaning further back in his chair and clasping his hands behind his head. His body language was saying, *This is gonna be good!*

"No kidding," Ron assured him. "Wanna see?"

"Sure." Joey laughed and winked at me. Joey would've been perfect as a thug in *Goodfellas*.

Ron unbuckled his belt and pulled down his thick corduroy pants. He had not acquired his nickname yet, "The Hedgehog," because he wouldn't start to get fat for another decade. He wasn't a bodybuilder or anything, but he was fit enough that he was proud to show off his body.

I felt like an extra in a lost Hollywood film: *Ron's Penis Doesn't Live Here Anymore*. Maybe if Total Impact hadn't been so tacky, with a bright orange shag rug and "modern" office furniture, maybe if Joey Asaro hadn't been such a sleazy stereotype, or maybe if Ron wasn't lying there on the rug, stroking his huge dick, and throwing his legs over his head, forcing his crotch closer to his face . . . maybe I would've been grossed out.

But all that was going through my head was, *Jesus Christ, does this guy have balls, or does this guy have balls?* It was pure performance art.

I couldn't decide if Ron was incredibly brave, or a psychopathic narcissist, but decided it didn't matter and sat back and enjoyed the show. Ron was struggling on the orange rug, grunting and squirming like a shelled armadillo, until his hips were directly overhead, and he lowered his big prick into his mouth.

"Uh-uh." Joey shook his head. "Ya gotta suck it. That was the deal . . ."

Ron bobbed his head up and down; the veins in his neck exploding as his cock slid between his lips.

It was a puerile freak show, what most porn films became after a very short period of experimentation. But his "oral gratification" was really impressive, and he later did it a bunch of times on camera.

I don't think Ron came in his own mouth during his audition. I would've remembered that, or maybe I turned away and missed it. But I don't think that was the point. He wanted to show he could suck his own dick and prove he'd do anything for the gig. That was it. And since it wasn't particularly sexy, the money shot was unnecessary.

But for all his superhuman contortions on the orange shag rug, Ron didn't get a part in *Blow Dry*. Jamie Gillis, another '70s and '80s porn icon, was in it, and so were Helen Madigan, Crystal Sync, and a few other adult-film veterans. But Ron Jeremy? Sorry, pal. Better luck next time.

The last time I saw Ron Jeremy for many years was the sight of him pulling on his clothes and leaving the "audition," pausing only to jot down his contact info with Joey Asaro, who literally told him, "Don't call us, we'll call you . . ."

I would've been pissed if I'd just sucked my own cock and didn't get the part, but Ron didn't seem particularly hurt, which I found amazing—just very professional and polite. And then he was gone. That was that. Goodbye and good luck in your new career!

But what I didn't know at the time was that I'd just witnessed one of the master hustlers in the multibillion-dollar-a-year business of exhibitionism at the start of his rise into the pantheons of American pop culture. Do you know how many people asked me to get them autographed Ron Jeremy photos when I was working on the porn book *The Other Hollywood*? Dozens!

It's decades later, and Ron Jeremy, a man who could suck his own cock, has since been charged with sexually assaulting numerous women.

But as we've all learned, truth is much, much stranger than fiction. Take *Blow Dry*, for example. By this time I'd stuck around Total Impact long enough to become an assistant director, and I took the nom de film Eddie Haskell, Wally Cleaver's fuckup friend who was always running afoul of Ward and June on *Leave It to Beaver*. Around that time there was a rumor that Ken Osmond, who played Eddie Haskell, was actually enormously endowed porn star John Holmes, but I don't think I knew that at the time. I only wanted a suitably obnoxious alias.

Eddie Haskell actually had a dual role in *Blow Dry*; I was an AD behind the scenes, and a grunting and giggling mute pervert called Cyrus on screen, following rich, naïve brat Chastity Wadley around with a 16 mm camera wearing nothing but an oversized red football shirt.

Chastity was played by Kristen Steen, who appeared in lots of X-rated and soft-core films in the late '60s and early '70s, like *The Young, Erotic Fanny Hill*; *The Mind Blowers*; and *Alice in Wonderland: An X-Rated Musical Fantasy*.

In *Blow Dry*, our characters were inseparable on screen, even when she was coercing her mother's hairdresser and lover Warren Peace at gunpoint to fuck her in a horse stable. "Come on! Oscillate your pelvis!"

Kristen and I became friends, a friend I fucked only once; probably the worst sex of her life, but I was just so thrilled. I just fell in love with her. And though she wasn't my girlfriend, whenever I'd run away, a year later, in the *PUNK* magazine days, I'd wind up at her place on 14th Street and Avenue B, where we'd listen to *White Light/White Heat* by the Velvet Underground.

I'd always marvel at "The Gift," the fantastic short story by John Cale, told in his gorgeous Welsh accent, about lovesick Waldo Jeffers, who mails himself to his girlfriend and gets stabbed in the head as she tries to open the box.

I'd put "The Gift" up against Flannery O'Connor any day. Cale was expanding the parameters even further. The idea of corrupting the formula, the narrative, or the album as he did when he produced Iggy and the Stooges, Patti Smith's *Horses*, as well as Nico's solo albums.

Kristen Steen got me, got the Velvets, got the art scene. She was a beatnik chick, smart, funny, and incredibly sexy. She really taught me a lot about living in New York, which was hard, even if you didn't live in a closet. She was paying her own rent, and she was well-read. And more importantly, she encouraged artists to take risks.

For example, Kristen took me to a production of the Ballets Russes' *Parade*, which used Pablo Picasso's disorienting Cubist sets and costumes from 1917. It was just fantastic, all these people urging you to come into the circus. They were carnival barkers spewing out the wonders of the attractions inside, for just the price of a ticket. It was the urgency that appealed to me.

I thought *Parade* was a really marvelous premise for a ballet and was grateful to Kristen for getting me into the art scene in a way that I could understand, which was a gift.

Kristen also told me she had made it with Gay Talese, the author of *Thy Neighbor's Wife*, a 1981 bestseller about post–World War II sex in America. Kristen helped him out with his sex research, and amazingly she was able to talk about this stuff, talk about everything, actually, like it wasn't weird for her. It wasn't weird for me either, but it was still eye-opening to find someone who could be so open about the world.

Kristen was a porn star, but that's not doing her justice because she was much more than that. Porn was just one part of her personality; art and living well was a bigger part.

During the summer of 1975 I briefly returned to Cheshire to go swimming at the pond, behind Cheshire Academy, the prep school the entitled went to after getting thrown out of Choate. Cheshire Academy's pond had a giant rope swing to soar out high above the water, allowing swimmers to achieve great heights before letting go and dropping into the water.

Ged Dunn had started a house-painting business, and had an apartment in the center of Cheshire, and John Holmstrom showed up to work painting houses for Ged. Holmstrom wasn't having much luck catching a break in Manhattan and needed a summer job, and we picked up right where we'd left off. We were dating these gorgeous twins, the McCandless sisters, who later became *Vogue* models, and that turned into a competition about which of us scored the more gorgeous of the pair.

"*I've* got the better looking one," Holmstrom would say.

"Oh fuck you," I'd answer. "You can't tell 'em apart!"

Neither of us could actually tell them apart. One night my girlfriend came out of the bathroom, and when I put my arm around her she looked at me like I was a piece of shit. She was John's girlfriend.

Though I'd left Total Impact, I still had visions of becoming a filmmaker, and I started making a movie that should have never gotten off the ground. *The Unthinkables* was a gangster spoof of *The Untouchables*, the early-'60s TV series about the law enforcement agents who took on Al Capone and the Chicago mob, starring Robert Stack as Eliot Ness.

At the heart of *The Unthinkables* was a 1940s Ford my friend Tommy Hearn was supposed to fix up. It was really cool, with running boards and everything.

"You gotta get it done," I kept saying. And I was getting more and more pissed off about it. "You gotta fix it up, Tommy! *We need that car!*"

That's what was holding up *The Unthinkables*. But Tommy never fixed it up, so I decided to make the film without it. And it was a disaster. I got Holmstrom involved, and Tommy, and it was very slapstick. I was trying to make it like a Three Stooges comedy, but it wasn't funny. And I realized it wasn't just not having the car that made it suck; it was my writing. And I knew I had to take it more seriously if I was going to become a filmmaker. Though I felt like shit and cursed myself and everyone around me for my returning to Cheshire, it wound up being ground zero for everything that happened next.

It was right around this time that I first heard *The Dictators Go Girl Crazy!* and it changed my world.

Until that moment, whenever we were at Ged's house, Bob Dylan's *Blood on the Tracks* was on the turntable. And that's a brilliant album; I still love it. But I'd been working at Total Impact and everything there was a hangover from the '60s. Even *Blood on the Tracks* felt like that.

But then Holmstrom turned up with *The Dictators Go Girl Crazy!* and it was something completely new. That's what was so great about the Dictators. They weren't whining about lost love; these were anthems about getting drunk and getting laid on the weekend. It was relatable. It was revolutionary. "The Next Big Thing" opens with a round of applause, a boast, roaring guitars, a Neanderthal stomp. It feels like it's going to fall apart, like a subway train churning through a tunnel. It was excitement, and both Holmstrom and I were completely ready for it.

And almost immediately he was raving about the idea of manifesting that revolutionary spirit into a magazine.

The name: *Teenage News*.

"*Teenage News!*"

I was depressed, because *The Unthinkables* sucked. I was in a lousy mood, because my life wasn't going anywhere. And I was probably hung over, because I was always hung over. So when Holmstrom started raving about *Teenage News*, I just didn't get it.

"*Teenage News*?"

I wasn't sure which was worse: *Teenage News* or his first choice, *Electronic Comic*.

"Teenage News" was a New York Dolls song David Johansen called an "anthem for a generation" in a 1975 live performance, but I don't think it was ever recorded until it turned up four years later on Syl Sylvain's first solo album.

Anyway, the more Holmstrom explained his idea, the more it sounded like homework. I had NOT graduated from high school to do more homework!

But Holmstrom was always ahead of the curve, and I was always trying to catch up. That was the nature of our relationship, and not just because he was a few years older. Only this magazine wasn't an easy sell, even though he pitched it as a combination of everything we loved: rock 'n' roll, comics, rebellion, everything we heard and felt listening to *The Dictators Go Girl Crazy!*

. . . *Teenage News*?

The title reminded me of Scholastic's *Weekly Reader*, the educational newspaper for grammar school kids that was boring even when I *was* a grammar school kid. I only ever read it for the ads for thirty-five-cent mail-order paperbacks, and those would take six months to arrive, which by that time, you'd forgotten you'd even ordered them. Still, it was a big day when Scholastic books arrived.

Holmstrom said it would be anti-Scholastic, and he finally figured out how to get me on board.

"If we start a magazine, people will wanna hang out with us . . ."

"What, *really?*" My interest was piqued.

"If we start a magazine," Holmstrom repeated with his usual confidence, "people are gonna buy us drinks!"

We were nobodies. We were losers. We were punks. And that's what people had called me all my life, a punk. I had one leg longer than the other, so I always slouched, and it looked like I had a shitty attitude. And I *did* have a shitty attitude; I *was* a punk. But it was a physical deformity that fucked up my body *and* my mind.

"*Teenage News* sucks. We can't call it that . . ."

What are we? Broke losers with tons of ambition and no money to see it through, failed hippies who could barely get laid.

Holmstrom asked, "What would *you* call it?"

I just said, "*PUNK*!"

And that was it. Holmstrom never mentioned the word "punk" when we discussed the title for his new magazine, "*Teenage News*," until I suggested it. Period.

Besides, that's what I'd been called all my life, so I might as well use it, right?

But Ged, probably wary of getting involved with something so blatantly dumb, suggested we call it *The Punk Journal*, and I think Holmstrom and I groaned loudly. We were barreling down Interstate 95 at the time, in Ged's old Chevy station wagon, with the fake wood paneling on the side, the only thing holding it together.

"I'll be the editor," Holmstrom said, "and Ged will be the publisher."

I didn't understand what either of those roles actually meant, but all I cared about was my job, anyway.

"And you can be the 'Resident Punk.'" Holmstrom laughed hysterically.

That sounded kinda cool—like Alfred E. Neuman, the gap-toothed mascot for *Mad* magazine, which I pored over at the Morton's Pharmacy lunch counter.

It was the role I was born to play.

"What's in it for me?"

"Whaddya want?"

The negotiations were brief.

"Make me famous and buy me a pack of cigarettes a day."

"Okay," he agreed, and we shook on it.

PUNK's startup would be partially funded by selling Christmas trees, or at least that was the plan. Of course, after we spent an entire day cutting down about forty or fifty trees, they were stolen when we went to dinner. Fucking Connecticut sucks!

Miraculously a backup plan materialized when I earned a thousand bucks fucking a well-heeled older lady in Connecticut. I wasn't a primo gigolo or anything; she wanted to help us get "*my career*" off the ground. Had she known I was also fucking her daughter she might not have been so generous.

A grand could go a long way in 1975, even in New York City. There were apartments in the East Village going for $150 a month, big enough that we could have run our whole operation from the living room. But for some reason, Holmstrom spent $195 on a shitty fucking abandoned used auto parts store at 30th Street and Tenth Avenue in the middle of fucking nowhere!

Today, that corner sits in the shadow of a northwest curve along the High Line, a leafy elevated pedestrian trail built on a disused spur of the old New York Central Railroad that runs from Gansevoort Street up to 34th at the southern edge of the Jacob Javits Convention Center.

It's become a major tourist destination for everyone from families to social media influencers looking for the perfect urban angles. There's a Whole Foods and pickleball. Even the rats are respectable.

The only tourists around 30th and Tenth in 1975 were the late-afternoon bridge and tunnel crowd, looking for a blow job from a transvestite hooker before heading through the mouth of the Lincoln Tunnel—and back to the wife and kids in suburban New Jersey.

"The *PUNK* Dump" was our production headquarters and our home, and it was depressing and disgusting. We moved in on Halloween, an ominous sign. The previous tenants had disappeared, leaving behind their desks and file cabinets, jackets, half-filled cups of coffee, ashtrays with cigarettes burned down to the filter.

For some reason, the windows were painted pitch black. Other than the streaky beams that shot like needles where the windows hadn't been painted well enough, the only natural light that made it inside was when someone opened the front door. Perfect, since I avoided sunlight because my hangovers were so brutal.

Ged had told me he'd arrive at our new headquarters on November 1. He wouldn't turn up for two more weeks, by which time our money was running out. We wanted to talk about our plans for world domination, but the first thing Ged wanted to do was get drunk. And I didn't take much convincing, especially since he'd shown up with five grand.

Ged wasn't sure about the magazine idea and seemed more interested in financing a film company as the opening gambit in our global communications network. Even with *The Unthinkables* being a total bust, a year on the front lines with Total Impact had given me a lot of filmmaking experience and the confidence to match. But within a few weeks, Holmstrom's persistence—a publishing manifesto set to the music of the Dictators—had finally paid off.

But first, we focused on settling in at the *PUNK* Dump. Ged built a loft bed over his desk, with the promise of building one for each of us. You guessed it, he never got around to that.

He'd used up all the wood building his own, and we didn't want to risk stealing any more. And let's face it, I wasn't exactly handy, and I wasn't ever gonna build a fucking loft bed.

So I crashed out on the black office couch.

I was snug as a bedbug in a rug on that couch, until the night the waste pipe above me started to leak and I woke up to sewage dripping onto my head.

Plumbing wasn't our only issue: We had rats, giant rats, and I was definitely more scared of them than they were of me. They grew up in this neighborhood, and I'd just gotten there.

John Holmstrom, me, and Ged Dunn in front of the *PUNK* Dump in 1975.

Photo by Tom Hearn

The *PUNK* Dump had no stove, just a hot plate with a cord the rats chewed on, probably hoping to start a fire and drive us all out. The refrigerator door was held in place with a giant rubber band, and all we ever had in there anyway was an occasional six-pack of cheap beer—and leftover liver and onions.

Ged used to take us down to the meatpacking district and force us to buy tons of chicken livers and onions. “It’s because we drink so much,” Ged said. “It’s the only thing that’ll keep us healthy.”

I didn’t give a shit about health, and when Ged wasn’t loading us up on slop, I’d usually just go get a greasy slice of pizza, which magically soaked up the beer and the hangover.

Holmstrom had really hit the ground running, setting up his office and work area exactly as he wanted. He was already really great at layout, which was handy since he’d be doing every bit of every page himself, including hand-lettering, a time-consuming process that became partly what defined the magazine.

But even though he was buried under his own work, Holmstrom taught me how to write, and even more importantly showed me how to look at things from a different angle. He was always a contrarian, and even when I didn't agree with him, he always had an interesting point of view.

Holmstrom could always see stuff before anybody else, and he had a knack for making it commercial to hipsters.

From the very beginning, we knew we wanted the Dictators to be the cover stars for our first issue of *PUNK*, and Holmstrom suggested I change my name.

He thought it would be hysterical if we held a drinking contest between me and Handsome Dick Manitoba, the lead singer of the Dictators, because Manitoba appeared on their first album cover in a wrestling outfit. I guess Holmstrom didn't think Eddie McNeil was punk enough.

"How about Muscles McNeil?" he laughed.

"Nah."

"How about Arms McNeil?" he continued, as he went through my different body parts until he got to "Legs."

Now that one struck a chord . . . I mean, getting your leg cut off had to amount for something, right? So I said, "Yeah, I like that one . . ."

"Okay, then Legs McNeil it is," Holmstrom decreed, and that was it. Unfortunately the Dictators had broken up already, one of their many breakups, but we did eventually have the drinking contest at Club 82. That's where Andy Shernoff, chief Dictator singer and songwriter, pulled my boxing shorts down to my ankles, leaving me struggling to pull them back up with boxing gloves on, while everyone laughed.

Of course, Roberta Bayley got the photograph!

Roberta worked the door at CBGB but wasn't there the first night we arrived on the Bowery. Holmstrom had already been to CBGB and seen the Ramones in the summer of 1975. The club was holding a month-long Summer Rock Festival—*TOP 40 NEW YORK UNRECORDED*

BANDS—with Talking Heads, Blondie, Television, Patti Smith, Suicide, and Teenage Jesus and the Jerks among them. Holmstrom came away from the experience talking only about the Ramones: Ramones and Dictators, Dictators and Ramones.

Holmstrom told me, "Come on, Legs, we gotta check out this band at CBGB's, they wear black leather jackets and sound like the Dictators . . ."

"Okay, let's go," I said. All he had to do was mention the Dictators and I was in. We stopped by Total Impact to grab a photographer, and that's where we also picked up Mary Harron, who worked there preparing the hippie food. Mary was smart and very pale; she looked very unhappy and very British, so I figured she'd be a good writer. She was actually Canadian, but we couldn't let that stand in our way, we needed writers. I wasn't gonna write the entire issue. I couldn't; I wasn't good enough.

Holmstrom was very smart on the kinda people he wanted to contribute to the magazine, who he wanted as writers and artists. He took the idea of "inspired amateurism" literally. He encouraged and published so many artists and writers that owe their careers to *PUNK* magazine, including me.

CBGB was a dive Bowery bar, the place to go when the D.T.'s descended. It was a Hells Angels hangout, with dog shit littering the floors. Holmstrom paid the cover charge and we marched down the long bar to the stage, and on our way there, I saw that guy who released that horrible *Metal Machine Music* Holmstrom was always playing in the Dump. I said to John, "Hey, there's that guy you're always playing when I tell you to take that shit off!"

It was Lou Reed, sitting at a table with *Rock Scene* editor Richard Robinson, Danny Fields, and Lou's trans girlfriend, the infamous Rachel. It was so dark around the table, lit only by a candle sticking out of an empty Mateus wine bottle, it was hard to see who anyone really was, but I recognized Lou.

I approached his table, saying, "We're from *PUNK* and we're gonna interview you . . ."

"Yeah," Holmstrom said, "we'll even put you on the cover . . ."

Without missing a beat, Lou deadpanned, "Your circulation must be fabulous."

We didn't linger around Lou as the Ramones were about to take the stage, and we hurried to the front where about twenty people had gathered.

The Ramones hit the stage like the SS arrived, looking more like a gang of thugs than a rock 'n' roll band. Dee Dee counted off, "1, 2, 3, 4," and they all began playing a different song. It sound like a louder version of *Metal Machine Music*, and Lou Reed was laughing at his table as the Ramones stopped playing and began arguing with each other on stage. As quickly as they arrived, they were gone again.

My mouth was hanging open, like, *What just happened?* You never saw a rock 'n' roll band display such raw honesty onstage. It was usually just show biz, razzmatazz, like, *"Hey everybody, it's great to be here in New Haven!"*

Fuck that shit, it was never great to be in New Haven!

Then the Ramones hit the stage again, Dee Dee counted off again, and they played the loudest version of "Now I Wanna Sniff Some Glue," and I knew I was home, even though I never sniffed glue, but my best friend Tommy had.

As the Clash's Joe Strummer said about seeing the Ramones for the first time, "You could barely slip a razor between one song to the next, the band was so tight."

Exactly. No bullshit tuning up nor tedious guitar nor drum solos, no talking about writing a song in the garden of your Hollywood Hills home, but lead singer Joey Ramone standing at the microphone, shouting, *"You're a loud mouth baby, you'd better shut it up! Hit it, Dee Dee!"*

With every song, I fell more in love with the Ramones.

After "I Don't Wanna Walk Around with You," the Ramones launched into "Blitzkrieg Bop," and I was in ecstasy.

Danny Fields arranged for us to interview the band after their set climaxed with "Today Your Love, Tomorrow the World," and we all gathered around the band by the pool tables in front of the stage. We didn't know if they were Nazis or gangbangers or what.

Holmstrom and me with the Ramones in New Haven.

Photo by Tom Hearn

But they were just like us! They got the joke! They were just writing songs about their real lives instead of Captain & Tennille's "Love Will Keep Us Together," which was number one on the *Billboard* Hot 100 singles charts for 1975.

No, this was definitely different—but possessed the same sense of humor as us guys and gals at *PUNK* magazine. A match made in rock 'n' roll heaven!

After the set the drummer, Tommy, answered most of the questions, which seemed unusual at the time. Johnny was also very outspoken. Dee Dee was so animated onstage, and the singer, Joey, was . . . well, he was the singer. But the two of them were silent, Joey eating a chicken sandwich and nodding his way through the interview, conducted by Mary Harron.

Mary Harron: Did you hear the Monkees are getting back together?

Tommy Ramone: Oh, one of the highlights of our life. And 1910 Fruitgum Company, "Yummy, Yummy . . ."

In 1975, no musician on the planet wanted to admit that "Yummy, Yummy, Yummy, I've Got Love in My Tummy" was an influence on them! The 1910 Fruitgum Company's bubblegum hit was so retarded, it was hip! The Ramones were exquisitely redefining hip in front of our eyes! And we were all on the same page! Hey Ho, Let's Go!

Unfortunately we did have to go, as Holmstrom pulled me and Mary away from the Ramones to tell me Lou Reed was going over to Mickey Ruskin's new club, The Locale, right next to The Bottom Line. And we were invited to interview him there. Holmstrom was overjoyed.

I wanted to stay and hang out with the Ramones. The lead singer, Joey Ramone, fascinated me. He seemed the most interesting, even though he didn't say a word during the interview. Just giggled into his chicken sandwich.

I mean, *my god,* ***that voice!***

We took a taxi over to The Locale; I was in a particularly bad mood, having been pulled away from the Ramones, to interview an art asshole. I was hungry, thirsty, and the more I gazed at Lou eating this huge, juicy cheeseburger, the more I hated him.

I was a complete obnoxious creep, like I was playing a role, to add some punk credibility. Instead of talking about it, we had to be it!

Even if I'd been in a good mood, The Locale was full of pretentious and intimidating artist types. I didn't make any secret about not wanting to be there, and Lou, who was sitting with his trans girlfriend Rachel Humphreys, was getting off on antagonizing us, taking even bigger bites into his cheeseburger. I think we could only buy one beer that we had to share, which didn't help.

Lou called me an asshole, and I agreed with him, and that summed up the whole fucking night. Starving and cranky, I dragged myself out of The Locale and onto the street.

Mary Harron wasn't in a great mood either. She was shocked at how amateurish we were and how badly the interview had gone, and she was probably regretting ever getting involved with us in the first place.

Holmstrom, though, was over the moon, jumping up and down shouting, ***"We got Lou Reed for the cover! We got Lou Reed for the cover!"***

I said, "Yeah, but did you see that chick he was with?"

The night after the Ramones/Lou Reed experience I went back to CBGB on my own. This time I saw Talking Heads, and their twitchy front man David Byrne introduced every song with his nervous, fey voice: "The next song is called 'The Girls Want to Be with the Girls.'"

I thought, *Wow, there's really something special going on here.* Not just the Ramones, but there's this band, too, and they're fantastic. All the bands were exquisitely different, but they all had this quiet cool, which is something people miss when they argue about what is or isn't punk. It's not just a sound. It's an idea. And everyone at CBGB was just being themselves, which was fantastic, because you never saw that with stadium rock.

But at CBGB, there were real rock stars in a small room who weren't playing hour-long guitar solos. And they were a lot more interesting than Emerson, Lake & fucking Palmer!

That second night at CBGB, listening to "Psycho Killer" on my own, that's when I started feeling like maybe we were onto something. *PUNK* magazine could actually work.

That became even more clear after I saw what Holmstrom had done with the Lou Reed interview, which he turned into a comic strip. And it was hysterical. When Lou was talking about different comic books and artists, Holmstrom drew him in that style, which I thought was just brilliant. And for the cover, he depicted Lou as Frankenstein's monster in the studded leather jacket he wore on the sleeve of *Lou Reed Live*.

Holmstrom had gone from explaining it to me to showing it to me, and I was all in from that moment on.

It was during the making of that first issue of *PUNK* that I caught on to just how much work Holmstrom was doing. And everything Holmstrom did was meticulously cut and pasted by hand onto art boards before it could be reproduced. Millions of zines have done it like that, and many of them stole Holmstrom's aesthetic. And Holmstrom's graphics were just fantastic.

People have tried to duplicate that, and even now they still can't get it.

Holmstrom designed a flyer to promote the magazine: ***WATCH OUT! PUNK IS COMING!!*** and we spent much of December plastering New York City with them. Of course I didn't have gloves, and it was fucking freezing, the wind howling down the street. I'd slap wheat paste onto a flyer, then try to stick it to a lamppost before the paste froze.

It felt like a brilliant guerrilla marketing campaign. Nobody knew what *PUNK* even was, never mind why it might be coming. But they were seeing it all over the place. And they were talking. Probably.

On New Year's Eve we were going to celebrate with the Ramones and the Heartbreakers at this fifth-floor loft club, the Sea of Clouds ($7.50 cover, including champagne toast). After we'd collated the first issue of *PUNK* by hand, I left Perez Printing with ten copies, fresh off the press. Holding it in my hand, it solidified everything. It felt like we were going to take over the world.

I was walking up Broadway to the Sea of Clouds, and as I got closer people were grabbing them out of my hands on the street. I had a few copies left when I got there, and I handed one to Danny Fields and Joey Ramone, and they opened it up to Mary Harron's Ramones story. In Mary's story, Tommy Ramone was talking about how the 1910 Fruitgum Company was a big influence on the band

Danny and Joey opened our magazine to the Ramones centerfold. They were just staring at it and smiling. And at that point, Danny turned to me and said the magic words: "Legs, can I get you a beer?"

There was a night when the enormity of what we'd created actually hit me. We were uptown in some fancy mid-Manhattan restaurant, the kind with fancy dining booths, with curtains you could draw when you wanted to get intimate. Holmstrom and I were there attending some ridiculous press party for the free food and booze that corporations pumped into the publicity machines of bands and movies no one ever heard of. We ate dinner at a different press party every night. Lots of R&B and soul bands, so many that I got tired of eating fried chicken every night, and I went up to a fat Black musician, resembling a linebacker for some pro football team, and said in a low voice, "Don't you think it's a bit racist that all they give you guys is fried chicken?"

He laughed and put his arm around me, then whispered in my ear, *"Any night you're eating dinner for free; you're doing alright! You'll learn, you'll learn!"*

At this fancy uptown press party, Holmstrom and I picked up two sisters and convinced them to hide with us in the booths when they locked the place up at two or three o'clock in the morning. We had the whole place to ourselves—the bar, the private booths with the curtains. After we had intense make-out sessions with the sisters in our own private booths, I went behind the bar for a pack of matches to light my smoke when a janitor came through the door, rolling his mop and bucket.

"Do you know how long we've been locked in here!" I screamed at him. ***"Does your director of publicity know you've detained important members of the press for five hours? We're talking major lawsuit!!!"***

The guy looked like he was gonna cry as he held the door for us. Holmstrom could barely contain his laughter. That was the night we realized the city was ours. We could do whatever we wanted to. I didn't realize that "with great power comes great responsibility," to quote the first *Spider-Man* movie, until after I stopped drinking. But that night was not about stopping for a second but going straight to the Toppermost of the Poppermost!

"Hey Eddie?" Holmstrom asked me, as we walked outside into the kaleidoscope of midtown lights.

"Yeah?"

"Can you feel it?"

"Yeah, yeah, *I can . . .*"

"Me too . . ."

"We're from *PUNK* magazine and we get in for free . . ."

It's the only time I ever used that line, but I was feeling very confident on the success of the first issue. And why shouldn't we be proud? The magazine was great!

The person at the door that we had to get past was Roberta Bayley. She was no pushover. Roberta was absolutely drop-dead gorgeous, and of course, I got a wicked crush on her. So did every other male who met her, and it became so regular that it became a joke.

"What's his problem?"

"He's in love with Roberta . . ."

"Nuff said . . ."

As Roberta tells the story: "Terry Ork asked me to work the door at CBGB's . . ." Terry Ork was Television's manager who Roberta knew because she was Richard Hell's girlfriend.

"He just thought it was a good idea to have a girl on the door. That's when the take at the door was two dollars, but somebody had to sit there and get the two dollars, so it was me."

I led the charge against Roberta.

I said, "I'm Legs McNeil and I get in for free!"

She said, "No, it's two dollars, you have to pay me."

I said, "No, I get in for free."

She said, "Well, okay, give me a copy of the magazine."

I said, "No, it's fifty cents at the bar."

She said, "Alright, that's pretty cool, you go in for free . . ."

Roberta told me later that she went to the bar, paid her fifty cents, and got a copy of the first issue. She took it home with her and read it after work and thought, *Man, I gotta work for these guys, this is incredible!*

Roberta became like an older, wiser big sister, with excellent taste. Always a necessity.

Roberta would say to me, as she sat at the desk at CBGB's door, "You haven't read *Last Exit to Brooklyn? **If you haven't read Hubert Selby, you're an asshole!***"

I was so humiliated I went out and bought a copy of *Last Exit to Brooklyn* the next day and lost myself in the Brooklyn docks flooding with sex and violence.

I'd always enjoyed gang-related books. Because I was too much of a wimp to join a gang, I really loved reading about them, Nicky Cruz's *Run Baby Run;* Piri Thomas's *Down These Mean Streets;* Iceberg Slim's *Pimp;* and, of course, S.E. Hinton's *The Outsiders* and *That Was Then, This Is Now*. Stay Gold, Ponyboy . . .

But *Last Exit to Brooklyn* was the ultimate gang book, because it took you further and imagined what happened to all these gangbangers when they got older. Selby laid out all the racism, sexism, alcoholism, and sheer brutality of the lower classes. Something I was familiar with. As poet Allen Ginsberg said in a pull quote on the paperback, "It will explode like a rusty hellish bombshell over America and still be eagerly read in a hundred years."

Roberta was usually dead-on with her recommendations. She was also a fan of film noir and turned me on to movies like Sam Fuller's *Pickup on South Street* and *The Naked Kiss,* and Nick Ray's *They Live by Night* and *Knock on Any Door.*

In fact, Nick Ray started hanging out at CBGB, fueling the rumors that Richard Hell was going to be the star of Ray's remake of *Rebel Without a Cause.* Although I never really believed it was gonna happen because Ray was a hopeless alcoholic with one foot in the grave, I hoped he would consider me for the role of Plato, James Dean's wimpy sidekick that was played by Sal Mineo, though I had limited acting ability and not much discipline.

Roberta laughed at my aspirations. I don't blame her.

Later, in the pages of *PUNK* magazine, I'd play Richard Hell's sidekick in *The Legend of Nick Detroit* that Roberta so expertly shot, along with

Debbie Harry's photographer boyfriend, Chris Stein. But more on that later.

So fuck Nicholas Ray! Who needs him! Besides, I hated *Rebel Without a Cause*; James Dean overacted his way into the grave . . .

We were all feeling pretty optimistic heading into Christmas 1976 and looking forward to our first real yuletide party at the *PUNK* Dump. I'd found a pathetic tree on the sidewalk so shitty, even Charlie Brown would have said, "No fucking thanks," and we decorated it with trash from around the office, beer cans, and cigarette butts dangling from ornament hooks. The angel was the Debbie Harry "*PUNK* Playmate of the Month" centerfold, shot by Chris Stein for the July issue.

Johnny Ramone and his first wife, Rosana, turned up in the early evening, had a couple of drinks, then left. We were alone again, feeling like nobodies, just like when we moved in a year earlier. Our big party was a bust.

But at around ten o'clock, the doors opened and suddenly nearly everyone we knew from CBGB's and Max's Kansas City were there: Joey and Dee Dee Ramone, Richard Hell, Debbie Harry, Chris Stein, Johnny Thunders, Arturo Vega, Danny Fields, Lisa Robinson, and so many others. And suddenly it was a real party, and I guess the love I was feeling made me forget all the shit I'd been worrying about.

There were no orgies, nothing too bacchanalian. But it was a great night, a good time, a Christmas miracle. All the cool kids thought so.

At some point during the evening, somewhere along the road between just enough and far too many beers, I found myself in a conversation with a pair of writers, Victor Bockris and Jeff Goldberg. I thought they were hitting on me, particularly Victor, not just because he was so effeminate and had a British accent, but because I misread his interest in me.

Victor and Jeff invited me to their place later in the week for a dinner party, and though I figured they were a couple, I'd enjoyed talking to them enough that I went anyway. And they both knew and worked with other interesting people, like William S. Burroughs, Muhammad Ali, and Andy Warhol. In fact, in his 1979 book *Exposures*, Warhol wrote, "Victor Bockris is a brilliant young writer who only writes about three people: William Burroughs, Muhammad Ali, and me."

When I showed up for the party at 106 Perry Street in the West Village, the apartment Victor nabbed from Pat Loud, star of the hit Public Broadcasting series *An American Family*, I was surprised to learn that Victor and Jeff not only weren't a couple, they weren't even gay!

They were interested in me as a writer, a real writer.

And I really wasn't a real writer at that point, but I guess they saw something in me that said otherwise. It was really nice, and fuck, I needed it. Because I was always doubting myself. I still doubt myself.

I was uneasy about the monster I'd helped create, the Resident Punk, so until that night I struggled to imagine becoming a real writer. After *Nick Detroit* I was kind of getting recognized at CBGB, and I discovered I didn't like being famous. I was comfortable with them knowing who I was so they'd take me home. I liked people buying me beers. But I didn't like being mobbed, which was starting to happen more and more.

I was a rock 'n' roll fan, and I wanted to be a fan, not a spectacle. And I wanted to be a writer, and I was beginning to see the possibilities of what I later really explored, oral histories, doing different things with different mediums, mixing and matching, and seeing if they worked or not.

And I think that the best thing about working on *PUNK* magazine is that you realized that 99 percent of the stuff in America was crap. But even so, there were still some things out there worth looking at and appreciating. Like film noir, and Hubert Selby's *Last Exit to Brooklyn*, and Jim Thompson, who was fantastic. And here I was at a party with writers who moved in similar circles.

In 1974, Victor had co-written *Ali: Fighter, Poet, Prophet* with Andrew Wiley, based on his numerous visits to Ali's Pennsylvania training camp ahead of the "Rumble in the Jungle," the famous fight in Kinshasa, Zaire.

Ali shocked the world by talking shit and lying back in the rope-a-dope to coerce the bigger, stronger, younger George Foreman—then the undisputed heavyweight champion—into punching himself out. Ali won by knockout in the eighth round, and the fight, seen by an estimated one billion people around the world on a closed-circuit television broadcast, has long been considered one of the greatest sporting events of all time.

Jeff was a journalist who by 1980 would co-author the fascinating *Flowers in the Blood: The Story of Opium* with Dean Latimer. Eight years later he'd publish an in-depth study of endorphins, *Anatomy of a Scientific Discovery: The Race to Find the Body's Own Morphine*. Jeff was smarter and a better writer than me and Victor. Jeff was also nicer than Victor, which made him much, much nicer than me.

But everyone at the party was nice, and really smart, and interesting. And though part of me screamed *What the fuck are you even doing here?* they'd all made me feel so welcome that I pushed that voice down for the entire night.

Plus I immediately fell in love with Billie Bartlett, Victor's girlfriend, an editor at Knopf, one of the most prestigious publishers in the world. I thought, *I'm in love with this woman and this fey man cannot compete with that!* And when Victor went off to Australia for six weeks, she and I hooked up. Not just once, but for the entire time.

When I say I hooked up with Billie Bartlett, I don't mean we were fucking. She felt it would be a betrayal to Victor, someone she loved, to fuck me, someone she didn't love. She'd blow me, and I'd return the favor, and maybe stick a finger or two inside just to see what my cock was missing. But we didn't fuck. She drew the line at genital penetration, which sounds like a lyric from a lost Television song.

Later I found out she was writing letters to Victor, telling him about our affair. And she was also having an affair with Victor's best friend, and they *were* fucking. And Victor, being a gentleman, always said to me, for years and years after he got back from Australia, "Well, at least you didn't fuck her!"

FIVE

Joey Ramone and me pretending to read.

Photo by Tom Hearn

You doing alright, Legs?” Joey Ramone asked me one Monday night. We were hanging out at Arturo Vega’s loft right around the corner from CBGB. Arturo was the Ramones’ creative director, his loft their HQ. I’d just gotten dumped by Billie Bartlett.

Joey Ramone was the lead singer of the band lots of people on the scene thought would be the next breakout sensation from New York City. *PUNK* magazine believed they were the next Beatles. They were gaining momentum, getting tighter and faster every time they played CBGB, which was about every two weeks or so. Joey had one of the best voices in rock 'n' roll, and though he was an unusual looking guy—six feet, six inches tall and as skinny as me—he was also my best friend, one of the few guys I talked about real shit with.

"No, not really," I mumbled, nursing a Bud tallboy, floating in a sea of self-pity.

"Wanna watch Ted?" Joey asked, as we ambled away from the benzene stink from Arturo's silk-screen operation in the front of the loft to Joey's "bedroom"—a mattress right next to the bathroom in the back, with a small black-and-white portable TV and a hanging sheet for privacy. The lap of luxury.

"Ted" was our code word for *The Mary Tyler Moore Show*, because Ted Baxter, the clueless, knucklehead newscaster in a sky-blue blazer, was our favorite character.

Joey was nursing his own Bud tallboy. Arturo had given in to our whining and shoved a dollar fifty for two tallboys into each of our hands to shut us up. Arturo was an older gay Mexican artist who possessed a rare glow of immense possibility and made us feel like what we were doing was important. Arturo was a fucking saint.

"Yeah, okay, nothing better to do than watch Ted," I mumbled, sitting in the chair next to the mattress that Joey stretched out on. I put my feet up on the edge of the mattress, settling in for two half-hour episodes of *The Mary Tyler Moore Show*. I'd woken up quite a few mornings like this, and I figured one more wouldn't hurt.

"Whatsamatter?" Joey asked.

"Some chick dumped me," I told him.

"That sucks . . ."

"Tell me about it . . ."

"She *got* to you, huh?" Joey quizzed me, twirling his hair around his finger. He was constantly playing with his hair.

"Yeah . . ."

"That's the worst." He looked stuck, as if he was having a memory he couldn't turn away from.

"Yeah . . ."

Victor's girlfriend, Billie Bartlett, had her own apartment in the West Village, on one of those cute, little cobblestone streets that no one I ever knew lived on. Her apartment was lovely, a one-bedroom unit that definitely had a woman's touch: Scarves were wrapped around the base of antique lamps, jewelry was laid out on an antique dresser, clothes were neatly folded or hung up, except for a few cashmere sweaters lying on the bed. Nice, sexy, girlie stuff. Everything smelled fresh and sleek. Just like her.

I was pretty drunk as usual, but I let her pour me a Campari and soda to enhance my feeling like a sophisticated, urbane quasi-intellectual. Even if I had nothing to talk about except rock 'n' roll, comic books, television reruns, and massage-parlor pamphlets.

The last thing that I'd read that was any good was Hubert Selby, Jr.'s *Last Exit to Brooklyn,* which made everything else pale in comparison. Billie wanted to talk about *PUNK* magazine making the "Talk of the Town" section in *The New Yorker* magazine, but that was the least impressive feat among our latest achievements. Besides, I *hated The New Yorker*: They would never run an excerpt from *Last Exit to Brooklyn*. Their short stories never ended, and the articles were a snooze fest. The cartoons sucked, too, always clever—an excuse for not being funny.

"*The New Yorker* is boring as shit," I said, wrapping my arms around her, as Billie put the soda back in the fridge.

"Oh hush," she laughed, turning around so she was facing me. "It's a superb magazine. Truman Capote, Shirley Jackson, John Hersey . . ."

But I wasn't listening; I was just staring in her eyes, dying to kiss her. Then she pecked me on the lips. It was as if she could read my mind, though it wasn't that difficult, and then she ducked out of my grasp.

"It's a sea of type," I continued our argument, "and it makes me seasick every time I see the pages blowing in the wind. Haven't they ever heard of graphic arts?" I was very proud of Holmstrom's graphics in *PUNK* magazine; the entire issue was hand-lettered like a comic strip, affording us the freedom to make individual words ***pop***. Or drip. Ooze. Explode!

"It's their style," Billie said, nervously folding a cashmere sweater on the bed, as I came up behind her and put my arms around her again.

Billie turned her head and looked at me.

"You really turn me on," I whispered. Not the most original line, but an honest one. As I said, I was drunk, and I did nothing to disguise the boner in my pants.

"Obviously," Billie quipped, then tried to lower her head, but my mouth was on hers. And we were locked in a deep kiss, grinding up against one another. And then we were lying on the bed, still making out. And then we had some of our clothes off, she was clutching me, as I kissed her belly, making my way down to her naked triangle . . .

I rolled down her panties and Billie had the most gorgeous little slit, which silently screamed *I'm why you put up with all this shit, why you put up with a stupid name like Legs, with being the Resident Punk, with living in a slum of an office, with sleeping in a crusty old sleeping bag on a broken-down couch, with eating liver and onions twice a day, with getting paid shit wages, with never enough cigarettes—I'M WHAT MAKES IT ALL WORTH IT!*

And her pussy was right.

I took Billie to CBGB and Max's Kansas City to see the best bands of the day, the Ramones, Blondie, Suicide, the Dead Boys. She liked being escorted around town by the Resident Punk of *PUNK* magazine. It gave her street cred, and it was a lot more exciting than poring over manuscripts in her small office at Knopf. She found our time together exciting and liberating—but ultimately not something she wanted to subscribe to full-time.

One night as we were coming from Max's, I was drunk, sniffing the vapors from a small vial of amyl nitrate, getting incredible rushes as we walked hand in hand. I could see Billie eyeing me, as she said, "You might want to cool it with that, Buster . . ."

She always called me "Buster" when she wanted to emphasize a point. I should've listened, but I couldn't hear. Our affair continued until Victor came back from Australia, and she stopped taking my phone calls. I thought it would continue on and on, but Billie decided to put her money on herself. She broke up with her boyfriend, and as I later learned, took up with another one of his friends, who it turned out she'd been seeing the entire time she was with me.

That little minx . . .

"It's bad when you let 'em get inside," Joey mused, still watching the black-and-white TV. It wasn't a very good *Mary* episode—it was the one where Mary and Rhoda join the Divorced People's Club in order to be eligible for the club's cheap plane tickets to Europe, even though neither of them were divorced—and there wasn't much of Ted Baxter in it, so Joey and I just kept talking . . .

"You ever been in love?" I asked.

"Yeah, after I got out of the bin . . ."

"The bin" was our shorthand for the nuthouse. Joey was referring to his short stay in St. Vincent's Hospital a few years earlier.

"Whycha hafta go in?" I asked.

"Oh, ya know." Joey smiled that cryptic smile of his.

"Not really . . ."

"Well," he thought, then smiled even broader and said, "'cause it was—*time.*"

"Time for what?" I giggled.

"Green Jell-O," Joey snorted, "and TV till ten."

We were both laughing. Hard.

"Yeah, green Jell-O and TV till ten," Joey hummed. "That's the way the bin 'as always been . . ."

Joey always liked playing with words, like they were ricocheting around his brain, trapped inside until he could distill them into his own language.

I think it had something to do with his OCD, but why it happened didn't matter. Joey was always a lot of fun.

"Doesn't sound so bad?" I suggested.

"Yeah," he snorted, "it was—*very therapeutic, ha, ha, ha!*"

We laughed some more and sucked on our beers, both lost in thought.

Joey was receiving SSI, Supplemental Security Income, a kind of public assistance, because he'd been deemed "nuts" after his stay in St. Vincent's. So he had some money coming in. "Crazy Money" is what he called it.

Joey was so generous he even took me down to Wall Street one morning and tried to get me signed up for "Crazy Money," too, but the Social Security functionary insisted on seeing a note from a psychiatrist. I was too afraid to go see a shrink, thinking they'd mistake my ruse for reality and lock me up for a monthlong stay in the nuthouse too. So I never went back to the SSI office.

Mostly Joey and I were partners in adventuring to the end of the night, every night. The blistering night was all that mattered. Fuck the daytime: That only served to do some work and watch the clock until the sun was ready to retire. It seemed as though every night was another chance to live out our fantasies—whatever they were at that moment—and to taste the whim of sex, drugs, and rock 'n' roll again. Joey and I would inevitably get drunk, try to pick up some chicks, and see where the darkness led us . . .

But every now and then, we'd take a Monday night off and stay in at Arturo's and watch TV.

"I hate fucking Monday nights," I said, counting and recounting the number of Marlboros I had left in the pack. "Mondays always feel like Sundays used to feel . . ."

"Hey Legs, I wonder if ten years from now," Joey deliberated, "will Tuesday nights feel like Monday nights feel now?"

"Good question." I snickered. It made sense. As weird as Joey behaved sometimes, he always made perfect sense. He was a complicated but profound thinker.

"Like how Friday nights used to feel in the bin, ya know?" he added, his OCD not letting go of the thought.

"So who was the girl you fell for?" I pressed.

"Just some chick," Joey shrugged, getting moody, still playing with his hair. "But I let her *in,* ya know?"

"Yeah . . ."

"If only you could fuck 'em, and not fall for 'em," he laughed. "That would be *great* . . ."

"*Yeah* . . ."

"It really sucks when you're sitting around wondering what she's doing, ya know? Like that Boyce and Hart song, 'I Wonder What She's Doing Tonight?' That song says it all, ya know?"

"I know, man . . ."

Joey was an incurable romantic who believed in the concept of a perfect love but didn't mind indulging in the tasty treats that hung out at CBGB while he waited. We were just starting to get really hot chicks on a regular basis, but we still had to take what we could get, and sometimes that was nothing—like tonight. Sometimes that was nursing a Bud tallboy and watching reruns of Ted.

"I wonder if *they* ever sit around wondering what we're doing, ya know?" Joey mused. "Like, if they're out there watching Ted, thinking, 'Hey, what's Joey and Legs doing tonight?' I wonder if their hearts hurt as much as ours, ya know?"

"I'd like to think so," I griped, "but I doubt it . . ."

"*FUCKING CUNTS!*" Joey burst into hysterics. "Why? Just 'cause we *fucked* somebody else?" He was doubled over, holding his stomach, laughing so hard at the absurdity of his argument. I couldn't help it; I was in hysterics along with him.

It was hard to imagine that this tall, long-haired, instinctive genius was the forerunner of a cultural movement that would shake the world and change the course of rock 'n' roll history. I mean, Joey couldn't even find his fucking sneakers.

I think that was the key to the Ramones' eventual success: They made it look so simple, they inspired the world.

I spent most of my time with Joey drinking at CBGB, since it was literally around the corner, and stumbling around the Lower East Side looking for one of Joey's long-lost girlfriends.

"I met her in the bin." Joey giggled. "She didn't have a phone . . ."

So we'd wander around the Bowery until Joey came to a familiar-looking building and we'd scream out the girl's name at the top of our lungs until the people in the tenements above emptied their trash on us.

We'd never find the girl, and we wound up passing out in front of the late-night Ted reruns instead, waking up the next afternoon in the same bed, fully clothed in our black leather jackets, wondering who'd hit us over the head. Joey'd look at me first thing and disappear into the bathroom for two hours and then reappear and spend the rest of the afternoon searching for his sneakers, finding them just in time to hit the bars.

I don't know how Arturo put up with us. But he loved us, and we loved him. Even if we didn't always totally see eye to eye.

"*ABBA?* Really Arturo? *ABBA?*" I shook my head in disbelief as I entered his loft, where the latest chart-topper by the Swedish pop band blared from the record player. The sound was coming from the corner of a table on which sat the Ramones' entire silk-screen operation.

On the counter was a wooden silk-screen frame, cans of white acrylic paint, and stacks of black T-shirts. Arturo made another pass with the squeegee over the latest model of the new Ramones logo, with the names of Johnny, Joey, Dee Dee, and Tommy encircling an American eagle with a baseball bat clutched in one talon and an apple-tree branch in the other. It would become their most famous design ever.

"Aren't they wonderful?" Arturo beamed at me, looking up from the T-shirt.

I couldn't tell if he was talking about the music or the T-shirts.

Arturo was never self-conscious about his musical guilty pleasures.

Let's face it: Even though ABBA was spectacularly popular, no one would ever accuse them of being hip or figure they'd be on the stereo here at the epicenter of punk, the Ramones' loft at 6 East 2nd Street.

But that was the beauty of Arturo. He would combine elements that didn't fit and make it actually work. Though, I wasn't so sure hearing ABBA in the Ramones' loft was an experiment that worked.

"ABBA is like some Satanic bubblegum that you can't stop chewing, ya know?" Arturo explained, noticing my displeasure. "Es like what you think happiness should sound like, right?"

"I don't know about that," I said, considering his theory. The Swedish pop music was way too loud, way too jovial. Way too ABBA.

"*You are the dancing queen, young and sweet, only seventeen . . .*"

"That's happiness?" I scowled. "Give me the fucking alternative . . ."

"Happy, happy, happy!" Arturo chuckled, using a line from the Ramones' "Gimme Gimme Shock Treatment," as he pulled a freshly printed T-shirt out from under the screen and replaced it with another.

"Happy, happy, happy" became sort of a mantra around the Ramones, especially whenever things weren't looking too good for the band, which was pretty much all the time.

Arturo would smile that inviting smile of his and, overflowing with irony, say "Happy, happy, happy!" Then everyone would kinda snicker, suck in their gut, and keep on going.

Sometimes a line from a song is all you have to go on, a rallying cry. It was their version of the Beatles' "To the Toppermost of the Poppermost!"

Arturo held the freshly screened shirt up for me to inspect. "Isn't it beautiful! Es so . . . so . . . so *majestic*! Like, the awe of the presidential seal combined with 'Beat on the Brat' honesty, right?"

He wasn't just pleased with his new design, he was thrilled. It really was already an iconic symbol. "Wow, really cool," I said admiringly. "Can I have one?"

Arturo rolled his eyes. "Donchoo ever have any money? Doesn't

Holmstrom pay you? You know, Legs Muck Neil, maybe you should be looking for another job?"

"Doing what?" I moped, knowing that now wasn't the time to hit him up for a pack of smokes and a tall boy of Bud. I only had three Marlboros left. Shit. At least the ABBA album finished, and Arturo didn't restart it like he usually did. So that was a plus.

"I don't know. There's gotta be something you can do." He thought hard before breaking out laughing at the absurdity of his own words.

"Never mind! Of course you can have a shirt, but you gotta wait until we get back from London, this has to last us the whole time!"

"Why are you guys going to England, anyway?" I griped, not seeing any benefit to the Ramones' upcoming weekend in the UK. I knew about Malcolm McLaren and the cool rock 'n' roll fashions coming out of the King's Road, but I didn't think there was much happening musicwise in London. Maybe Dr. Feelgood.

Besides, who was I gonna hang out with over Fourth of July weekend? Holmstrom and Ged were fighting again, so not much fun to hang with.

Though I wasn't aware of it at the time, the English punk rock explosion was waiting for the Ramones to show them how to detonate the bomb. It would only be a matter of days before the shit hit the fan. I continued griping. "Come on, England sucks. There's nothing going on there! I mean, warm beer—you call that civilization?"

"You'd rather we stayed here and played My Father's Place?" Arturo deadpanned, referring to a shitty nightclub out on Long Island that was a hangout for the mullet set that were becoming the Ramones' staple. There weren't many places that welcomed the Ramones outside of Max's and CBGB. It was a pretty desperate situation all around; none of us could understand the resistance to the world's greatest rock 'n' roll band.

"I think we should take over a radio station," I offered, growing excited. "We could, like, barricade ourselves inside and just blast the Ramones for twenty-four hours until everyone realizes how great they are! You know, like that DJ did in *The Buddy Holly Story*, how he just locked himself in and played 'That'll Be the Day' over and over."

Arturo just smiled at me. "You're such a child, arenchoo? You know, they do have SWAT teams now, ha, ha, ha! You'd be dead before 'Today Your Love, Tomorrow the World' finished!"

"Well, at least it was an idea," I mumbled, defending myself. "There's gotta be some way of getting the music out there."

I was interrupted by Joey Ramone bursting through the door, happy and excited for his upcoming weekend in England. He was gushing and fired out a machine-gun greeting: "Hey Legs, what's happening? What's going on? Where's the party?"

Joey was carrying a few packages, and he dumped them on the kitchen counter before joining us around the silk-screen operation. His enthusiasm for England only made me sadder and lonelier.

"Hey," I nodded to Joey. "Where were you?"

"My mom had to take me shopping," Joey explained. "I had to get some shit for the trip, but when we went to get my vitamins, there was like this crazy homeless lady inside the health-food store who was screaming at the cashier. I thought she was gonna murder somebody, she was like really nuts. So we had to wait for the cops to come. I thought they were gonna pack her off to Bellevue, but all they did was take her name and address—and then they just left her there to continue her tantrum, man. The cops probably went back to get more doughnuts. So it was taking like hours, and it turned out all she wanted was a birthday card for her nephew. So I helped her pick one out, a real funny one."

"You shoulda mailed it for her," Arturo joked. "I can just see the headline: 'Twenty-Seven Massacred at Fourteenth Street Post Office, Little Boy Says His Aunt Never Forgot a Birthday.'"

"She wasn't that bad, for a nut, ya know?" Joey smiled as he looped a strand of hair around his index finger. He never stopped playing with his hair. Ever. "And she even paid me for helping her, she gave me a quarter!"

"Save it for her legal defense fund," Arturo quipped as he ran the squeegee over another T-shirt. "She's probably one of these eccentric millionaires who es gonna leave all her money to her cats."

"Maybe I can get Paul in her will too?" Joey quipped. Paul was Joey's cat. Joey loved Paul. He grabbed a shopping bag off the kitchen counter and pored over it, searching for something. Whatever it was, he couldn't find it. He was even worse than me, and I lose everything immediately.

Most of Joey's mornings at the loft were spent searching for shit—scraps of paper with girls' phone numbers on them, articles of clothing, a pair of sneakers—anything. Searching for Joey's stuff was a daily ritual.

"Yeah, she probably had millions stashed under her mattress," Joey laughed, abandoning the shopping bag. "That cheap bitch, she probably had thousands in cash on her. I shoulda frisked her, but she wasn't smelling too good."

We all broke out in fits of laughter.

"So whatta we doing tonight?" Joey asked, as he stared at some of the finished T-shirts hanging out to dry. "And why does John's name always have to come first?"

Arturo ignored the question. He knew better than to open that can of worms.

"Johnny says he can't afford to pay me to go to England," Arturo explained, dodging Joey's query. He'd become an expert at navigating the Ramones' complex internal politics. "He said I can keep all the money I make selling T-shirts, so I thought I'd make a bunch of 'em to pay for my airfare and expenses. John said he didn't know why anyone would want to buy a Ramones T-shirt, but I was welcome to try and sell 'em."

"Yeah," Joey snorted again. "Always the optimist, ain't he?"

Joey was already tired of Johnny Ramone taking all the enthusiasm out of the Ramones' creative possibilities with his excruciatingly practical approach to band business.

"I think they look really cool, ya know?" Joey said, admiring the T-shirt design, pretending to get past the order of names on the shirts. But Joey could never let anything go. "It's like one of those presidential things, ya know? That they hang on his desk whenever he speaks? What are they called? Emblems?"

"Presidential *seals*," Arturo corrected him as he dropped the needle on ABBA again.

"Uh-oh," Joey cracked. "I feel a 'Dancing Queen' about to rape me! You know this is crap, right?"

"Es happy music!" Arturo laughed, singing along with the record. "I was telling Legs, es what happiness is supposed to sound like!"

"No one was ever that happy," Joey cracked. "Except you."

"Oh, go on and be the big, bad punk rockers," Arturo told us, glowing. "It makes me happy, and es all that matters, right?"

"Happy, happy, happy!" Joey laughed, mesmerized by Arturo's assembly-line production as he silk-screened the shirts. Arturo fell into a faster pace, bolstered by the Swedish pop music.

We just stood over him, watching him work.

"It would be really cool if we sold some shirts, ya know?" Joey mused, looking at me and dreaming. "Imagine how great the Ramones' presidential seal would look stretched across a big pair of breasts! And then maybe we can afford to eat breakfast, ha, ha, ha!"

And we were all laughing again.

SIX

"I'm gonna make you millionaires!"

Anyone says that, you're probably gonna listen. But in this case it was Tom Forçade, who looked like an Old West outlaw, which in a way he was. Forçade wore what was probably the first pair of cowboy boots to ever set foot in the *PUNK* Dump, and he arrived with promises of wealth and fortune.

He showed up midway through 1976, when *PUNK* was getting plenty of attention, but we still didn't know how to pay for the next issue, never mind our own survival.

Forçade made his first fortune as a drug dealer, quickly learning how to fly between Arizona and both Mexico and Colombia so he could run the entire operation himself. After connecting with the Underground Press Syndicate, later the Alternative Press Syndicate, collective, he grew their membership from several papers to hundreds.

In 1970, Forçade was called before a Senate subcommittee during the President's Commission on Obscenity and Pornography, showing his disdain for the whole enterprise by hitting Chairman Otto Larsen in the face with a pie.

Just two years before moseying into the *PUNK* Dump, Forçade founded *High Times*, a monthly magazine devoted to celebrating and legalizing marijuana, activism, sex, and other countercultural ideals. It was an instant hit, and by 1976 *High Times* had a monthly circulation of over half a million and revenues of around $10 million.

Forçade said he was gonna take over our distribution, and in return we'd all get rich. Before he left the *PUNK* Dump, he gave each of us a brand new one-hundred-dollar bill. It was happening just like we'd imagined it would, though Holmstrom seemed unsettled by Ged's dollar signs, but who gave a shit, our dream was finally being realized!

With our hundred-dollar bills, John, Ged, and I all took our respective girlfriends out to dinner at Pete's Tavern for a proper celebratory dinner. I was seeing the most gorgeous Puerto Rican banker, Kiki O'Brian, who was blessed with the most gorgeous skin and the perkiest small breasts that turned me on, constantly. All we did was fuck.

And here we were having a food fight inside a private dining room inside Pete's Tavern, and we were fucking signing a major publishing deal with one of the true outlaws of the counterculture: Tom Forçade!

This scheme of ours was actually working! No more worrying about where the money was coming from! No more fucking pizza for breakfast, lunch, and dinner! No more worrying how many smokes were left in the pack! No more worrying!

And I was having sex with a beautiful woman who was into me as much as I was into her.

Tom Forçade had a huge loft above a bakery in Greenwich Village, and he invited us over under the guise of getting to know his new partners, but what he meant by that was showing off his stereo system, with speakers so tall I had no idea how he even got them into the place.

Bonding for Tom Forçade was playing a record so loud it liquified my organs and ground my bones into dust.

Holmstrom was skeptical of our new benefactor and his open paranoia, but Dunn was impressed and believed in Forçade and *High Times*, imagining himself lighting cigars with hundred-dollar bills by the end of the year. Me, I was caught in the middle, philosophically agreeing with Holmstrom, but hooked on the idea of diving into a swimming pool full of money like Scrooge McDuck.

Forçade and Dunn came to an agreement about doing an eight-page *PUNK* insert for *High Times*, and Holmstrom was like, "Why are you giving me more fucking work?"

There always seemed to be tension between Holmstrom and Dunn, like two raccoons in an alley fighting over a moldy ham sandwich. And like always, I got caught in the crossfire.

Even with the promise of *PUNK* sucking at the golden teat of the *High Times* empire, Holmstrom was already stressed-out about putting issue #6 together. Because he did so much of the work himself, he was held together by chewing gum and tension. But throwing a glossy eight-page insert onto his personal dumpster fire put him on the edge. So that was probably the worst time for me to pitch my idea for a fumetti series called *The Legend of Nick Detroit* starring Richard Hell.

SEVEN

Besides hanging out with Joey Ramone, I was also good friends with Richard Hell, who I went down the Mississippi River with in 1985 during flood season, to celebrate the one hundredth anniversary of the publication of *Adventures of Huckleberry Finn.*

The river was nineteen and a half feet deeper than normal.

Instead of being a half mile across, it was now two or three miles across.

Every island, farmland, or forest within two or three miles of the Mississippi was under water. Barge traffic was suspended, as well as all commercial shipping.

We were traveling in three rubber rafts—and Hell was in one of his rare overzealous, "Let's play pirates!" moods.

I was trying to quit drinking, while eating Valium like M&M's. (Don't try it, it doesn't work.)

Right before we got on the river, Richard made a call to his wife, rock star Patty Smyth, who'd had the hit single "The Warrior" with her band, Scandal. Richard had decided, for the sake of "authentic journalism," that we should document every moment of our trip.

So I was standing next to Hell inside a phone booth in Hannibal, Missouri, just off the river, holding the tape recorder as Richard said all the things to Patty Smyth all newlyweds purr: "I miss you, honey, I love you," "Me too," "I can't wait to see you . . ."

As soon as he hung up the phone, Richard was shouting, ***"Why did I get married? Why? Why? Why? What the fuck was I thinking?"***

He was shouting at me as if I were to blame.

"Yeah, Richard," I finally asked, bewildered by his frantic mood swing, "*Why did you get married?*"

"Shut the fuck up, Legs!" Richard shot back, and I believe that was the basis of our relationship. I was easily dismissible to Hell, except I had connections with magazine editors.

This scam was being funded by *SPIN* magazine, since Halley's Comet was coming round the bend again and had a huge impact on authentic American folklore and literature, as it only came around every seventy-five years or so.

Mark Twain was born two weeks after Halley's Comet's closest approach in 1835, prompting him to declare in 1909:

> *I came in with Halley's Comet in 1835. It is coming again next year, and I expect to go out with it. It will be the greatest disappointment of my life if I don't go out with Halley's Comet. The Almighty has said, no doubt: "Now here are these two unaccountable freaks; they came in together, they must go out together."*

Unaccountable freaks. Pretty cool, right? That summed up me and Richard to a T.

Although I always loved *Tom Sawyer* and *Huck Finn,* I much preferred Twain's *Life on the Mississippi*, since it's Samuel Clemens's (Mark Twain's real name) true account of his younger years spent as a riverboat pilot. In the book, he remembers navigating between every sandbar and shallow strait, describing every half-hidden clump of tree stumps and sunken logs with the same beauty as T. E. Lawrence describes every rock and sand dune in *The Seven Pillars of Wisdom,* where he brings the desert alive in Technicolor.

Of course, Richard Hell, being a sensitive, sensualist poet, spent his off hours writing poems about deer and fawns, that I hated, but that made the girls fall in love with him even more. Which is why Richard got the cooler name for the title of this swindle, "The Adventures of Huckleberry Hell and Legs Sawyer" for *SPIN* magazine's November 1986 issue.

Richard was playing his part to the max. He showed up for a publicity photo shoot with a straw hat and a long piece of straw hanging from his mouth.

As with all Richard's schemes, he thought this might be the big one to get him out of working for a living—and if not, it was a chance to play pirates and find buried treasure! There are not too many people you can dream out loud with, but Richard Hell was one of those generous explorers who invited me inside his fantastic illusory bubble—overflowing with outlandish possibilities.

In 2015 while promoting his new book of essays, *Massive Pissed Love,* Richard was asked about our Mississippi odyssey by Iowa literary magazine *Little Village*.

"That was a blast," Richard gushed. "I thought, 'This is the life, you just think of something interesting to do and approach some editor and get them to pay for you to do it—and not only that, but then they pay you more to write what it was like?!' That looked promising."

Richard in a bad mood is a nightmare. A solipsistic, stubborn, unforgiving cunt.

But when he was fun, he was a riot.

Which led to Hell's harebrained scheme of floating down the Mississippi like Tom and Huck on plastic rafts during the one hundredth anniversary of the publication of *Adventures of Huckleberry Finn.*

Except when we finally arrived in Hannibal, Missouri, we discovered the Mississippi River was completely flooded, and we were gonna have to spend the last hour each day paddling to find shore before the sun went down. And we never knew where we were sleeping. One night at a car wash. Another at a dog kennel or an all-night laundromat.

All of this thrilled Huckleberry, who wrote in our *SPIN* article, "*I'm forever amazed at how much fun it is to leave. Arriving has its points, but leaving is inexhaustible. And what better opportunity for leaving could there be than a drift down a river, because what does a river do but leave?*"

Richard was especially tickled that it was a law on the Mississippi River that any floating craft that sailed down to a lock had to be lowered to the next water level, no matter how small the boat. Even plastic rafts.

When we arrived at US Lock and Dam 22 near Saverton, Missouri, Huckleberry delighted in watching them fill these gigantic locks with water until they reached our river level—just for us!

Then they opened the lock doors and we sailed on, laughing hysterically as they slowly let the water out. It would take almost an hour, and we'd float around as the water drained, excited that these blue-collar longshoremen would indulge our Huck and Tom fantasy! We really were on the Mississippi River, on fucking rafts, having a true adventure.

Richard has that weird knack of getting strangers to do things for him. Usually without even asking them to. That's when the Mystic Huckleberry Hell emerged. On the night we spent at the all-night laundromat, we had to cross some railroad tracks, and Huck spotted a dead black cat.

He said, "We gotta put the dead, black cat into a tree stump at midnight if we want to get good luck on the river and find buried treasure!"

The way he said "on the river" was creepy, an *Apocalypse Now* sacred reverence to how everyone we came into contact with owed their livelihood to this wild river that did what it wanted.

And everybody we met was as broke as us.

Yeah, Richard was into it, but I had him beat—when the next night we slept on top of a levee and the next morning I ran into a bear. The flooding everywhere had the animals freaked out. I heard this tremendous *ker-plunk*, and saw this black, extremely fat, shaggy dog waddling to the top of the levee. Suddenly, I realized it was a bear, and the beast just glanced at me like, *What the fuck are you looking at?*

Then it waddled down the other side of the levee, and loudly *ker-plunked* back into the water. I heard the bear crashing through the smaller treetops sprouting out of the water, searching for more solid ground, until it faded away.

Richard was pissed he didn't get to see the bear: "No really, tell me the truth, you didn't *really* see a bear?"

We fought about that all morning, until Huckleberry Hell walked down to the levee where I'd seen the black bear, and then came back a half hour later and said, "You didn't *really* see a bear . . ."

Oh fuck you, Richard, I did too.

My biggest fear on the Mississippi was being swallowed up by one of the huge barges that were docked all along the river. Barge traffic was prohibited during flood season, but who was to say when they'd be allowed to move again? We were trying to make it to St. Louis from Hannibal, Missouri, about 120 miles away, so we'd be on the river for a week or so. The barges were like giant train cars, with as many as forty barges being pushed by a tiny tugboat, which was about nine or ten football fields behind them.

And what would happen if they suddenly started moving again? What would happen if we rounded a bend in the Mississippi and spied one of those monsters barreling down on us? We'd be dead!

It's not like they had a guy in the first barge looking out for two knuckleheads in rubber rafts! In fact, the barges had no crew members on board. They were all on the tugboat, miles behind the trains!

As one river rat at Lock and Dam 22 told me, "A standard Mississippi river barge is two hundred feet long and thirty-five feet wide, and a typical tow includes as many as fifteen barges. Give 'em plenty of space to maneuver."

Give *them* plenty of space? Fuck you, what about us?

The scariest thing about the barges were their gigantic mouths that ate up everything they soared over! Their open mouths seemed about a hundred feet high and had a menacing glare—like a gigantic catamaran with only two skinny hulls on either side of its huge gaping jaws. Yeah, we'd be dead alright. No matter how furiously we'd paddle, they were just too big, and we were just too small.

Richard was completely unconcerned about the possibility of barge traffic resuming.

"Barge traffic has been halted, so what are you worried about?"

"What happens when they get going again?"

"Then we'll get out of their way."

"Do you see how big they are?"

"Legs, who knew you were such a wimp?"

"I was fearless when I was drinking . . ."

Time for another handful of Valium.

Richard and I had made a pact before we arrived in Hannibal that neither of us would drink or take drugs while we were on the river. Richard seemed drunk on the freedom; I kept having nightmares about the barges swallowing us up. I sure could've used a couple of beers; instead I kept sneaking vitamin V's from the big bottle I'd brought from New York.

Richard and I were never known as the most sober guys you'd ever meet; in fact, just the opposite. Richard was the first person I ever saw shoot up heroin in front of me. It was very quick, and he didn't seem high, just normal, and I thought, *Geez, does he have to do that every time he leaves the house?*

It never occurred to me to realize I always needed a few beers before I left the house. Brilliant, right? I never liked hanging out with junkies, like Johnny Thunders or Nancy Spungen, but Richard was different; he had a magical presence that was mostly smart and funny.

As Richard wrote in our *SPIN* story:

Legs and I go back a long way. He and his friend John Holmstrom were responsible for applying the name "punk" to the music we slum folk were playing at CBGB's, in '76. Punk promoted the beery white, cartoon, high school version of rock 'n' roll cherished by its founders. Legs was famous for being obnoxious, but only if he knew you well enough to try. A guy frequently forced to apologize, though not frequently enough, sort of like a court jester.

Maybe Richard wasn't so funny after all.

I don't know how we started hanging out; I usually just showed up and bugged people until they let me in. Hanging with Richard probably happened because Roberta Bayley and Richard had been lovers, and Richard was Roberta's best friend, and Roberta used to ask me if I wanted to hang out with them. I guess I amused them, or I just invited myself along.

I was inspired hanging out with Richard to write *Nick Detroit*, because he was so cool-looking. I mean he looked like Clint Eastwood; you couldn't take your eyes off him. And Hell acted like he really didn't care, because he really *didn't give a fuck about anything*—except the next get-rich-quick scheme so he wouldn't have to work for a living. Richard Hell was one of the laziest babe magnets I'd ever met. He always had very hot girls around him. Usually skinny, French junkies, or they looked like junkie wannabes. It took twenty years before junkie chic finally caught on.

Even though Richard reminded me of Clint Eastwood, there was also something very Humphrey Bogart about him, and I thought he'd make a great star in a private detective movie. Like Rick of Rick's Café, in *Casablanca,* probably because Richard Hell had that same type of "I couldn't give two shits about anything" attitude. That bored, cutting Bogart personality before Ilsa Lund comes walking into Rick's Café, only Richard Hell wasn't acting.

He hated being a rock star because it was hard work, and he only wanted the perks of being a star. The girls, the drinks, the meals, the drugs, and the adventures. I never once saw him rehearsing with his guitar, and every time he played live he looked like he was learning the chords for the first time, so it always sounded very frantic—the way Richard looked.

One day I was with Roberta, walking up St. Mark's Place or 14th Street, and we were on our way up to Andy Warhol's Factory, because I'd usually drop off the new issue of *PUNK* magazine to Andy when it came back from the printer. Holmstrom told me to get a picture of Andy holding the magazine the next time I dropped the new issue off. I usually did what Holmstrom told me, otherwise he wouldn't buy me a pack of cigarettes a day.

Anyway, Roberta and I ran into Richard and invited him to come to the Factory with us. She was glad when he agreed so she'd have someone more interesting to shoot than just me and Andy.

Roberta, Richard, and I were just dazzled by Andy and his paintings, and we were just laughing and giggling at the goings on at the Factory. Andy was working on his giant black-and-white silk screens of skulls that I thought were just beautiful. The large studio reeked of that sweet, fresh paint smell since silk screens were littering the floor, drying everywhere.

As John Cale said in a 2002 interview with *The Guardian*, "It wasn't called the Factory for nothing. It was where the assembly line for the silk screens happened . . . Every day something new."

Andy was a serious worker but always seemed happy to talk about his work while he was actually doing it.

At some point Andy would pick up the new issue of *PUNK*, always very slowly and very carefully studying it. Then he'd say, "*Oh, oh, oh, oh, oh, this is so great! You guys have all the ideas! I don't have any! I wish I had ideas like this!*"

The sad thing was, I think he meant it, for the Factory was the place where art and commerce really collided. All these guys in Brooks Brothers suits, looking like real adults, guys like Vincent Fremont and Fred Hughes, glaring at you. And then you'd see Brazilian soccer star Pelé dressed in a full ermine coat, surrounded by two gorgeous models, chatting away with writer Bob Colacello or artist Ronnie Cutrone.

So Richard, Roberta, Andy, and I all just got to talking, and we forgot about taking the photo of Andy Warhol reading the magazine. Instead, Roberta asked us to stand in front of one of Andy's skull paintings, Richard, me, and Andy, and clicked the shutter. It's such a great photo; it truly captures the spirit of the moment. Yeah, this *PUNK* magazine could really go places, literally and figuratively.

Richard Hell, me, and Andy Warhol in front of one of Andy's fantastic skull paintings.
Photo by Roberta Bayley

And yeah, there was really something we could do with Richard Hell, he was such a presence, as was Blondie's Debbie Harry, scenester Anya Phillips, New York Doll David Johansen, Joey and Dee Dee Ramone, Patti Smith, Lenny Kaye, Talking Heads, etc., etc., which prompted me to say to Holmstrom, "I feel like we're surrounded by all these movie stars, *but no one knows who they are yet!*"

That's when I first told Holmstrom about the idea of shooting a movie on paper, like a photo comic of Will Eisner's *The Spirit.* I was heavily influenced by *The Spirit,* and Holmstrom actually knew Will Eisner and another famous cartoonist, Harvey Kurtzman of *Mad* magazine, as his teachers when he attended the School of Visual Arts. I mean, how cool is that? Holmstrom even arranged for me to interview Will Eisner and I just sat there in awe, but the tape was stolen before I had it transcribed.

But instead of Eisner's friendly superhero, Denny Colt, my superhero would be this protofascist, psychopathic killer named Nick Detroit, played by Richard Hell. In my version, Nick Detroit gets rehired by the police chief, played by Bob Quine, the genius guitarist from Hell's new band, the Voidoids, and the only bald guy I knew.

The chief tells Nick that the city's leading mobsters are getting bumped off one by one, and he wants Nick to find out who's doing the killings. Turns out the murders are being committed by a gang of Nazi Dykes, or, if you prefer the politically correct term, "Fascist Feminists," who are pissed off that the male mobsters always get to be the bad guys—and never the women! So they are on a mission to wipe out the mob and take over the city's rackets, and dare I say it, "Rule the World!"

I didn't want Nick Detroit to be the entire issue of the magazine. My first suggestion was that it could run four or six pages, every issue. "*See who gets murdered next month, will it be David Johansen or the Talking Heads? So join us as we present Chapter Seven of* The Legend of Nick Detroit*!*"

Kind of like a serialized photo-comic book version of *Rock Scene* magazine, the hippest rock rag on the East Coast, that was all backstage photos, usually by Bob Gruen, which Lisa Robinson edited and had funny photo captions written by Lenny Kaye.

Holmstrom was exhausted from producing the first five genius issues of *PUNK,* and he suddenly had to produce an eight-page *PUNK* insert for *High Times*. John was burnt the fuck out!

He had to paginate the entire magazine on one of those circular slide rulers, used for mathematical calculations before computers. He had to make sure the color separations for the cover were exactly on register. And he had to hand-letter, and get me to design T-shirt ads, among other hassles.

I could tell just how strung out Holmstrom was when I again brought up serializing *The Legend of Nick Detroit*:

He said, "Make it the entire issue. I have to recover from the last six months. I really need you to do this . . ."

"The script's not finished . . ."

"C'mon Eddie, help me out . . ."

"Will I have a budget?" I asked.

"Yeah, how much?"

"Like five hundred bucks?" I said. That was a lot of cigarettes at seventy-five cents a pack, and that was a lot of beer for $2.99 a six-pack.

"You can only have $250."

"When's it due?"

"Two weeks for you to shoot it, then another week or two for us to lay it all out."

When I got the money, I was buying drinks and asking every early band member from CBGB to be in it. I got Lenny Kaye being machine-gunned in a telephone booth. I got Talking Heads getting machine-gunned in a barbershop. I got Robert Gordon and the Tuff Darts getting ambushed as they climb out of their limo. I got Holmstrom's girlfriend, Judy LaPilusa, to play Nick Detroit's love interest. Judy was one of the most gorgeous and sexiest women I'd ever seen. Judy looked like a cross between a thinner Lauren Bacall and the sexiest and skinniest raven-haired model from *Oui* magazine, *Playboy*'s sexier and hipper alternative.

I mean, come on, who wouldn't want to see that movie!

Roberta Bayley shot most of *Nick Detroit,* with some help from Chris Stein, Debbie Harry's long-term partner and collaborator. My favorite moment on the *Nick Detroit* shoot was standing at the turnstiles at the Staten Island Ferry as I dropped a quarter into the slot so another of the hundreds of malcontents from CBGB could board. It was probably the biggest expense of the entire shoot, hundreds of dollars in quarters.

Unfortunately, Judy LaPilusa was developing a dope habit, and she wasn't just Holmstrom's girlfriend, she was also with Richard Lloyd, the genius guitar player from Television.

Eventually Holmstrom and Lloyd traded fists, and then it seemed over. Judy was still around, but I could never tell if she was with Richard Lloyd or with Holmstrom. It got too confusing, so I steered clear. Instead, I concentrated on the costumes for the Nazi Dykes.

I even designed their logo: the female sign, the circle with the cross coming out of the bottom that are actually contractions of the Greek names for Mars and Venus, with a swastika inside it. The swastika in the middle of the circle made for a pretty startling graphic. There was a costumer I was having an affair with, and she made me Nazi Dyke armbands for the girls to wear. The lesbian kingpin was played by the muscular Helen Wheels, who had her own band but made money writing songs for Blue Öyster Cult.

I was having an affair with Helen early on, but then her Hells Angel boyfriend knocked on the door and I had to hide in the closet. I was genuinely terrified, because he knew how much Helen loved to fuck.

Helen Wheels's lesbian lieutenants in *Nick Detroit* were Blondie's Debbie Harry and Contortions manager Anya Phillips, who looked like they really wanted to kill you. They could look so mean. The best bad girls ever!

The climax of *Nick Detroit* comes when Nick tracks the Nazi Dykes to the Staten Island Ferry, where the big shoot-out occurs. Holmstrom's

Me, Anya Phillips, and Debbie Harry shooting *The Legend of Nick Detroit* on the Staten Island Ferry.

Photo by Chris Stein

special effects—his cartoon drawings over Chris's and Roberta's photos—really made this movie on paper come alive.

When I saw the final reproductions, I said, "John, you can't have Anya getting shot in the *tit*!"

"Why not? She'll love it!" John shot back, and, of course, he was right.

Debbie Harry was the easiest rock star that I ever worked with. I asked her to do some pretty wacky photo shots, like, "Can you climb on top of this car, and act like Nick Detroit just punched you in the face from his open window? And look like you're seeing stars? While hanging onto the roof of the car? Great, that's perfect, now can you cross your eyes . . ."

Without hesitation, Debbie would do it, and more importantly, make it hysterically funny. Debbie was so beautiful that people couldn't imagine how funny she was, but she was hysterical! And Debbie had a car and would give us rides back to the *PUNK* Dump from CBGB.

Debbie and Chris were *PUNK* magazine stalwarts; they were always around, as well as Roberta, Elin Wilder, who I was "dating," and a bunch of Holmstrom's cartoonist friends from the School of Visual Arts.

As I said, Richard Hell was the laziest motherfucker I'd ever met, and he soon grew bored with *The Legend of Nick Detroit* after the first week of shooting.

"*Why do we hafta do this shot?*"

"Because we need a shot of you going out the door on your way to the Nazi Dykes' hideout . . ."

"*This is fucking stupid!*"

"Yeah, but we still need a shot of you going out the door . . ."

It would go on like this for five or six times a day for two weeks, and since I didn't have a script, just a hand-drawn layout, Holmstrom was laying out the photo cartoon as the pictures came in. We always had deadlines. Always. And worse, we had to meet them.

Chris did an amazing job with the big shoot-out on the Staten Island Ferry. That's where Debbie Harry and Anya Phillips get blasted to bits with Holmstrom's cartoonist pals adding the special effects over the photos as they just got shot; the bullets ripping through their bodies, under the cartoon lettering of "Rat-tat-tat-rat!"

I loved the project because it captures the youthful good looks of everybody in their prime in this fantastic story of people getting massacred.

In the end, even my character, "Little Norris," Nick's sidekick, gets shot in the face by a bored Nick, because Richard hated me so much by the end of the shooting.

This was one murder he was just dying to commit.

When *The Legend of Nick Detroit* came back from the printer, Richard Hell was furious with me. Maybe he thought it was gonna be like a *Vogue* fashion layout? I don't know, but I think he thought it would not be a photo comic book. Richard loved laying into me in his long soliloquies, breaking down my every character flaw in laborious scholarly detail.

"You wanna know what's wrong with you, Legs?"

I didn't, or at least I thought I already knew, but his thesaurus poetry act was just getting started. "You are an indolent, asymmetrical homunculus! You belong in a dusty jar in the back of a forgotten closet in a community college science classroom! Even an accidental glance at your malodorous mug makes me want to puke my guts all over the fucking floor!"

I didn't know all of those words, but I recognized enough of them to get the general idea. Of course that wasn't the end of it.

"You know what's gonna happen to you when you die?" he spat. "I'm gonna make a plaster of Paris arch that spells out the word 'mediocre' over your gravestone so that whenever it rains, it'll drip plaster of Paris onto your grave until it becomes one big puddle of off-white calcium sulphate that ignores what an unexceptional person is buried here."

I knew *The Legend of Nick Detroit* would fail miserably. It was too bizarre to be commercial, and no one at the 7-Elevens knew where to stock it—with the rock magazines or the comic books? Here was a tabloid magazine called *PUNK* with a swastika on the cover; I mean, who wouldn't want to buy that?

Magazines need regular features and some identifiable context so the customer knows what he's buying. *The Legend of Nick Detroit* had none of that.

I think the problem, besides Holmstrom being so burnt out, was that he was hanging out and listening to Lou Reed's advice that each issue of the magazine had to be an art piece on its own, independent of anything that had ever been seen before. Yeah, *real commercial!*

Magazines depend upon ad sales, which depend upon circulation numbers, and that ad revenue was supposed to pay our salaries. But after *Nick Detroit* we had very few ad sales, if any. So things were looking kinda bleak after bundles upon bundles of *Nick Detroit* were returned by our distributor. Besides, Holmstrom and Ged were starting to argue even more than normal. I just avoided them.

As Richard later wrote in our *SPIN* article, "The Adventures of Huckleberry Hell and Legs Sawyer":

> *But who is this wimp I'm with, who gargles Kool-Aid (it's for people who want to be more Kool) for his oral hygiene and breakfast in one and when the going gets tough the tough goes to sleep? It's happy-go-lucky Legs McNeil, my old pal and parasite, who likes to let me insult him. The perfect travel companion.*

No Richard, I didn't enjoy your insults. I tolerated them because you were fascinating. I think Richard and I got along because we never talked about music, just writers and movies and pop culture. Once Richard said something that stuck with me . . . well, he said a bunch of things that have stuck with me, but this one was one of the cooler things; he said, "Legs, can you imagine if we created a monster that would live forever? Like Frankenstein or the Creature from the Black Lagoon?"

We were always having conversations like these, with Richard cooking up some "what if?" scheme. But I was overwhelmed. I mean, what a fantastically cool thing to dream up!

Richard was excited by the idea: "We'd be like Mary Shelley creating

Frankenstein, or Bram Stoker creating *Dracula*! And then Universal Studios could transform our monster into one of the coolest horror films ever made! I mean, we'd be like the coolest guys on the planet!"

We were in hysterics.

Richard snickered, "It'd be like, '*What do you do?* Oh, I created Dracula, *I don't hafta do anything!*"

Richard's schemes always involved doing the least amount of work for the largest amount of bucks. I think that was his major goal in life—to do something so fantastic, he'd never have to do anything again. Which he kinda did, but it took so long for people to recognize it, Richard already moved on to the next arcane thing.

Still, he kept going: "See those zombies over there? *Mine!*"

I shook my head. "No, zombies belong to George Romero, he took those outdated ghouls and turned them into one of the most terrifying members of the Famous Monsters collection!"

And I'd have to say, "*Night of the Living Dead* single-handedly reinvented the zombie, and all the zombies that came after George Romero should be paying him a royalty, you know? The zombie is probably the only monster that has been reimagined and remade in our lifetime; all the rest are originals from the last century . . ."

"No." Richard shook his head. "I know an original monster that's been created, from start to finish, in our lifetime . . ."

I said, "Which one?"

He said, "Godzilla!"

I said, "Oh my God, you are *so right*! But Godzilla is so fake looking, I mean knocking toy trains off train tracks, and crashing through scale-model buildings, and then they explode cheap fucking firecrackers! Not the scariest monster I've ever seen, more like monster camp!"

"That's your problem, Legs," Richard sighed. "You have no imagination!"

"Still." I shook my head. "Godzilla; very lame."

Richard finally succeeded in his monster scam since Malcolm McLaren, the Sex Pistols' manager, told me about what he found in New York City after the New York Dolls self-destructed in Florida.

Malcolm said, "I just thought Richard Hell was incredible . . . I don't think it was a safety pin there, may've been, but it was certainly a torn and ripped T-shirt and this look, this image of this guy, this spiky hair, everything about it was something I knew I could bring back in my mind to London."

And so, Richard Hell was the inspiration for Johnny Rotten, probably the greatest rock 'n' roll monster ever created. But Richard Hell was the original monster of rock 'n' roll, the slumming Dracula. Richard actually got his dream come true by being the guy whose attitude inspired Johnny Rotten.

"Those were the images I brought back to London," Malcolm McLaren continued telling me. "I was like Marco Polo or Walter Raleigh, you know? These are the things that I brought back; I brought back this distressed, strange thing called Richard Hell. And I brought back this phrase, 'The Blank Generation.'"

I think Richard Hell felt like he'd done it all after he'd written "Blank Generation," a perfect rock 'n' roll song, but not the album version, that one sucks. The true version of "Blank Generation" came out as a single on Ork Records, which was owned by the late, great Terry Ork, a short, curly-haired gnome. Terry possessed the charming magic as the film expert at Cinemabilia bookstore, was the manager of Television, and was the only guy who would always buy me beers at CBGB.

The Ork version is fantastic, but leave it to Richard to fuck up his masterpiece by rerecording it for the album. It's a horrible train wreck of Hell trying too hard, and, unfortunately, only five people in the world have heard the Ork single—the slower, "wonderfully bored wail of a drained, dirty hungry vocal in a torn T-shirt," so that when he sings, "I can take it or leave each time," you really believe him.

I was over at Roberta Bayley's apartment on St. Mark's Place the night Richard called Johnny Thunders and said he was quitting the Heartbreakers.

Richard had stopped going to Heartbreakers rehearsals, and it was finally time to come clean, sorta.

Richard was finally forced to call Johnny to tell him he just got out of jail and that's why he hadn't been to rehearsal.

Richard and Roberta exchanged smirks as Richard told Johnny some elaborate story about not paying his Con Ed bill, and the girlfriend of the day paid with her credit card, and the card turned out to be stolen, and they arrested Richard, even though he didn't know the card was hot. "Oh what a terrible web we weave . . ."

It was a bad lie, and Johnny probably knew, but he wished Richard luck anyway.

I loved Richard in the Heartbreakers. Watching him and Johnny compete for attention was a spectacle. You didn't know which one to look at. They were the only other band at CBGB that was as good as the Ramones and the Dictators. And Richard loved Johnny's authentic rock 'n' roll style, his songwriting, his hair, his clothes. So I asked him why he was leaving, and Richard just sorta grinned and said, "Oh, you know Johnny, he's brilliant, but half the time I don't know what he's singing about, some girl on the phone, nobody's home . . . I mean, then *why's the phone ringing if no one can hear it*?"

Richard was a writer, a decent poet, but he had very little patience for redundant pop songs.

Even "Blank Generation" is a fucking novel compared to Johnny Thunders's "I Wanna Be Loved." Richard was a bit more complicated than Johnny, that's why he was leaving the Heartbreakers; and, if the truth be told, rock 'n' roll bored Richard Hell.

Sure, he liked the sex and the drugs, but the monotony of performing music seemed like a waste of time. Richard wasn't a trouper, like Debbie and Chris and Clem and David Johansen and Patti Smith and the Ramones. To Richard, rock 'n' roll was just another get-rich-quick scheme, only this one worked! And besides, he was good at it!

I think Richard articulated his enthusiasm for punk rock in his memoir, *I Dreamed I Was a Very Clean Tramp,* when he wrote:

It can't be overstated, that initial rush of realizing, of experiencing, what's possible as you're standing there in the rehearsal room with your guitars and the mikes turned on, and when you make a move this physical information comes pouring out and you can do or say anything you want. It was like having magical powers.

That's why I put up with Richard's insults, because there were times when he could so profoundly articulate the chaos. Nail to the wall the hectic messes that were our lives.

And what was I myself but chaos? Or at least living a chaotic life. I slept on a couch where overhead a sewer pipe leaked on me while I was sleeping. There was no shower in the Punk Dump. I had just killed a giant rat with a layout table stool. The refrigerator door was kept shut by a giant rubber band. I had no clothes except a pair of jeans and an endless supply of *PUNK* magazine T-shirts, a pair of sneakers, not even cool ones, and a black leather jacket.

I was paid thirty dollars a week and came to hate my daily slice of pizza and exchanged it for Jamaican beef patties; they were a quarter more than a slice, and took longer to cook, but they were well worth the wait.

Not having a shower proved to be a godsend when it came to picking up girls: "Hey, we don't have a shower at the *PUNK* Dump, think I could use yours?"

When the girl said yes, I immediately moved in, because the line usually worked.

The only time it didn't work was on Anya Phillips, one of the Nazi Dykes who gets blasted with Debbie Harry by Nick Detroit on the Staten Island Ferry.

I think Anya took my "we-don't-have-a-shower" line as a sex come-on, instead of a quest to cleanse myself.

When we got to her apartment Anya pointed to the bed and asked me, "Do you want me to tie you to the bed and stand over you while I masturbate?"

"Not really," I said, stealing and lighting one of her cigarettes. "I'd rather have a peanut butter and jelly sandwich? Got any white bread?"

I sat in her bathtub eating my PB&J, enjoying the suds and smoking her cigarettes.

Anya threw me out after I asked her, "Do guys really get turned on being tied to your bed while you jerk off over them?"

Needless to say, I knew nothing about S&M.

Decades after our journey down the Mississippi, I was part of a group reading: William Burroughs, Allen Ginsberg, Kathy Acker, Richard Hell, and me. Within months of one another, the participants died.

After Allen Ginsberg passed away, Richard called me up and asked, "How are you feeling?"

When William Burroughs finally expired at eighty-three, Richard called me up and asked, "How are you feeling?"

After Kathy Acker died of breast cancer, Richard called me up and asked, "How are you feeling?"

I told him, "Fuck you! Stop trying to give me your father's heart attack! I'm in perfect health! And I'm gonna live forever once I quit smoking!" I didn't even want to answer the telephone anymore!

Later, Richard got so health conscious that he once turned up at my place with a tennis racket and a suntan! The first person I ever saw shoot up wouldn't even let me light a cigarette in his apartment anymore. The place hadn't changed in the forty years since I'd last been there. I mean not a thing. It still looked like a fantasy Bob Dylan album cover circa 1965.

After we sent *PUNK #6*, *The Legend of Nick Detroit*, to the printer, Holmstrom and I were invited to be guest stars at the First Annual World Sleaze Convention, held in Wilmington, Delaware, chemical capital of the world. We were second billed to "Edie the Egg Lady" from John Waters's *Pink*

Flamingos, and the crowd, such as it was, reflected this. Still, it was our first chance to make a frontal attack on the heartland of America.

I drove down to Delaware with Mark Jacobson, who was writing a feature about me for the *Village Voice*, "Legs McNeil: Teenage Hipster in the Modern World." Mark and I hung out a lot on that trip, and he was writing some really great shit at that time. He had his finger on the pulse of popular culture.

Debbie Harry and Chris Stein from Blondie came to the Sleaze Convention with Anya Phillips to see what was going on, meeting us at the Del-Mar, a scuzzy hotel popular with junkies, along with hookers and their discerning clientele. What was going on was nothing. Marty Thau, New York Dolls manager, bubblegum-rock promoter, and general adviser to the scene, arrived the second day of the festivities, took one look around, and decided everyone needed a drink.

There were no punk bars in Wilmington, but there were regular bars, and in 1976, a beer in a regular bar in Wilmington was like twenty-five cents a glass. I paid for around ten bucks' worth and stacked the full glasses in a pyramid, and we got thrown out when I knocked them over and made a big mess. It was time to leave. It was always time to leave when I was around.

Our next stop was a gay disco. In 1976, gay discos were everywhere, even in Wilmington. Within minutes I'd found the only straight girl in the place. She worked in a massage parlor blowing guys all day. She was really hot. Like countless others had done before us, perhaps many on the same unwashed sheets, my new friend and I left the gay disco to go fuck each other into oblivion at the Del-Mar Motel.

What I didn't realize was that by bailing on the gay disco to fuck a stranger, I'd pissed off everyone I was with. Never mind that we were in town for a Sleaze Convention, and I was being sleazier than everyone else put together. Apparently nuance meant nothing, so they cooked up a revenge plot.

"That motherfucker ditched us!!!" Anya spat out.

"Yeah, and what are we gonna do about it?!?" Debbie and Chris demanded.

"LET'S GET LEGS!" Holmstrom exploded. He was always looking for ways to "get" me, often succeeding.

There I was, fully naked, on top of my date, banging away, when the hotel room door burst open. Suddenly, four masked figures raced in and threw ice water all over me and my new friend. I don't know which one of us screamed the loudest, but I didn't stick around to find out. I leapt from the bed fully naked, grabbed a chair and a belt, and chased Holmstrom down the street. Which in that neighborhood was not an uncommon sight.

The rest of the Sleaze Convention didn't live up to its billing. The media didn't give a shit about it, or its guest stars, and barely anyone turned up. At one point Holmstrom was attacked by some guy tripping on LSD and nearly thrown out a second-story window, and then he had to stick around and judge the Miss Sleaze Beauty Pageant, with drag queens for contestants.

Having reached our fill of Wilmington and the Del-Mar bedbugs, the rest of us had already returned to New York by then. We were halfway into the first year of establishing our global media empire, and the rot was already setting in.

If Holmstrom was dead by late summer of 1976, I wasn't far behind after the emotionally and physically draining experience pulling *The Legend of Nick Detroit* together. And for what?

Nobody read it. Nobody cared. I'd tried to get them to serialize *Nick Detroit* instead of filling a full issue with it, but I still kept hearing from Holmstrom and Ged that if *PUNK* sank because of "Legs's folly," it was all my fault. And just because I was used to getting the blame for everything, that didn't make it true.

After just a few issues, people from *Time, Newsweek, The New Yorker*, and a shitload of other foreign and American journalists were knocking at the

PUNK Dump demanding access into this newly discovered "perverse, decadent world of black leather and white noise."

I'd tell them all they had to do was watch reruns of *Bullwinkle*, *Green Acres*, and the Fonz. But the press never likes simple answers so I'd make them take me out for beers and ramble about teenagers being the master race, McDonald's versus Burger King, and "cars, girls, surfing, and beer." They'd all nod their heads sincerely, while writing down quick notes as if I'd said something profound.

Mostly I was drunk a lot, playing the mascot for a cultural revolution that had no redeeming social value except to corrupt the vast corporate structure of the entertainment industry, and let everyone be who they needed to be. Make the world bigger, in a real way.

The only high crime was boredom, punishable by death.

Even with the early success of *PUNK*, Ged and Holmstrom were arguing all the time over the same shit: money, or lack thereof, and workload.

Ged hated me because I was too lazy to do laundry, so I'd just help myself to a fresh *PUNK* T-shirt every day. I figured it was within my job description as Resident Punk to be a human billboard for the magazine, showing up at Max's, CBGB, and wherever else I could run a tab. But Ged didn't see it that way, insisting the T-shirts were for *PUNK*'s readers, who'd send in $4.50 (or $3.75 with a subscription!) from Pismo Beach to Poughkeepsie.

We were also showing up on magazine racks at 7-Elevens, right next to *Rolling Stone* and *People* magazines, which was too surreal to even comprehend. Who knows? We might have even turned up in dentist's office waiting rooms stuffed between copies of *Highlights* and *Ranger Rick*!

Ged also hated me because I was getting laid and he wasn't. I was already finding it increasingly difficult to constantly maintain the chaotic Resident Punk façade. But as long as people were buying me beer and cigarettes, and I was getting sloppy blow jobs in greasy-spoon bathrooms while being treated to a grilled cheese sandwich, I was more than happy to be a cartoon character.

Ged finally had enough of me for something that happened in the *PUNK* Dump when he was back in Cheshire visiting his family. I met two *PUNK* fans at CBGB, and on the long walk home realized it wouldn't be gentlemanly to defile them both on a tiny sofa marinated in sewer water.

Ged's office was on the left of the *PUNK* Dump, his huge loft bed overhead. Holmstrom's space was down the hall from Ged's, a small bed, a stereo, some improvised bookshelves—and a giant drawing board he was usually hunched over. The entire issue of *PUNK* was hand-lettered, and Holmstrom's cartoon-style print was distinctive, personal, and a joy to read, but it was incredibly labor intensive

Owner of CBGB Hilly Krystal throwing me out of the club in a posed photo for *PUNK* magazine.

Photo by Roberta Bayley

With Ged out of town for the weekend, his loft was gonna be my loft. And I was gonna commit unimaginable horrors in that loft.

I was just starting to feel like somebody around that time. I mean, suddenly it mattered that I was here on the planet, 'cause overnight there was possibility, like seemingly endless possibility.

CBGB was the perfect club because it seemed like no one was in charge. Well, maybe Merv the bouncer, 'cause Hilly Kristal, the owner, was always passed out on the couch after ten o'clock, and after finishing his last vodka and Fresca.

As long as Hilly's ex-wife wasn't around, everything would be cool.

On this night she wasn't. Only Merv the bouncer, in his customary yellow hard hat, who just rolled his eyes when he saw me. I was used to that.

I was clutching the first issue of *PUNK* magazine, the one with Lou Reed on the cover. You know, the cartoon of Lou looking like Frankenstein?

You never saw it? Well *fuck you*. But these two skinhead girls noticed I had the magazine in my hand and came up and asked me, "Do you think Lou Reed will show up here tonight?"

I laughed. It was dead. I looked around the club and saw only the moths. You know, the "moths"—badly dressed fans drawn to mediocre bands. Moths.

"There's no way Lou's gonna be here tonight," I said to the skinheads, one with blonde stubble, the other with red. "With bands like Auntie Moon, it'd be unspeakable torture . . ."

"Then what are *you* doing here?"

"See *this*?" I flashed *PUNK* #1 at 'em. "This is *my* magazine . . ."

"Yeah, we read it," the blonde skinhead girl smirked. "What do you think we're doing here looking for Lou . . . ?"

Wow, cool, people really are reading us. This is wonderful!

The skinhead girls were kinda cute, kinda Goth, with thick, black eye makeup circling their enlarged pupils, just to accent their concentration camp look, years before it became chic.

"Sorry it's such a dud night," I flirted, "and sorry you didn't bump into Lou . . ."

Seeing how bored they were, desperate for something to happen, anything, I added, "But if you got a car, I can take you on a tour of the *PUNK* magazine offices. It's a dump, but it's also got the unedited transcripts of our Lou Reed interview from issue #1 . . ."

Did I really say that? I did.

"Really?" the redhead nodded. "That'd be cool, nothing going on here . . ."

It worked! I guess Holmstrom was right. And not only will people buy us beers, they might go home with us too. Two at a time. My first threesome!

On the way uptown, after we picked up two six-packs of beer, I told the story of killing the giant rat with a layout table stool, and how I wanted to get the rat stuffed but we couldn't afford it. Then we turned onto Tenth Avenue and into true film noir.

Overhead, the remains of ancient railroad tracks framed the street in an iron-and-concrete cave. Huge, ugly, metal pylons shouldered the train tracks, providing the perfect opening shot for any big-city crime drama.

To one side, Manhattan's largest post office, a huge slab of concrete occupying an entire city block, sat before dozens of tractor-trailer trucks fighting with each other to back their screeching eighteen-wheelers into the next vacant bay. Twenty-four hours a day.

"*Neither rain, nor sleet, nor the Westies . . .*"

Across the street from the humongous post office, on the opposite corner, sat a small three-story building. On the first floor was a storefront, the glass splattered in black paint, with only the small poster, ***"Watch Out! PUNK Is Coming!"*** to identify it as the *PUNK* Dump. It looked dangerous. But then, *everything* in New York City in 1975 looked dangerous.

The only cool thing in the *PUNK* Dump was Will Eisner's desk that Holmstrom had gotten from the "Father of the Graphic Novel" when he drew bricks for the cover of one of the *Spirit* reissues.

The two skinhead girls were thumbing through the most recent issues of *PUNK*; the Patti Smith one; the Ramones one; the Iggy one; and giggling at the articles. The first few issues were perfect, and most importantly, *funny.*

I popped open a Bud and invited them to check out Ged's loft bed, saying, "*It's huge,*" well aware that Ged told me I could never use his loft bed when he was away. Ever.

Fuck you, Ged, where's my loft, motherfucker? I thought as I eyed the badly built ladder. *Asshole! You told us when we were stealing lumber from suburban construction sites for your bed that our loft beds were going to be built next, you lying fucking weasel!*

But when Ged is away, the Resident Punk will play, and after I grabbed a bottle of maple syrup from the refrigerator, we climbed into *PUNK*'s publisher's loft. I didn't think I was being decadent enough, and I thought of the line "Put jelly on your shoulder, baby" from "Some Kinda Love" by the Velvet Underground as pretty decadent. We didn't have jelly in the *PUNK* Dump, but we did have maple syrup, and that seemed really decadent. I really wanted to be hedonistic.

Yeah, it felt delicious crawling up the ladder and across the king-size mattress and pulling the blonde on top of me. The redhead, at the other end of the mattress, unhooked her black brassiere, showing tits so white I went snow-blind.

After what seemed like hours of filthy physics-defying sexual contortion, I paused and marveled at actually living in the kind of erotic fantasy I masturbated to during puberty. But this fantasy was actually happening to me.

All that's missing from this is maple syrup, I thought, opening the bottle and emptying it onto our writhing bodies as I drifted away into dreamland.

When I woke, I was glued to the sheets. Half my face was pink from having to tear the sheet from it. When Ged and Holmstrom came back on Monday morning, they were fighting again, so they didn't notice I was up and trying to get the fridge door open. It was a complicated procedure 'cause it was kept shut by a giant rubber band. I was praying there was a Coca-Cola inside the fridge . . .

Shit! There *was* a Coke!

Coke was the only thing that'd cut through the residual alcohol sludge stuffed down my throat every morning, and I found two Marlboros left in the pack, and *my God* did that first smoke of the day taste exquisite! Combined with the Coke fizz burning through my throat mud, I was coming alive! Yeah, that worked, when so many other things didn't.

"*I'm hand-lettering every fucking issue by hand, by myself, and I need some help!*" Holmstrom yelled.

Incredibly, another investor turned up at the *PUNK* Dump in 1976. He said his name was Tom Katz, and he wanted to unload a $20,000 insurance windfall he'd received after his Detroit police officer brother was shot and killed in the line of duty. I think he felt guilty, like he wasn't entitled to the money.

Katz said he had seen a poster for *The Legend of Nick Detroit* and instantly knew what he wanted to do with his money. He was given the title of assistant publisher, and one of his primary roles was to keep an eye on me, the Resident Punk. I was a living cartoon mascot drawn around bad behavior, but it only worked until it got out of control. I don't think either of us believed we could get along, but we became really good friends.

"Assistant Publisher" was an honorific, because Tom knew nothing about magazines. He'd given *PUNK* $20,000 in capital, and I think Holmstrom consulted with him, but it was like handing out an "Executive Producer" title for helping finance a movie.

Later, I moved into an apartment with Tom Katz in Staten Island. Manhattan was a nightmare, and I liked the peacefulness of Staten Island. Even though I couldn't wait to leave Cheshire for New York, I always wanted to be comfortable. And the *PUNK* Dump was a hovel, and crashing at other people's apartments was anything but comfortable.

One day I was looking around the apartment for some money to buy cigarettes, and I found some documents that revealed that Tom Katz's real name was Kent Atchison, and he'd been a driver for Ronald Reagan when he was running for president. They'd even been in an accident.

I couldn't believe Tom Katz had another name and another life and I hadn't known anything about it. When Holmstrom heard, he thought Katz was working for the CIA, but John was always so fucking paranoid. I loved Holmstrom, but I was getting along much better with Tom by then.

I just thought Tom Katz was a great guy. I didn't think he was a spy, and I didn't care what his real name was. I think he might have changed it because he thought everyone in publishing was Jewish, and Tom Katz sounded more Jewish than Kent Atchison. I called him Tom Katz; I called people whatever they wanted to be called. He didn't even ask me to.

He had this cool car, a black Lincoln Continental, and we'd just drive around and he'd tell me about military history. Once we drove to the Aberdeen Proving Ground, a US Army facility in Maryland, and he taught me all the different parts of the tanks.

But living on Staten Island was a nightmare because I'd always pass out on the ferry and wake up as we were leaving Staten Island! I'd miss my stop! So I'd have to rerun the entire sequence of events again, and again, 'cause I'd always wake up as we were leaving my stop, like a nightly loop of *Groundhog Day*, until I finally got the message and started staying at Victor Bockris and Jeff Goldberg's apartment at 106 Perry Street.

At my first dinner party at Victor and Jeff's place, I noticed that Jeff had the most wonderful artwork above his desk—a hand-drawn poster of an artist's night of drunken debauchery.

The poster was broken into four panels like a comic book—there was the artist lying in the gutter as a taxicab almost clipped him; there was him getting thrown out of a bar for vomiting on the floor; there was him stumbling out of an abandoned tenement as the morning sun rose in the sky—all the great humiliations of amateur alcoholism in one picture.

But it wasn't a cartoon, more like a hip graphic novel. Since we were all into the "graphically real" then, reading *Last Exit to Brooklyn* and Andy Warhol's *Popism*, we were all searching for new ways to express what life was like for the new artist. And I knew this poster artist had hit a nerve. He was telling the truth. And he was also a friend of Victor's and Jeff's, who I'd meet the next time they invited me over.

I didn't like Duncan Hannah when I first met him. He was a rich kid. And maybe too good looking.

It happened at one of Victor and Jeff's more horrifying dinner parties—I once saw Victor dish out a canned ham that was more spam than ham to Burroughs and Warhol—and we immediately got into a fight about music.

Duncan was wearing an ascot when we met, at least that's how I remember him, even if it's not true; it probably is. He seemed that pretentious. He was cut from ascot-wearing cloth, and I was cut from cheap leather and empty cigarette packs. We were exact opposites, as our first argument proved: I was pro-Monkees, Duncan was anti-Monkees, which was a big deal, since music defined almost everything about a person in 1970s New York City.

"They don't even play their own instruments," Duncan spat.

"No band in LA plays their own instruments, it's always the Wrecking Crew!" I shot back, referring to the nickname of the best studio musicians in LA that played on virtually everyone's record, from Frank Sinatra to the Byrds.

Duncan professed to love the Stooges, Bowie, Marc Bolan—and Roxy Music, perhaps the most pompous band on earth. Bryan Ferry and Roxy Music canceled out any of Duncan's punk credibility in my book, and I quickly dismissed him as a conceited ass.

Still, our long nights at CBGB, Max's, and the Mudd Club—and our shared love of great rock 'n' roll, booze, and women—brought us together in an uneasy alliance. And our recognition that we were complete opposites proved more interesting to each other than not and made us closer somehow. And as I got to know him better, Duncan also bared a hysterical sense of humor. Goofy funny, even.

I believe it was over drinks at Duncan's girlfriend's apartment, the noted dominatrix Terence Sellers, author of *The Correct Sadist,* that I started calling him "Dunc." He responded by calling me "Legsy," and then it was time to go see whatever band, or party, or art opening we were attending.

Terry Sellers said, "Wait a sec," and walked over to a large armoire in the corner of the room, opened the closet door, revealing a little old man tied, gagged, and blindfolded inside, and casually said to him, "I'm going out, I'll be back late . . ."

The guy didn't dare reply. Or couldn't. It was like an X-rated version of that scene from *A Hard Day's Night,* where the Beatles find a hotel butler in his underpants and sock garters hiding in the closet because Paul McCartney's grandfather stole his tuxedo to play baccarat and ogle women at Le Circle Club.

Eventually I moved in with Carol Overby, more about her later, and resumed my childhood obsession of collecting snakes, pythons to be precise, and Duncan was fascinated with my menagerie. In the early 1980s, Duncan quit drinking and joined the Sober Sailors Society and was even more charming to be around. He even gifted me a beautiful portrait of a king snake, and his painting career really started to take off. I wished him well but had no use for sobriety at the time, and Duncan never mentioned it, much to his credit. As he told my girlfriend, "He'll call me when he's ready."

When Carol left me for a photo-realist painter from Arizona and threw me out, Duncan took me in. I went to meetings. I got my job back at *SPIN.* And I kept asking my ex-girlfriend, "A photo-realist painter? But how can you fuck someone so mediocre?"

I guess, for her, it was more about looks than substance, and I took it as a personal insult that she was sleeping with such a lousy artist. While I was complaining to Duncan, he'd just sigh exasperatedly and say, "Legs, you've been here for two weeks, can't you even wash one dish?"

To flash forward some more, I eventually married my ex-girlfriend, got divorced, left *SPIN*, and started working on a book that became *Please Kill Me: The Uncensored Oral History of Punk*, and I knew Duncan was one of the guys I had to interview for it. There were all these people in the punk scene who were stars already, people like Duncan Hannah, Terry Ork, Bebe Buell, Cyrinda Foxe, Philippe Marcade, among others who no one really knew much about, but who needed to be exposed to the world as the fabulous characters they were! I was determined through *Please Kill Me* to put them on the map. They deserved to be on the map. All I had to do was edit it in a way that was cohesive, chronological, and funny, when it wasn't being horrifying, like life is.

So I brought my tape bag up to Duncan's pad on West 71st Street, and pushed play on the record button and Duncan did the rest. It was a delightful afternoon with us both in hysterics as we skipped back to the '70s, and not only did Dunc have an amazing memory, he also possessed the ability to recall the events in the same mind frame as when they were happening. He had no filters during our interview.

DUNCAN HANNAH: I was hanging out at Max's with Danny Fields at his usual booth. We were having a couple of brandies and in walks Lou Reed with the Maltese crosses sculpted into his head. It was 1973, and Lou comes over and says, "Hey, Danny!" Danny says, "Oh, Lou, sit down, sit down." So it's the three of us. And I'm introduced and Lou goes, "Hey, he looks like David Cassidy, you know that?"

And I said, "Oh, I don't really like David Cassidy." And he goes, "Yeah, you look just . . . doesn't he, Danny? Doesn't he look just like David Cassidy?" And then they started talking about me in the third person, "Doesn't she look like David Cassidy?"

That goes on for a while and then they started talking about Raymond Chandler. And I'd just read all of Raymond Chandler. So I'm thinking, Hey, I know about this, and I'm sitting with my hero,

> *Lou Reed, and we're going to have an intellectual conversation about Raymond Chandler. All right!*
>
> *So Lou is making some point, talking about a scene that was in* The High Window. *And I said, "Oh no, that's in* The Little Sister.*" He goes, "Wha?" I said, "That's in* The Little Sister. *I just read that, too, it's great, I know that piece . . ."*
>
> *So Lou turns to Danny and says, "Hey, Danny. She speaks. Does she think? I guess she reads, huh?"*
>
> *I thought, I get it. I'm just a dumb blonde.*
>
> *So Lou says, "Hey, Danny, what does she do anyhow?" And Danny says, "Oh, she's an art student." So Lou goes, "Oh, an art student." And it was horrible. It's horrible being with your heroes when you're an art student. It sounds like nothing. So I got the message: Be seen and not heard. I'm a bauble. I'm an accessory. Oh, great. Here's my hero, I finally meet my hero! And I can't talk.*
>
> *So then Danny goes to the bathroom and Lou turns to me and says, "Say, are you Danny's?" And I said, "No, no, Danny's my friend." He said, "So you don't belong to Danny?" And I said, "No, you know, he's my friend." Lou goes, "Well, will you be my David Cassidy then?" I said, "Uh, no, I don't think so." And he said, "Well, look, why don't you come back to my hotel with me?" I said, "And?" He said, "And you can shit in my mouth. How'd you like that?" I said, "I don't think I would like that."*
>
> *I was really ashen. And Lou started whispering, like it was supposed to make me hot, and said, "Does that, does that repulse you?" I said, "Yeah." And he said, "Well, I'll put a—I'll put a plate over my face, then you can shit on the plate. How'd you like that?"*
>
> *I said, "No, I don't think I'd like that either."*
>
> *From Please Kill Me: The Uncensored Oral History of Punk.*

As I said, hysterically funny. *Please Kill Me* came out and was a hit because of Duncan Hannah's voice and all the amazing others, and "Dunc" became the famous artist he will always be remembered as, and for being the accomplished author of *20th Century Boy*, his diaries from the 1970s that are a must read. Don't even think about it, just pick up the book and dive in.

I mean, in the photo Duncan was stunning. I mean head-turning stunning. He looked like a girl, so feminine, yet with a weirdly masculine vibe. And I didn't want to hang it in my apartment and have every girl that spent the night say, "*Who's that?*"

Yeah, thanks Danny, you could've ruined my sex life with that one photo!

Instead, I gave it to Duncan, he had to have it, it was the best photo—out of the millions of movie-star photos of him—I'd ever seen. He seriously looked like a god in the photo, and it was too hallowed for me to possess.

Dunc had it all: the charm, the clothes, the looks, the brains, the talent, and more importantly, he was not an asshole. He didn't need an entourage, he enjoyed going to see his friends' work, and he enjoyed explaining why he liked something or did not like it. He was extremely accessible, and his take on "the work" was inspiring. And his manner was classy, in an unpretentious way, more Midwest down-home. And his smile was infectious.

On New Year's Eve 1976, Holmstrom and I left the *PUNK* Dump with no plan, but within a few minutes we ran into Clem Burke and Jimmy Destri from Blondie on the street. They were heading to Bethesda Fountain in Central Park to play a New Year's Eve show, and asked if we wanted to be their roadies as the ball dropped.

Holmstrom and I were real tight then. Blondie didn't have any vinyl out yet and were pretty unknown.

Holmstom said, "We should go!"

I said, "John, it's seven degrees out!"

John said, "Debbie and Chris have been really good to us."

He always had to remind me of shit.

"Yeah they have. Let's go . . ."

We got up to Central Park, and there was just a tiny crowd. I guess Bethesda Fountain wasn't a New Year's Eve tourist destination.

Blondie began playing to a small gathering of people.

Suddenly a crowd spilled down the stairs and through the tunnel as Debbie sang a cover of "Time Is Tight" by Booker T. & the M.G.'s, and Holmstrom and I were on stage go-go dancing, doing drunken versions of "The Jerk" and "The Swim" and "The Mashed Potato," and other dance faves.

Debbie and Chris had urged us on stage and all of us were laughing hysterically; Debbie, Chris, Clem, Jimmy, and me and Holmstrom, though I was always a better dancer than John.

EIGHT

Mick Jagger once said: "Never wear a new pair of shoes in front of him" about David Bowie. At least I think he said that. Anyway, it's stuck with me for a long time, because Bowie really was a thief. He was a thief of ideas, of trends, of fashion. He'd see the cutting edge coming and elbow you out of the way to get the credit, so you never wanted to give him a chance to one-up you with some *ultra-hipper-than-thou, trend-setting status.*

Be the first on your block with a new red-rooster unisex cut and ten-inch sparkling platform shoes!!!

That's what Bowie's career was truly about, and he turned it into an art, taking whatever he could to create the future before our eyes and ears. Sure, Bowie's future sometimes looked like cheesy '50s sci-fi schlock, but he also made some really great rock 'n' roll. All the best people steal, but it was funny how desperate Bowie was about it. And I think that's what Jagger meant, because by the time he and Bowie crossed paths, the Rolling Stones were past their prime, and people thought Bowie was hipper than they'd ever been.

But David Bowie was a regular thief, too, a guy who'd take something that didn't belong to him, not to make art out of it but because he wanted it. Because he fucking could.

I had a run-in with the regular-thief version of Bowie sometime in the year of *Low* and *Heroes* when he was mostly over stealing cheap soul music and had moved on to brittle darkness.

Somehow word got out that Bowie was going to be at the Factory, and Holmstrom in *PUNK* editor-in-chief mode shoved me out the door of the *PUNK* Dump with a cheap cassette recorder and told me not to come back without an interview.

On my way to the Factory, I checked in with Marty Thau, producer of the new Suicide album. Weeks earlier, Thau had played me the rough mixes, and Alan Vega's vocals were so buried beneath the savage organ of Martin Rev that they were unintelligible. I yelled at Marty to fix it, and he actually did! I mean, they were still unintelligible, but you could at least pretend they weren't. I'm sure Alan Vega said the same thing—"*I can't hear me, Marty!*"—but as a huge Suicide fan I was proud of my little contribution. To prove he'd taken my advice, Marty gave me a test pressing of the album.

I wanted to find someplace to listen to the *Legs mix* of the Suicide album. But first I had to go find Bowie at the Factory.

Big fucking mistake.

Bowie was surrounded by a crowd of people as he glided through the Factory to the back room where Andy was waiting to receive him, surrounded by his own coterie of supporters and sycophants. It was like *West Side Story* when the Jets and Sharks set the rules of the rumble, but here all the hangers-on were trying to attach themselves to either Andy's or Bowie's good graces rather than making a case for knives or chains. I'm sure Andy was relieved by the whole scene, because that meant he didn't have to say anything himself. Andy seldom had much to say, ever.

Meanwhile, I loitered by the receptionist's desk for close to an hour for Bowie to reemerge from the Warhol war council, and I was really bored because all the gay guys who worked for Andy were real fucking snobs and too important to talk to me. I tried to hit on the only girl in the place, beer heiress Catherine Guinness, and though she found me amusing, she definitely wasn't interested.

Me interviewing Andy Warhol at his Factory on 33 Union Square West.

Photo by Roberta Bayley

Finally, Bowie floated out of the back room, still surrounded by his minions, whose numbers seemed to have doubled. As he turned to bid Andy a fond farewell, I slid beside him and said, "Mr. Bowie, I was wondering if you might be willing to do an interview for *PUNK* . . ."

Bowie glanced at me, grabbed the Suicide test pressing from my hand, and was swept along the hall by his entourage into an elevator and then his waiting limousine.

I didn't even have time to yell **"GIMME BACK MY FUCKING SUICIDE RECORD, YOU FUCKING ROOSTER!!!"**

A few weeks later, Bowie turned up at CBGB with Bianca Jagger, which was only strange because it was an off night, middle of the week, with some shitty band playing and only die-hard drunks like me, Cheetah Chrome, Joey Ramone, Robin Rothman, and a few others in there.

Hahaha, this ain't no Factory or Studio 54, asshole, I thought to myself as Bowie and Bianca walked the obstacle course of dog shit left by Hilly Kristal's saluki all over the floor.

I didn't throw a bottle at Bowie. I didn't storm up and grab the ridiculous lapels of his tailored jacket and scream, *Where's my goddamned Suicide record, you thieving piece of shit!* while I shook the life out of him. Instead, I got my revenge in the most Resident Punk way I knew how.

I went outside and stole the hubcaps off Bowie's limousine.

Later I would read in the *New York Post*'s "Page Six," Manhattan's daily dish of juicy gossip, that Bowie's limo suffered a flat tire on his way home from CBGB, and Bowie and Bianca had to hail a cab surrounded by Bowery bums looking for a handout. I could just imagine Bianca cursing out Bowie, "***You said we were gonna have fun!!!***"

The furious antics of punk didn't get real until 1977, when Patti Smith fell off a stage in Tampa, Florida. Up until then, it had all been cartoon violence, like a *Tom and Jerry* episode. When Iggy Pop fell off stage, he always got up, showing off his bloody wounds like some grinning, battle-weary Viking cartoon—and kept going.

But those days were over. Now life was foreclosing on our accrued promises of endless possibility.

I had first met Patti when I was sent to interview her at the Record Plant while she was recording her new album, *Radio Ethiopia*. I made the mistake of asking her, "Uh, is anybody from Aerosmith playing on your new record?"

Someone from the *PUNK* magazine office told me to ask her, and since I was so drunk and unprepared when I showed up, Patti really laid into me for asking her such a stupid question.

Patti forgave my drunken interview, though, and a few weeks later sent me a note asking me to call her. When she fell off that stage, she'd broken her collarbone, and she was recuperating at home at One Fifth Avenue in the apartment she shared with her boyfriend, Allen Lanier, the rhythm guitarist in Blue Öyster Cult. Patti's assistant, Andi Ostrowe, would spend the day taking care of her; she was a lot more banged up than the press reported. Andi would leave at around five, and most nights Patti needed someone to keep her company until Allen came home from his gig. I was enlisted to help her out, in exchange for a six-pack of beer.

I knew that some people had a hard time with Patti, claiming she was nothing more than a gold-digging bitch who had used her boyfriends to get where she was. But I wondered if that wasn't some kind of blatant sexism.

In a 1977 interview for *Sounds*, Mick Jagger was quoted as saying, "I think she's so awful. She's full of rubbish; she's full of words and crap. I mean, she's a poseur of the worst kind, intellectual bullshit, trying to be a street girl when she doesn't seem to me to be one—I mean, a useless guitar player, a bad singer, not attractive. She's got her heart in the right place, but she's such a POSEUR! She's not really together musically. She's . . . all right."

Thanks, Sir Mick "I'm-Not-a-Fucking-Poseur-I-Just-Like-Hanging-Out-with-Royalty" Jagger. I mean, when a guy behaved the same way as Patti, he was called a stud. Accolades for the men, disparaging remarks for the women. It didn't seem fair. Patti was truly a usurper in the male-dominated world of rock 'n' roll, and even though I was a pussy hound, I was smart enough to see the writing on the wall.

Before Patti, women in rock were nothing more than disposable trinkets to be used and abused and never taken seriously. Yeah, there were a few—Janis Joplin, Grace Slick, Tina Turner, and Marianne Faithfull, who were all undeniably talented—but they never changed the equation. They were just ear candy, no matter how rebelliously they behaved.

Patti was the first female rock star that guys imagined being. Until I met her I never understood how difficult it was for a woman to be replacing a man as the new rock god. I still didn't know—it just seemed to me that women could finally be whoever they dreamed, at least at CBGB, which was pretty much my entire universe.

I was naïve.

Still, for all her androgynous posturing—spitting, swearing, and sneering—Patti had a girlish playfulness that was infectious, a kind of "let's dress up and pretend to be stars" quality that I found wonderfully attractive. She was funny, intuitive, and for all her babbling about art and artists, she could gush about TV reruns, comic books, and old rock 'n' roll songs with as much enthusiasm as she held for William Blake and Jean Genet. And I especially loved that Patti could be a real smart-ass . . .

"See, Legs, ya don't roll it in joints," Patti explained. "Ya give everyone their own pipe, 'cause it's cooler that way. It's how the Moroccans do it . . ."

"But I hate pot," I told her.

"No, no, no," Patti protested. "It's better for ya than all that beer . . ."

"But I always get paranoid when I smoke pot," I hedged, trying to think of a way to escape another trip to Paranoiaville.

"Aw, don't be such a wimp . . ."

"It doesn't have any angel dust in it or anything?" I asked nervously.

"What kind of punk are you anyway?" Patti griped. "Sheesh, ya sound like somebody's mother . . ."

She filled the little ceramic pipe from the big bowl of ganja sitting on the mattress and handed it to me with a look that said *Smoke it and shut the fuck up!*

I was out of beer, and Patti hadn't been to the bank for a while—unfortunately, that day she had spent the last of her cash on groceries to make couscous, a foul-looking concoction, for a late lunch. These being the days before ATMs, it didn't look like she'd be buying me my usual six-pack, my standard payment for babysitting her.

Even though Patti was already a rock 'n' roll legend in that spring of 1977, she didn't fully appreciate the "wonders" of beer and was always trying to convert me to the heightened spiritual experience of marijuana, that stupid green weed that smells worse than my sneakers. But Patti wouldn't roll it into joints—she kept the big bowl of ganja always within her reach—and provided her guests with ceramic pipes to fill from her bottomless bowl of buds. Patti didn't like sharing.

I was usually successful in finding excuses for not smoking her shit, but that day I had run out of them—as well as the beer.

"See, it's good for ya . . ."

Ten minutes after I finished the pipe, my brains were running out of my ears. This stuff was so potent it didn't need any extra ingredients. We were watching *Mothra*, the ridiculously bad Japanese monster movie about a giant moth controlled by two miniature geisha girls who live inside a clamshell and always speak the same singsong sentences in unison. Whenever Patti would see the giant moth, she'd tell me about shopping at Bloomingdale's for cashmere sweaters and running into this snotty salesgirl who gave her a hard time, and telling the bitch she'd take them all—and how good it felt to show that she was somebody.

And I couldn't take any more.

"Patti, what *is* this shit?" Whatta stupid question. I could *see* the words coming out of my mouth.

"Whatta ya think?" Patti groused, wiggling her neck brace since she couldn't shake her head. "That I'm gonna smoke some homegrown bullshit?"

Patti was disgusted with my lack of cool, and very disapproving of my eyes dripping out of their sockets and bouncing off the floor while different clumps of brains shot through weak points of my skull. Then booster rockets fired—and long spaghetti threads of my cerebellum shot up to the ceiling, where they sat like molten spitballs, grew eyes, and stared down at me. The "me" who was still sitting on the cushion on the floor—*melting*. My fingers dripped off. My sneakers were grinning at me. But worse was that Patti was lying there, giggling at my drug-induced hysteria.

"I think my *head's* shrinking!"

"Then ya probably need it," Patti nodded. "Ya know what William Burroughs said about his trips on yage, the psychedelic drug from South America . . ."

The blood in my head was rushing and running. I stared at Patti and said in desperation, "What I need is a beer . . ."

"Aw, don't start . . ."

Realizing that Patti couldn't sympathize with my whacked condition, I understood that I was on my own. I looked around the sparse luxury apartment and noticed a portable stereo record player on the floor next to Patti's mattress.

What I need is some music, I thought as Patti went on about a dream she had about running naked through the desert with Haile Selassie, the emperor of Ethiopia . . . There was a copy of her first album, *Horses*, lying on the floor next to a turntable and speakers. I grabbed it up and put the needle down . . .

"JEZZZZUS DIIIED FOR SUUMBODY'S SINS, BUT NOT MIIINE . . ."

Suddenly, my body stopped dripping and came to attention. My brains were still out there but started giving orders to my body. Fuck this pot bullshit, I wanted to kick some ass.

Man, oh man, it was all there on that record.

I was gone again—fists clenched; arms straight out in front, pulling and tugging; mouth leering and sneering; legs spread and poised in belligerence; and my hair flopping in my face, *just right!* Yeah, I was becoming Patti on stage, even if it was just in my own mind. Yeah, the Patti who captured the cool so expertly—that skinny little girl from South Jersey who wanted to be Keith Richards.

Patti wasn't so much a dancer as she was a strutter. All the best ones know how to strut, and I learned to strut by watching the best of them live, onstage.

But I was so stoned that I forgot I wasn't in my own bedroom listening to tunes, posing in front of my mirror. I took my head out of the speakers to see Patti lying on the bed in her neck brace and a sweaty gray sleeveless T-shirt. Her entire body was convulsing in laughter as she witnessed my imitation of her.

"LEGS, LEGS, STOP IT! I CAN'T LAUGH! IT HURTS MY NECK!"

Patti's head was bouncing in hysterics as I spelled out every letter with my hand, daring her to take 'em away. "G - L - O - R - I - A . . ."

"STOP! STOP!"

"Where's the beer, Patti?"

"STOP! IT HURTS!"

"I think we need more beer!" I taunted her. "And not just any beer, but sixteen-ouncers!"

"STOP! STOP! STOP!"

She was still cackling in hysterics.

". . . DO YA KNOW HOW TA PONY? LIKE BONY MARONEY?"

I don't remember if she ever bought more beer. I only know that Patti Smith kicked ass so hard she knocked down the whole fucking wall.

Patti was the first woman in rock 'n' roll that guys aspired to be. She was the first woman to get it down so good that it didn't matter what fucking planet she was from. Patti kicked gender in the balls. In the process, she opened the door for every woman who looked up on the stage and refused to imagine herself down on her knees, blowing the rock god—and instead saw herself firm on her feet, becoming one.

John Holmstrom and Ged Dunn were still constantly falling out with each other and fighting. And he might not talk about it, but I think the final straw might have been when Holmstrom slept with Ged's girlfriend. Not long after that, Ged was fired from *PUNK*. He'd driven a wedge between us and blown through Tom Katz's $20,000 investment in a matter of months. Rather than accept a demotion he took the nuclear option, shouting on his way out the door that we'd regret it.

Once we fired Ged, we ran into constant problems with the printer. Holmstrom thought Ged had told them that we weren't good for the money we owed, and that's why they stopped being so reliable, but I don't know anything about that.

We also abandoned the *PUNK* Dump around that time for an actual office space at 225 Lafayette Street, which was the original home of EC Comics and *Mad* magazine. It was our cultural destiny.

But we were still broke, and even with Tom Katz coming up with more money, we had no way of publishing our next issue. So we came up with the idea of a benefit concert, and Hilly Kristal blocked out two weeknights at CBGB in early May for a *PUNK* fundraiser.

The Ramones were on tour in Europe, but it was still a huge success. Blondie, the Dead Boys, Richard Hell and the Voidoids, Suicide, the Paley Brothers, and the Cramps were among the bands who showed up. But the highlight was the Patti Smith Group.

This was the year that, in January, Patti had her fall during a show in Tampa, Florida. She hadn't played since then, but we were friends and I asked and she said yes. I think she really wanted to get out and play again.

Still wearing her neck brace, Patti dedicated her set to all fanzines. In the absence of the Ramones, the Patti Smith Group covered "I Wanna Be Your Boyfriend."

At the end of the second night, Hilly Kristal cut us a check for over $2,000, and the next day I met with Holmstrom and Tom Katz for a slice of pizza. Tom had the check in a folded-up newspaper for safekeeping, and we smiled through our greasy slices at how well the *PUNK* benefit concert had gone, how much love we'd been shown from the bands and fans; we gushed about this new beginning for the magazine.

And on our way to the bank, Tom realized he'd thrown the newspaper in the trash.

Fortunately it was still there when we went back, and we immediately deposited it in the bank.

My relatively idyllic life in Staten Island ended when our apartment was broken into and the thieves stole everything I owned. I moved back to New York and crashed at Arturo Vega's to figure out my next move. It turned out my next move was detox.

NINE

I went to detox for the first time in 1977. I'd been staying at Arturo Vega's place, and my brother, Craig, came to New York to visit me; Holmstrom had helped get tickets to see Led Zeppelin at Madison Square Garden, which Craig wanted more than anything. I was really skinny, and I was born skinny, but I wasn't eating or sleeping, just drinking constantly. I must have looked like a ghost. Craig went back to Connecticut and told my mother about it, and she made the arrangements. They even came from her house to pick me up.

The hospital was in a continuing care unit of Hartford Hospital. It wasn't the kind of detox you see now, where you dry out in a swimming pool in the desert. It wasn't a spa. It was cold turkey, plus they wanted to give me pills and I thought, *I'm not fucking taking any of those.* I was just drinking beer at that time, and I didn't think I was that bad.

My roommate thought he was Jesus Christ. Really; a really nice guy, but I'd never have guessed he was Jesus if he hadn't told me. He didn't have long hair or a robe or sandals. He didn't turn water into wine or seem particularly pious. He just looked at me and said, "You know I'm Jesus Christ, right?"

"Alright, Jesus. Just don't smother me with a pillow in the middle of the night. Amen."

The timing of my trip to detox was really inconvenient, because I was still writing for *Hit Parader* and I was on deadline. It seemed really important to me at the time, but I can't remember now what it was even about. I was writing all the time, and being stuck in a hospital got in the way.

The hospital wouldn't let me go to work, because I guess they didn't trust me to take care of myself. They'd let Jesus Christ leave on day passes, and one day when he was out he committed suicide. ***Jesus!***

It started to feel like the walls were closing in on me until a friend of mine who was a cop put me in handcuffs and "arrested" me. We jumped on his motorcycle and I felt like Steve McQueen in *The Great Escape*, only I got away.

"Do you wanna go to a bar?" my friend yelled back to me as we roared away from the hospital. He was a nice guy, and funny too. We didn't go to a bar.

Instead, I got a job for a few months writing for *The Observer*, a local newspaper in Southington, Connecticut. I wrote two or three articles a week about things like programs for people recovering from heart attacks through the YMCA and other dull community shit.

I was still writing for *PUNK*, and for *Hit Parader*, too, though they didn't have any money. But I liked coming up with my "Legs McNeil Famous Detective Stories," like the one where Elvis Costello's manager hired me to find him after he'd abandoned the Attractions and ran away to become the human cannonball for the Bungling Brothers Royal Razzmatazz Circus. I saved the day and rock 'n' roll by pulling out my trusty .45 and shooting the cannon's controls so Elvis would land right outside his manager's office, Riviera Global.

I don't know how many of these I wrote between 1976 and 1978; it was a lot. But *Hit Parader* took so long to pay me that the money was already spent by the time I got it.

After a few months covering community news, I left *The Observer* and Connecticut and went back to New York City, where I immediately started drinking again.

Meanwhile, Tom Katz had broken his leg and moved back to Detroit and got some high-paying job in the automobile industry, maybe with General Motors. He was a really smart guy, so I wasn't surprised.

Tom and I kept in touch. In the early '80s I had a girlfriend in Detroit, and I flew there just to fuck her. Yeah, she was that good, and I was that horny. At some point I took a break from our weekend fuck-a-palooza to come up for air and visited Tom, who, incredibly, was staying in the same apartment building as Patti Smith and Fred "Sonic" Smith. Fred was one of the founders of the MC5, Lincoln Park, Michigan's electrifying proto-punk pioneers. Patti moved with Fred to Detroit in 1979, and they were married a year later.

I went and knocked on Patti's door and Fred answered.

"Hi Fred, it's Legs; is Patti here?"

But he was really cold, and I don't know if he just wanted to keep Patti away from what she'd left behind in New York, or if she just didn't want to talk to me. I guess it didn't really matter.

That night, Tom and I went for a long walk through his neighborhood, and as we smoked cigarettes, he told me the entire plot, in great detail, of *Doctor Zhivago*, Russian writer Boris Pasternak's sprawling epic. I was just mesmerized as he covered in graphic detail this epic story.

Then I went back to my girlfriend's and we did it some more.

As far as *PUNK* went, if I wasn't looking over Holmstrom's shoulder I might as well have been on the moon. Not long after *The Legend of Nick Detroit* I wrote another photo comic called *Mutant Monster Beach Party*.

It took forever to get going, and Holmstrom kept asking me for revisions. It didn't wind up in the magazine until issue #15, Spring/Summer 1978. By then Holmstrom had taken over directing it and made a mess out of my script, adding all these plots that weren't in the original script. Like Joey Ramone's brother, Mickey Leigh, as an alien landing in a spaceship. What the fuck was that all about?

Me at the New Haven train station bringing my older brother's old surfboard for the shooting of my next fumetti, *Mutant Monster Beach Party*.

Photo by Tom Hearn

TEN

Los Angeles is a city of crap. That's where they make it. I once asked Danny Fields what the most influential American city was, expecting him to say New York City, but he surprised me by saying Los Angeles.

"Undoubtedly, LA, because of the movie and television industries," Danny said. "Just think how much your world has been formed by movies and TV!"

Probably my favorite time with Danny was when we were hanging out one lazy afternoon, smoking a joint, watching TV, and *The Simpsons* was on. It was the episode that parodied William Golding's novel *Lord of the Flies*, where Bart and Lisa are on a class trip, and the school bus crashes off a bridge, and all the kids get stranded on a desert island. Bart sends the kids out to gather food, but only Lisa comes back with some purple berries.

Ralph Wiggum, the seemingly mentally challenged kid in Bart's class, eats the berries, falls to the ground clutching his stomach, and squeals, "They taste like . . . burning!"

Danny and I collapsed in laughter.

Yeah, LA was the city that had corrupted us the most. Consider animated anarchy like *The Simpsons*, *South Park*, *Archer*, and *Rick and Morty*. Never mind all the great '60s and '70s shows like *Mister Ed*, *The Munsters*, *Green Acres*, and *Happy Days*!

We used to stop work at the *PUNK* Dump every day at 11 PM to watch two half-hour episodes of *Happy Days*, starring the Fonz, and Holmstrom even had a big poster of him hanging on the wall! We loved the Fonz!

I figured wintering in LA was cheaper than buying a new winter wardrobe, as those winds coming off the Hudson River were so fucking cold—like wind tunnels on the crosstown streets—so I got *High Times* magazine to pay for my LA trip!

Like everyone else, I had the fantasy version of Los Angeles, *Gilligan's Island* reruns on a permanent loop. *How we love our crap!*

I was staying at the Tropicana Motel on Santa Monica, the one with the Orange Julius stand three blocks away, selling the fast-acting cure for a hangover: a large Orange Julius!

But don't leave the motel room without your sunglasses! *Oh shit, forgot 'em again! Dammit!* You end up squinting down the three long city blocks to heaven, the Orange Julius stand!

Luckily the Tropicana was hopping! Tom Waits and Chuck E. Weiss lived in back, on the other side of the office and pool. The "Trop" was where everybody stayed. I kept calling back to New York so *High Times* would wire me more money, so the motel wouldn't keep putting that huge clunky door lock on my room door. And I kept calling Holmstrom and asking if Harvey Kurtzman had talked to Hugh Hefner about letting me interview him for *PUNK* magazine.

Cars, girls, surfing, beer, nothing else matters here!

It would be my *masterpiece!*

Unfortunately, who knew that the Playboy Mansion at that time was the unclassiest joint in town? With all the coke, speed, 'ludes, and orgies going on, the last person Hef wanted to talk to was a journalist from *High Times,* America's premier drug magazine.

Hef had the perfect setup. A god worshipped by gaggles of horny men. Narcissistic paradise! He didn't want a nobody from *High Times* fucking it up for him.

While I was busy trading phone calls with Holmstrom and *High Times,*

I started hanging out with Jonathan Paley of the Paley Brothers, who were also signed to Sire Records, along with the Ramones, Talking Heads, Dead Boys, and Richard Hell. Jonathan and I already knew one another from CBGB, and we became pals when the Paley Brothers played their debut performance at the *PUNK* magazine benefit at CBGB, then went from CB's to playing Madison Square Garden, opening for Shaun Cassidy.

Jonathan and his equally handsome brother, Andy, comprised the Paley Brothers, a brother rock act like the Everly Brothers. The Paley Brothers played catchy commercial bubblegum, but apparently not catchy enough, at least not until Andy went on to write the songs for Warren Beatty's *Dick Tracy* and music for *SpongeBob SquarePants*.

Jonathan happened to be extraordinarily pretty—the kind of guy you want for your wingman when you're cruising for women. Plus we had opposite tastes in the ladies, so there was never competition. In Los Angeles, Jonathan had a rental car, so we were all set.

"Shit, there's no press party tonight," Jonathan lamented. "You should've been here for Stigwood's *Sgt. Pepper's Lonely Hearts Club Band* movie! Now that was a fucking party!"

The Paley Brothers had appeared in *Sgt. Pepper's Lonely Hearts Club Band* and always knew where the best parties were. Robert Stigwood also produced *Saturday Night Fever*, and *Grease*, and also founded RSO Records, so he had boatloads of money to throw around. Andy Paley sure knew which side his bread was buttered on.

Meanwhile, back at the Trop, Jonathan moaned, "Shit, no press party, and I got this car and everything . . ."

I snapped, "That's all we need!"

"Whattaya mean?"

"Jesus Jonathan, didn't you see the movie *American Graffiti*? That's all they do is cruise around in their cars! That's how they pick up girls out here! We just cruise Sunset Boulevard or Santa Monica Boulevard until we see two hot babes, and we ask them if they got a light at the first stoplight."

"You gotta talk to them . . ."

"Sure," I said, "I'll do all the talking, just gimme a cigarette . . ."

Within a half hour we had an ongoing conversation with two sexy girls at every stoplight for ten blocks, until they finally pulled over and the big-busted blonde joined Jonathan in our car, and I joined the brunette in their car. Back at the motel we fucked like bunnies. Jonathan didn't turn up at the Trop until the next morning.

Jonathan was usually busy fucking Damita, the famous muse and groupie from CBGB, who was also staying at the Tropicana. Meanwhile, I hung out with Chuck E. Weiss and Tom Waits. Chuck E. was signed to the William Morris Agency, the biggest talent agency in Hollywood at that time. Chuck E. had just had a freak hit with his pastiche of Paul Simon's hit record "Fifty Ways to Leave Your Lover," transformed by Chuck E. into "Fifty Ways to Have a Hit Song." So William Morris owed Chuck E. fifty dollars, and he invited me to the talent agency to pick up a check.

Chuck E. was a combination of a hipster con man and gypsy musician, who hung around with Waits like they were Batman and Robin. Every night they'd get in Tom's big black Cadillac convertible and spend the night scoring dope and chasing Mexican girls.

"No, no, no," Tom hacked when he saw me approaching the car, with my look that said, *Take me with you!*

"You're too young for this shit," he said very paternally. Tom was a decent guy, but I kept waiting for him to clear his throat. His voice was *that* gravelly, even as a young man.

"Tell ya what," he said kindly, "we'll do the interview tomorrow at noon, inside the office?"

I said, "Okay, but I'd really like to see your room, I hear it rivals the CBGB's bathroom . . ."

"Someday, someday," Tom chuckled gruffly, Chuck E. grinned, and the Cadillac sped off into that warm California night.

That fucking voice gave inspiration to every young alcoholic out there, like me, with his cult hit "The Piano Has Been Drinking" off his first album, *Small Change*, after David Geffen signed him to Asylum Records.

There was nothing dishonest about Waits, except that he may have exaggerated stuff when I interviewed him, but I was so enchanted with the story he was telling, and the world he was creating, that I urged him on.

Chuck E. at the William Morris Agency was a scream; we'd walk the hallways, drinking beer, and Chuck E. would walk by some junior agent's office. The guy would be sitting back at his desk, feet up, and Chuck E. would bark, ***"GET YOUR GODDAMN FEET OFF THE DESK!"***

And the agent would take his feet down every time! We'd just collapse in laughter, giggling madly in the hallways, the passersby too disinterested to give us a second look.

Chuck E. is the guy Rickie Lee Jones wrote about in her hit record "Chuck E's in Love," of which she says, "And whatever it is that he's got up his sleeve / Well, I hope it isn't contagious . . ." Chuck E. was one of a kind.

Tom Waits arrived in the Tropicana office the next afternoon at noon. It was tiny, with a guy behind the desk, and a very small couch and chairs in a minuscule reception area. I had my tape recorder set up on the couch while Tom sat in one of the chairs across from me. It was one of the best interviews I've ever done. I asked him, "If you wrote a cheap, sleazy paperback novel what would the title be?"

"Love Wears Shades," Tom said after he thought it over. I thought that was the best title I'd ever heard. It conjured up so many different meanings. *Is she the woman who can't be trusted and betrays her gangster boyfriend in the end? Or do aliens take over her body and force it to attack the army base?*

This is the part Waits lied about: Tom told me his parents worked in the film business. He said his father translated films from English into Spanish. It made me think about how Universal Studios filmed *Dracula* in 1931 and simultaneously filmed a Spanish version at night, when Tod Browning, Bela Lugosi, Helen Chandler, and Dwight Frye went home. At night, director George Melford shot the Spanish-language version on the same sets, with Carlos Villarías in the role of Conde Drácula.

I could just see Tom Waits's dad on the sound stage providing Spanish translations for this Spanish-language version of *Dracula*. I was tripping on old Hollywood and falling through the *City of Nets*. Tom gave me a conversational tour of old Hollywood, from a middle-class family's take on it; the camera and lighting rental companies, the recording studios, the tailors in costuming, the edit bays, the back lots, and the cheesy bars where the different crews hung out—all those middle-class jobs that Tom might've exaggerated about.

But who fucking cared? Waits's world was so real, you could tell he'd been around the block a few times and discerned for himself what was interesting and what wasn't. And he wasn't interested in sanitized excrement. He's an authentic hooligan with a poet's soul.

Just as we were getting to the most interesting part of the interview, a kind of skanky girl opened the glass office door.

"Tom, Tom, I gotta talk to youuu . . ." she begged.

"Not now, honey, I'm doing an interview," he replied graciously.

"No Tom," she marched to the couch. "You gotta see these spots on my legs . . ."

She pulled her skirt up to her panties—and her legs were sprinkled with open sores, greenish-purple pustules, each about double the size of a quarter.

Tom was shocked. "Oh darlin', you gotta take care of yourself, you gotta go to the hospital and have 'em looked at . . . they look infected . . ."

The advanced case of syphilis lesions made both Tom and me gag. It was all on tape.

The piano had been doing more than just drinking.

And so had I, as I lost the tape. A tragedy, but life was so chaotic then. And I never lost another tape again.

I was shocked later when I was watching a Cal Worthington commercial: "If you wanna better car, go see Cal / If you wanna better car, go see Cal," wherein Cal rode some exotic beast—a camel, a buffalo, or a cow—through his used car lot—and I heard a knock on my door.

I opened it and Tom Waits and Chuck E. were standing there, grinning.

"You said during the interview you didn't know how to shoot craps," Tom explained. "So we're here to teach you," and they marched right in my room and got down on their knees.

Tom brushed my cigarette ashes off the rug, then rolled the dice.

I just thought, *How cool is this, Tom Waits and Chuck E. are teaching me how to shoot craps!*

I think they brought beer with them; I'm not too sure now, but Tom and Chuck E. and I discovered we all drank from the same well. We were all influenced from the same sources: Lenny Bruce; William Burroughs; Jack Kerouac; Rod Serling; Hubert Selby, Jr.; Cal Worthington; as well as the entire gamut of crime noir authors: Dashiell Hammett; Jim Thompson; David Goodis; to name a few.

We talked about Jim Thompson's little-known novel, *Savage Night,* about a hit man who moves into a boarding house so he can kill one of the lodgers, while having an affair with a one-legged maid. Shades of Flannery O'Connor. As author Dennis Cooper wrote about *Savage Night,* "Rare are the endings who live up to their stories, but with Jim Thompson, this isn't a concern."

Jim Thompson, the most notorious crime noir writer of the '40s and '50s, once said, *"Life is a bucket of shit with a barbed wire handle."*

It doesn't get any blacker than that.

As for why he and Chuck E. lived at the Tropicana Motel, Tom said, "You almost have to create situations in order to write about them, so I live in a constant state of self-imposed poverty." It probably had more to do with the dope and Mexican girls.

Duke's, the coffee shop that was attached to the Tropicana, was always closed when I was there, so I never got to meet Rickie Lee Jones, who Tom and Chuck E. had breakfast with most mornings. Tom was dating Jones at the time, though I didn't know it.

According to the legend, Waits was talking with Rickie Lee on the phone and she asked, "What's up?"

Tom said, "Chuck E.'s in love," and a hit song was born.

Unfortunately, Waits's and Jones's relationship didn't last due to dope addiction, though I was never sure whose. It didn't seem to matter. Heroin always wins. "*Small Change got rained on with his own .38.*"

Staying at the Tropicana felt like a Tom Waits song come to life, with Tom right there narrating the entire thing. Even the girl I picked up with Jonathan Paley at the stoplight lived like she just walked out of "Pasties and a G-String," as she turned out to be a prostitute who started coming to my door at two in the morning after she finished turning tricks.

I'd be passed out in front of the portable color TV with reruns of *The Twilight Zone* on—and her pounding on the door brought me back to life. At least she brought cigarettes.

The girl Jonathan picked up gave him a dose of hepatitis, and Jonathan had to fly back to Boston to recover. Jonathan's brother, Andy, always blamed it on me and told Jonathan to stay away from me, that I was a bad influence, even though I wasn't even there with Paley and his girl, and had no idea what had gone down. I think Jonathan was corrupted long before he met me.

Like I said, I always get blamed for everything . . .

My time in Los Angeles was about to come to an end, with or without a Hugh Hefner interview, and I was about to head north to infiltrate enemy territory: San Francisco, home of the hippie.

Though the Ramones were undoubtedly the first wave of attack in the punk Panzer division, the Sex Pistols were readying themselves for a breakout that would rival the Wehrmacht at the Battle of the Bulge. After Malcolm McLaren left his official role as the New York Dolls' manager and general instigator, he returned to London and opened a trendy clothing store. It became a hangout for tomorrow's stars, and its name changed as fast as the styles, the most memorable being SEX. It was here McLaren regrouped his forces and reviewed his tactics, all the while promoting new punk fashions. He'd rant and rave about the threatening appeal of the Dolls; the ever-exciting rawness of inexperienced, arrogant, on-the-dole teenagers; and Richard Hell's haircut, style, and warp-ten alienation.

Before Malcolm could catch his breath, he met a disgusting smart aleck the world would come to enjoy under the name of Johnny Rotten. This nasty, vile jerk with a keen mind and a whiplash tongue goaded Malcolm on, never laughed at his jokes, and viciously ridiculed him for trying to find fame and fortune in America only to wind up a trendy clothing-store owner on King's Road at a ripe old age. It's a sure bet Malcolm had met his match—this street-smart kid would never let up on him except to guzzle another beer and light a cigarette.

As the legend goes, Malcolm spotted the genius of Rotten's acid contempt and auditioned him for his concept of the perfect rock 'n' roll group—"perfect" meaning most dangerous and threatening—and Rotten lip-synched Alice Cooper's "I'm Eighteen" on the store's jukebox and passed the audition with flying colors. Inspired by Rotten, McLaren combined his instinctual understanding of the press with his knowledge of the music biz from working with the Dolls in order to cause the Scandal of the Decade.

Malcolm was well aware the Sex Pistols would never get attention unless they demanded it. He understood that prime-time airplay on the BBC was reserved for boring American disco groups and decrepit stadium cock-rockers. The only way to break through would be to generate enough horrible press that the public's natural curiosity would cause them to buy a single or two. Everyone loves, or at least can't look away from, a freak show.

Malcolm McLaren would force the Sex Pistols down the BBC's throats, and if they banned the band, it would only prove his point. Either way he couldn't lose.

With the help of London's tabloid dailies and a well-timed swearing match on national TV, the Sex Pistols became a household word. Malcolm's muddled politics and Rotten's anti-everything stance and rhetoric created an exciting phenomenon, selling the world a spitting, slobbering, vomiting, drunk bill of goods. Kids bought it and swallowed it whole at expensive retail price tags, and overnight everyone everywhere knew that punk was another crazy English rock 'n' roll invasion. It was no use telling anyone different. Punk was ugly kids vomiting and pissing onstage. No journalist was about to admit the New York scene had ever existed.

The more that was written about punk rock and its subculture, the less anyone knew. So why the hell should anyone care at all? Nobody in the real nine-to-five world gave a shit, but journalists sometimes run short of bad copy. It was happening, so why not write about it? Being mostly attitude and image, Malcolm's politics, the Sex Pistols' hysterics, and the bad shape of England made much better copy. It had all the ingredients for a good feature: anarchy, sex, violence, discontented working-class kids, politics, and a musical blitzkrieg through the English class structure. In the good ol' US of A, it was just some pale, skinny weirdos in black leather jackets. For some reason, no one took "Now I Wanna Sniff Some Glue" as seriously as Johnny Rotten's sinister laugh at the beginning of "Anarchy in the U.K."

Even my mother called me at the *PUNK* Dump and said, "I just heard punk started in England . . ." Thanks, Mom!

Though it happened in both countries almost simultaneously, its evolution would produce something as different as day was from night.

Somehow it meant more to the press that the English scene was populated by working-class kids, highly visible to even the most cloistered member of the British Empire. The English kids translated their frustration into a classic weapon of defiance—hair, dress, and music—and went looking for anyone who disagreed with them. They were pissed off, and so were we. But we didn't want to take ourselves too seriously, especially after the English punks started taking *everything* too seriously and threatening to ruin the whole thing.

But it was no longer our scene. The Sex Pistols became punk. No one remembered what came before; no one cared. Kids with short-cropped pink and green hair emerged out of the woodwork. Armies of the night were out on the move, slinking around in spandex with something to prove. Words like "poseur," "wanker," and "cunt," fueled by fake English accents, were dripping from the blackest suburban lips.

Nancy Spungen was the extreme case: scene maker, sometime stripper, and a neighbor of ours on the West Side. She'd come by the *PUNK* Dump once in a while, read the latest issue and listen to the latest underground singles, and talk about stripping. It is most likely she learned about the Sex Pistols from the first American interview we published in *PUNK* issue #6. After we finished work, she'd let us take showers at her apartment, make us scrambled eggs, and would talk about the best bet for music that evening.

As word of the English scene grew, Nancy Spungen disappeared from New York and emerged in the UK as a hard-ass punk rocker with a fake English accent. The English press called her "Nauseating Nancy" after she became Sid Vicious's girlfriend. Transformed by the bitterness of the English scene and riding high on her short-lived notoriety, her ultimate fate only proved just how dangerous taking yourself too seriously can be.

Punk was polarized by then, and while the English jumped headfirst into the muck of class wars and politics, the American groups held on to their upbeat heavy-metal pretensions of the first English invasion. While those foreigners tried harder to loosen the shackles of an earlier generation of their own countrymen's contribution to rock 'n' roll, the Americans embraced the simplicity of that bygone era.

America and England were more than just an ocean apart, but the confusion was good for both teams as journalists worldwide were assigned the problem of sorting it all out. And since they never got it right, the myth grew. A hell of a lot of records got sold, and after all the bullshit of tearing down the corporate structure, isn't selling records still the bottom line? After all, no one gave them away.

It couldn't be more the opposite, as Johnny Rotten proclaimed: "We're not here for your enjoyment, you're here for ours." If anyone was giving anything away, it was the fans throwing money, cameras, full beer cans, and other expensive antipersonnel weapons onto the stage during a typical concert on the Pistols' American tour: Atlanta, Tulsa, San Antonio, San Francisco. It was supposed to be a voyage to every place no one would ever play, in order to fuel the confusion. It worked.

I finally got tired of waiting, and tired of Holmstrom nagging me over the telephone to join him and Roberta Bayley in San Francisco to see the Sex Pistols' Winterland show. So I showed up at the *Playboy* offices on the Sunset Strip and met the receptionist. I was there as a last-ditch effort to interview Hugh Hefner for *PUNK* magazine. Harvey Kurtzman was lobbying on our behalf, but Hefner, being the control-freak asshole he was, kept blowing us off.

I went to the *Playboy* office to figure something out, and when I got there I met this tall, gorgeous, really skinny receptionist with black hair who had a wicked crush on me. Sometimes you can just tell.

I told her I was heading up to San Francisco to cover the Sex Pistols' show, and when her face lit up I asked if she wanted to go. I arranged to pick her up at *Playboy* the next day.

My last night in LA, I was invited to a party on the other side of the Tropicana. I got all showered and shaved and thought, *Tonight's the night!* Beautiful nymphs with long blonde hair, plump breasts, thick golden-tanned thighs that melt down into a perfect slenderly wrapped pair of legs. Oh baby, oh baby, oh baby . . .

Much to my horror, when I arrived I found out it was a punk party specially equipped with now-negative girls, all foul, their tans stripped from them with Easy-Off oven cleaner. Their beautiful long hair was cut to the skin with razors and dyed purple, pink, green-blue, and those creamy complexions were accented with acne, cigarette burns, and safety pins. I felt cheated.

You fucking Sex Pistols, why couldn't you come next year!

Turns out, the Sex Pistols did in ten days what the New York scene hadn't been able to manage: make punk a four-letter word across America.

An extremely unattractive teenage girl who resembled a forty-year-old matron in a women's prison rather than a young woman fresh on the road to self-discovery approached me.

Knowing that I co-created *PUNK* magazine, she erupted in a verbal assault at the pretense of the New York scene. I didn't want to hear it. I was already pissed off enough that no one here looked like Julie, the hot blonde girl from *The Mod Squad*, but she got nastier and kept on insulting me. I told her she was ugly and to leave me alone. She spat beer in my face and the alcohol burned my eyes. As soon as I wiped it out and my vision cleared, the first image to take focus was this snarling girl still glaring at me. I told her the beer didn't help; she was still ugly. She belted me in the nose. I told her, yes, she was still fucking ugly.

Three seconds later, I was surrounded by hideous monsters who were probably nice kids before the local NBC news devoted the feature story on their prime-time show *Weekend* to an in-depth study of English punk. The kids were acting like they were on the dole when most of them probably lived in comfortable homes on a healthy allowance and gasoline credit cards for their very own car.

"Go back to New York!" is all I remember hearing as I left the disintegrating party. Instead, I went back to my motel room alone. I locked the door and watched TV and wondered why Hollywood was called "Sin City." The bars closed at quarter to two, the drinking age was twenty-one, and no one liked to have fun. I sat sulking and slowly it dawned on me.

Who could blame these kids? LA sucks and they know it. It must get pretty depressing knowing your town's biggest cash crop is *Charlie's Angels* or Rona Barrett. In a city that constantly reminds you that if you're nobody, you really ain't anybody at all, it must get tedious dodging limos, Rolls-Royces, and Mercedes as you make your way to the unemployment office. It made sense that they found their salvation in punk, the best defense being a good offense. If you had to walk around all day looking at a bunch of bimbos with Farrah Fawcett haircuts and nipple boners giggling about the antics of their blow-dried polyester disco boyfriends, you'd want to vomit too. But there was no use trying to communicate. The Sex Pistols were due in San Francisco at any moment, and punk rock in America was about to climax.

Frustrated and depressed that the buxom blonde California girls of my dreams had been transformed into ugly punkette mutants, I left LA and joined John Holmstrom and *PUNK* magazine photo editor Roberta Bayley in San Francisco.

I'd arranged a ride up to the Bay Area for me and the *Playboy* receptionist in a van with a couple of minor bands, eight hours of hard road with a bunch of assholes. I can't even remember who they were, I was just happy to be rid of them.

We got out of the van at the Miyako Hotel, one of the most luxurious places I'd ever seen. Every rock star rolling through San Francisco stayed there. At the hotel, John explained things weren't going so well with the Pistols. It seemed Sid Vicious kept trying to kill himself every free moment he had; Johnny Rotten was playing spoiled superstar and pulling Greta Garbo routines; Malcolm McLaren was disgusted by Warner Brothers fighting him tooth and nail on every creative idea he had for promoting anarchy in the States.

In addition to the Warner Brothers executives calling the shots from some penthouse on the Sunset Strip, a goon squad of Warner's thugs who reminded me of the Idi Amin babysitting service had surrounded Johnny and Sid, forcing them to travel for the entire tour in a Greyhound prison while Paul Cook and Steve Jones and McLaren flew. Malcolm seldom knew where the other half was. Divide and conquer.

But the Pistols still had an even more formidable enemy: San Francisco, the capital of hippie music. They should have gone straight to LA and played one set at the Whiskey a Go Go, causing a real riot on the Sunset Strip by the disgruntled fans who couldn't get in because of the small seating capacity. It might have been the birth of anarchy in the USA.

Instead, the ghosts of flower power rose from their graves and cursed the entire Sex Squadron with a thundercloud of paranoia from all the bad acid trips ever to hit Haight-Ashbury.

Me backstage after the Sex Pistols' Winterland show, standing behind Sid Vicious talking to the four girls he just pulled from the audience.

Photo © Bob Gruen/www.bobgruen.com

The Winterland gig itself was one of the most boring rock 'n' roll shows ever. Quite a hard task considering it was the Sex Pistols. Even Johnny Rotten knew it, scowling silently at the crowd while the other Pistols ground through a sludgy version of the Stooges' "No Fun." And it really was no fun.

Rotten finally broke his silence, famously sneering, "Ha-ha-ha! Ever get the feeling you've been cheated?" before stalking off stage.

Immediately after the set, Holmstrom handed me a backstage pass. At the party backstage, one of the local opening acts was having a food fight with the poseurs and celebrity curiosity seekers. It was very boring, so I went to the dressing room, sat down, opened a Heineken, and watched the Pistols. Sid had brought four girls from out of the audience back to the dressing room. "Who's going to fuck me tonight?" he asked.

"How about a kiss first?" a cute sixteen-year-old groupie asked.

Rotten sat alone on an old, overstuffed couch and grumbled to himself while Sidney entertained the four ladies. One of the girls got up the nerve to approach Johnny and asked, "How do you do?" This set Johnny off into a tirade about how "How do you do?" was an invalid greeting. The girl blushed and backed off. Rotten looked scared, naïve, and pissed off. I think he sometimes envied Sid for being an idiot. Dumb, but happy. But Johnny was cursed with the fame, the intelligence, and a low self-image that made him terribly shy, and that he made up for by being terribly obnoxious. I used that one too.

Legendary photographer Annie Leibovitz entered the room with all her flash equipment, umbrellas, and tons of cameras to take a cover photo for *Rolling Stone*. She wanted to get a picture of Rotten and Vicious together, but neither of them would join the other. Finally, Annie cajoled Johnny to pose for her in the bathroom, where she'd set up her gear. "Is my hair all right?" Johnny snarled loudly at her. No one looked like they were having fun. Even Sid, surrounded by four groupies, looked bored and unable to figure out what to do with the girls now that he had them.

I left the dressing room more depressed than ever, my jacket pockets packed with Heinekens, and bumped into notorious New York City groupie Damita, nine months pregnant, with a hole cut in her T-shirt to expose her belly. I ripped off my backstage pass, slapped it onto Damita's swollen stomach, and said, "Go get 'em girl!" happy to be done with the Sex Pistols.

I headed back to my hotel room with the *Playboy* receptionist, just wanting to get in the bathtub with her. The bathtubs were fantastic; you poured packets of this green shit into the tub that allowed you to float, and then ordered more crab meat sandwiches on English muffins, and the receptionist and I were in heaven. We were having so much fun, I didn't even want to go to the show. And as it turned out, I shoulda stayed in the tub.

The next day the Pistols would unofficially disband.

Although the Sex Pistols breakup in San Francisco wouldn't become official for a few weeks, the record companies who'd flirted with this new music and punk folly were not taking any chances. Since the Sex Pistols had become synonymous with punk, something drastic would have to happen if they expected to make any money selling their stable of new-wave groups.

Eureka, that's it! "New Wave."

Already as I arrived back in New York, music industry magazines like *Billboard* and *Record World* proclaimed: "Don't call it punk, call it new wave" in full-page advertisements.

Smart bastards, I thought. "Divide and conquer again." Separate the Pistols and their ilk from safer, more accessible punk rock groups. Was there a difference between punk and new wave? What was it? Confusion flourished again. It was a brilliant tactical move by the music industry.

Punk, of course, would be associated with vulgarity, vomit, and violence. New wave would be any of the new music that was commercial and accessible. Homogenized skinny ties.

Since the Ramones, Sex Pistols, Blondie, or Talking Heads never called themselves punks, the term "new wave" seemed okay—flashy and nebulous. But for American radio listeners and record buyers, it was an easier egg to swallow. "New wave" sounded hip and intellectual, like existential French movies. College kids could "relate to it" and, better yet, buy it.

The music business used the confusion to their advantage. It was a cultural coup. Groups like Queen, the J. Geils Band, and Bruce Springsteen cut their hair or shaved their beards and got back to basics. Cher wore leopard-skin leotards as she roller-skated around the recording studio in frustration, wondering why she hadn't recorded "Heart of Glass." Linda Ronstadt cut a few Elvis Costello tunes, pleasing his pocketbook but not his ears. The lead singer in most heavy-metal bands claimed to be the first punk.

Back at *PUNK* magazine, things weren't going so well. Because of the record industry's brilliant and profitable switch from punk to new wave, not too many record companies were interested in advertising in a magazine called *PUNK*. But even if we had become as popular as *TV Guide* or *Family Circle*, rags we'd shared rack space with for close to a year, it might have been the end of civilization as we knew it! Sweet old ladies in black leather motorcycle jackets causing riots at the Social Security office. TV newsmen in spiked dog collars and spiked green hair telling you, "Fuck off, go make your own news!" Every businessman in America quitting his job to join a band. Actually, it doesn't sound that bad if people didn't forget the joke.

Sid Vicious was anything but vicious when he replaced Glen Matlock in the Sex Pistols. Glen told me he wasn't kicked out of the Pistols, but left on his own accord. I don't blame him.

Sid forgot the joke and lived up to the romantic tragedy rock 'n' roll evokes. Nancy Spungen was murdered. Sidney overdosed. A new legend was born, and now the scene had its patron saints.

Move over Jimi and Janis—and tell Tchaikovsky the news.

Though it might never become apparent to most people through all the hype, bad press, sensationalism, bad taste, and loud music, a lot of good came out of the punk scene. Do-it-yourself records and magazines produced by kids with little or no money sprang up in almost every urban American center as nightclubs that once exclusively employed cover bands were connived into booking new bands who wrote their own songs. The idea that you could do something on your own and without a lot of money in corporationland was truly revolutionary, and hopefully rock 'n' roll would never again be worshipped as a religion but taken as a tribal rite in the next step to sane living. Whatever that is.

Meanwhile, the fallout from the Sex Pistols' tour had lasting repercussions. Covering the Pistols drove a wedge between me and the Ramones that Joey never healed from.

"It was Holmstrom's idea!" I protested, but he still blamed me. Joey was weird about his jealousies and thought of it as a betrayal. And maybe it was, because I was considered one of them, an ally, a friend.

"Joey, I *have* to go!"

"Aw, you just wanna go!"

He was such a baby about it.

The Ramones were touring with the Runaways at that time, which was a fantastic pairing. I'd much rather have seen them than the Sex Pistols, but Joey was unconvinced, even when I told him about my crush on Joan Jett.

"I don't wanna see the fucking Sex Pistols, give me a fucking break!" I told him, but he just drank another beer from the backstage cooler. I was impressed by the Runaways; so I just wanted to stay here and hang out with my friends.

I did end up seeing the Ramones with the Runaways when they played the Santa Monica Civic Auditorium a couple of weeks after the Sex Pistols debacle. And they were really fucking great. Much better than the Sex Pistols.

ELEVEN

I woke up late one morning in 1978 in the suburbs, where exactly I wasn't sure. It turned out to be Red Bank, New Jersey, and I was there because I'd been kidnapped from CBGB by a young punk band called Hard Attack. I was very drunk the night before, and though I hated their name, I was so intrigued by their sales pitch that I become their manager. The Sex Pistols sucked, but I found Malcolm McLaren charming and could relate to his bullshit.

Hard Attack saw me as a key to meeting their heroes, the Ramones, and it worked, because not only did they meet them, they also opened for them a lot. And later, their guitarist, Daniel Rey, produced a few Ramones albums.

But I was drinking a lot by this point, even by my own standards, and most of my memories of Hard Attack—who I renamed Shrapnel—are hazy, like trying to focus on something through an opaque ashtray filled with spilled beer and cigarette butts. So I asked my friend Geoff Shields to faithfully fill in some of the gaps for me, and as soon as he said, "There is no lie that could be worse than the shit that actually happened," well, I was kind of sorry I did.

A BRIEF TESTIMONY BY GEOFF SHIELDS, ROADIE/ ROAD MANAGER FOR SHRAPNEL, ROADIE FOR THE RAMONES, STUDIO CREW FOR BLONDIE

For Legs, that level of drinking was an extraordinary spike on the chart, but to us it was normal. That was our baseline. And it explains a lot of the decisions that were made or not made.

I recognized Legs as a drunk. I grew up in an AA house, because my dad apparently stopped drinking when I was born. At least, you know, that wasn't his reason for being. My dad got his shit together and made some money to improve the house. We had a basement, and there was always some fucking drunk down there.

I knew what a drunk was, and Legs was a drunk. They'd been at my dinner table many hundreds of times. It was always like, "Well, this is Mr. Matthews. He'll be with us for a little while." The guy would stick out this shaking hand, "How do you do," and my dad would be like, "You stay out of the mouthwash you lush!" All this is to say that I was not unfamiliar with the far shores of drunkenness.

The first time I met Legs it was at our guitar player's house. Daniel Rey—Rabinowitz, actually—had that perfect blend of cool parents who weren't fucked up, and they actually gave a shit about their kids. So they made a basement area where he and his friends could rehearse and stuff, and that's where I first met Legs was in that basement, because he'd formed some sort of arrangement with this band, who were my buddies.

Legs and I clicked because we'd both read something other than comic books. I'm not saying the other guys were stupid, they weren't. But they weren't reading actual books.

And Legs grew up in Connecticut in this weird morass of suburban homes and a fucking Louisiana-like swamp, which was familiar to me too.

But even with suburban roots, Legs was an animal of New York City. He didn't have a car; he didn't even have a bed. But I invited him over to our house, because I knew it'd remind him of home.

I grew up on this lake in the woods in New Jersey an hour from Manhattan, and my dad, through his post–World War II alcoholic fog and a GI loan, recognized like, holy shit, this place is great. Location, location, location! Our house was on a little dogleg of a street in the woods, and Legs came over and we sat outside and talked and he smoked all my cigarettes.

Then he fucked my sister and left.

I was watching him get driven away from our home after he fucked my sister and smoked all my cigarettes, and he turned to me and said, "Welcome to rock 'n' roll!"

I couldn't not laugh at that. And I teach college students now, and maybe when several fucked-up things happen at the same time, I'll say, "Welcome to rock 'n' roll!" Like, what did you think college was gonna be?

Hard Attack was on the right track even before Legs came along. They were sort of in this slot between heavy metal and punk, but there was a distaste for overproduction and overly long songs that became their ethos. Led Zeppelin were becoming dinosaurs, and Hard Attack were looking for something else.

They were also drawing inspiration from comic books. And they were edgy, and looking back, they were good-looking fucking seventeen-year-olds, except one of them was fourteen. Legs must have seen something in that combination when they approached him at CBGB, because suddenly he was in New Jersey.

Legs was only a few years older than we were, but he was much more mature. Not mature like a grown-up, but he sometimes gave the impression like he knew what he was doing.

And he was living a dream we'd all had, escaping the suburbs for New York City.

But he was also immature. Whenever he found out that I hadn't seen or read something he felt like I should've seen or read, he'd go, "Geoff, you asshole!"

And I'd think, *Alright, I haven't seen* Apocalypse Now *yet, but it doesn't make me an asshole.* We were all crammed in the van once, and I remember responding in the moment, "I think that's a little harsh." And everyone just started to laugh. And I laughed, too, but it wasn't like I had $4.50 to go see *Apocalypse Now*.

Legs was like a teenager with an old head that was stapled on top. He was rock 'n' roll skinny, right? But you could not get rid of his five-o'clock shadow with a fucking chainsaw; it was just part of him, you know?

He used to stay at Daniel's house, and Daniel came from kind of a traditional Jewish family. Herb Rabinowitz was his dad, who worked at Monsanto, and his mother was like really well read. She was home, she wasn't a housewife, if that makes sense. She was cool. And Legs would stay there a lot, and it was funny how he kind of like insinuated himself into the family unit. He was just irresistible. He'd entered the realm of the dinner table, and he's sitting there tucking into his free dinner while Mr. Rabinowitz tells his daily joke from work. Legs had established a beachhead at the Rabinowitz house.

Hard Attack already had a roadie who was probably way more capable than I was, and he knew a lot about electronics, but he was also out of control. And I had a 1964 Dodge van. And even though I cut school and drank and got high, I wasn't out of control.

Legs agreed to manage Hard Attack under the condition that they change their name to Shrapnel, and he convinced them to lean into the whole *Sgt. Rock* comic book army thing, with sandbags and rifles and explosions. But, you know, even if they hadn't been immediately on board with it, Legs had this way of saying, "This is what has to happen now," and you'd buy into it.

He was a good creative partner with the band. He would push them sometimes towards uncomfortable, kind of pop music realities. He'd say, "You need a song that makes the girls swoon. I'm not seeing that." And he'd kind of force them to write this like girlie, swoony song that they could put into the set just because it needed to be there in case there was an A&R person at the show. But he would always encourage more bombast, too, and encourage them to have a *fuck you* attitude ready. To be indomitable.

And that was Legs. He lived that. He was indomitable. He just keeps coming back. He's like some pesky fucking welterweight. Of course that brought in a huge amount of drama sometimes. He'd get into arguments with girlfriends on suburban front lawns, and that's frowned upon. It defies explanation to Mr. Rabinowitz.

Have you seen *Lawrence of Arabia*? Peter O'Toole is tossing this rock up and down and trying to figure out how to successfully attack the Turks with this ragtag band of guys. And as the sun is coming up, and he's still plotting, he grips the rock so tightly his hand is bleeding, and suddenly he says, "Aqaba!" Legs would say that whenever he figured out the next move. "Aqaba!"

And with Legs, "Aqaba!" meant something. He moved among famous people at twenty-one years old, and in New York, that's a form of currency. So we suddenly found ourselves having lunch at Andy Warhol's Factory. And Warhol was an interesting character. He was one of those guys who liked to make this cocktail from different people just to see what would happen.

The Factory had this giant, beautiful dining area set off from everything else, with this beautiful old Tuscan furniture, or some shit like that. And a sideboard with all these delicious dishes on silver platters. And it was us, Shrapnel, and Legs, and this beautifully tan family of Italian royalty that didn't speak English. But our bass player, Phil Caivano, spoke a little Italian, and he looked like a Greek god, which probably didn't hurt. And Warhol would just dance in and out and serve things.

Sometime in April or May 1978, there was some sort of punk extravaganza/art exhibition in Washington, DC. And we looked at the gallery and played the show and were hanging out in the bar. And I don't know how he did it, but Legs talked the bartender into giving us six-packs of beer to go, and Legs said, "Let's go to the Capitol Building!" Like, let's drink beer and walk across Washington to the nation's capitol.

Pennsylvania Avenue was completely empty because it was a Sunday night, and it was just streetlights and an empty boulevard. But then we lost

Legs for a minute, like where the hell is Legs? And it always felt like my responsibility to know where he was after a certain amount of drinking. And I found him staring into this expensive shop window at this hot mannequin. And he's trying to find the angle to look under her skirt. This was not performative. I don't even think he remembered we were there. That was just Legs.

So I grabbed Legs and we caught up with the other guys, marched right up the steps of the Capitol Building, and we turned and looked at the view. And it's corny, but we were all thinking how cool this was. And we started loudly singing these broken-down, bastardized American hymns.

Suddenly, from around the corner comes an armed cop. We looked at him, he looked at us, and we all started drunkenly babbling, "We're really sorry! We know you work hard!"

And he held both his hands out, palms down, to get us to shut up, almost like he was directing a choir. And he said, "It's okay, it's okay. This is your house. Just don't break anything."

All that happened because Legs said, "Aqaba!"

Another "Aqaba!" moment was this idea that we should play at Red Bank Regional High School every year and bring a special guest. And the first year was Joey Ramone. And suddenly, Joey Ramone is staying at the Rabinowitzes' house with Legs. And they had to be thinking, *This is different . . . Is that* Ramone*?*

And after that first show played by all these kids who'd either gotten thrown out or dropped out of school, or managed to squeak through, and who returned like conquering heroes, Legs recognized the potential. But Joey Ramone wasn't really well known outside of New York yet, and Legs turned into Ed Sullivan and felt like he really had to get a special guest, because the second year he got Glen Buxton, Alice Cooper's guitarist. And that was fucking cool. And he was gonna play the last song with Shrapnel, Alice Cooper's "School's Out."

The police were watching really carefully that night. I'm not sure why, they were just uptight, thinking something was gonna go wrong, the kids would get too boisterous, though they didn't strike me as overly boisterous. They were kids.

It was my job to run and fetch Glen Buxton from a faculty break room in the high school, and it smelled like coffee and dashed dreams, and there was Glen sitting in a high school like he probably hadn't since he was in trouble when he was actually in high school.

Glen was putting on his guitar, and this cop, who looked like the way Robert Crumb draws cops, burly, big, like an old-fashioned doughnut-eating kind, said, "You gotta shut this down!"

And I said, "I can't, it's the last song."

"I don't give a fuck!"

But I knew that it was a complicated setup, and there was no way this guy was gonna figure out how to throw a switch or pull out the right plug to shut it down, so I just ran away.

And Shrapnel introduced Glen Buxton and said, "Some of you might know this song," and the first chords are just so iconic. And the place just exploded.

Meanwhile, the cop found the lighting booth, and the lights went out. But the band was still playing, and then the kids were pulling out their lighters, and it was just this sea of lighters and lit matches illuminating the place, and it looked like ghostly figures were on stage roaring through "School's Out."

Then, the cop got to the sound guy, but he could only shut down the microphones, not the speakers. So he cut out the vocals, but he didn't realize that all the kids were singing the song, too, so there's no interruption. It's just the kids singing in the semi-darkness, and the guitars and drums are roaring away. It was just magical.

And I remember thinking, "Well, if this isn't good, I don't know what is." It was the kind of thing that if you saw it in a movie, you'd go, "Oh, bullshit." But it really happened.

Legs came on the road with us sometimes, which was kind of a mixed blessing. Because he smoked all our cigarettes but couldn't stand people smoking pot.

One time we were playing in Minneapolis or somewhere, and we're booked in this tiki bar with a bunch of angry Korean War veterans there. They were used to some guy with a Farfisa organ singing Bobby Darin covers. And we hardly made any money. So I had to make the announcement: "The choice is we get two rooms with no weed and some beer, or we get one room with a bunch of weed and a bunch of beer."

So we're all in our one room drinking beer and getting high in our tighty-whities, because it's summertime. And it had to be between three and four in the morning, and for some reason a couple of the guys were standing on the bed, and I might have been one of them. And suddenly the door opens really slowly, and in comes creeping this Black dude in full '78 disco regalia, huge green collar sticking out of a huge green jacket, emerald pants, patent leather shoes, big bag. And he clearly thinks he's going to see his girlfriend or someone lying on the bed. And instead he sees seven white dudes in their underwear standing on two beds, staring back at him. He just went. He looked up and he went, "Wow, I'm in the wrong room." He just did a little wave, backed the fuck out, and closed the door. And we couldn't stop laughing. And for days we'd repeat the line, "Wow, I'm in the wrong room."

After I started working for the Ramones, and we'd do these gigs in weird places, like Princeton, Legs would just show up to let me know he was there. It meant a lot.

Though he stopped managing Shrapnel after a few years, I think Legs had an impact on the guys. Three of them are still in music. Daniel Rey is a record producer. And Dave Wyndorf and Phil Caivano's heavy stoner rock band Monster Magnet has been going since the late '80s.

Legs and I kept in touch after Shrapnel, even after I moved to San Francisco. He came and stayed with me in the mid-'80s when Clint Eastwood was running for mayor in Carmel. Legs needed a base of operations to cover that for *SPIN* magazine, and even though Carmel is more than a hundred miles south of San Francisco, he chose my place, which I shared with my girlfriend, now my wife, for $660 a month. It was a big apartment, and we had a guest room.

Legs showed up and dropped his bags, then said, "I'll be right back, I've got a couple of things outside."

And he had a fucking Gila monster and a python. Not a parakeet or a cat, nothing a normal person would have. And we had two cats, who were like, "What the hell is this?"

So my girlfriend and I were going to work during the day, and Legs would be home working the phones or whatever and smoking nineteen packs of cigarettes a day. And one day I came home, and Legs opened the door and dashed by me with a contraption he'd rigged, like a mop handle with a loop on it that he'd made out of a tampon string, and he yelled over his shoulder, "Python's loose!" Meanwhile, the cats are flipping the fuck out and jumping straight up in the air like they're trying to launch themselves to the moon.

But Legs caught the python.

Another time I came home from working a late shift, and Legs wasn't around. Where was he? Upstairs, fucking my neighbor.

I never saw that motherfucker make a move either. Never. Suddenly it was, "I'm staying at Jackie's tonight."

I have four kids. I have a daughter and then I had triplet sons. And Legs had nothing to do with any of it. I hope, but you never know. But the things I remember the most keenly in my life after having my daughter, after triplets, there's Legs.

TWELVE

John Holmstrom was the guy really responsible for getting the Mudd Club off the ground. Steve Mass, the owner of the Mudd Club, used to hang out at Phebe's Tavern and Grill on the Bowery. Phebe's was for the off-off-off-Broadway crowd; about four or five blocks from CBGB, and most importantly, it took American Express credit cards. I knew that.

A rare commodity among the CBGB crowd.

The only guy I knew with an Amex card was this nerdy fellow, Steve Mass, who kept bugging me to be in this movie he was making. A movie I knew was never gonna get made.

Phebe's had floor-to-ceiling front windows, so you could see everyone walking from CBGB to Manic Panic, or Trash & Vaudeville, or Anya Phillips's apartment on St. Mark's Place. Or to Max's Kansas City up on 17th Street.

Since I knew Steve Mass had an Amex card, and I knew he wanted to talk to me about his movie, I'd go into Phebe's with half a pack of cigarettes and without a dollar to my name and just start ordering Heinekens, the premier German beer of the day.

Out the glass front windows, I'd see Debbie and Chris, or Arturo Vega and Joey Ramone. I'd see roadies and managers and publicity people, and I'd see tons of photographers—Roberta Bayley; Marcia Resnick; David

Godlis; and Bob Gruen on his motor scooter, with his cameras, having just gotten off the road photographing a Black Oak Arkansas tour in the Midwest—wondering, "Is Blondie opening for the Ramones tonight?"

They usually were, but who I was looking out for was that nerdy guy with the Amex card, to pay off my Phebe's tab.

I didn't even know what Steve's movie was about, nor did I care, as long as the Heinies kept coming. Notoriety brings out the strangest people to pay the bills.

Fast-forward a couple years later and there were rumors that this nerdy guy, Steve Mass, was talking about starting a nightclub. I think it was Holmstrom who told me, as he was furiously preparing for the first *PUNK* Awards Show, starring Lou Reed.

How Holmstrom got Lou to show up, I'll never know.

But I do know Lou was so humiliated by the *PUNK* Awards that he never spoke to Holmstrom again. Holmstrom couldn't organize an event to save his life. He was always the guy up on the ladder at every art show, hanging his artwork and complaining no one ever helped him, ten minutes before the doors opened.

The *PUNK* Awards Show was such a bomb that Holmstrom donated the hundreds of bottles of expensive liquor to Steve Mass to open the Mudd Club.

The Mudd Club had something for everyone, and everyone came including the gay crowd, the art crowd, the fashion crowd, the film and video crowd, as well as everyone cool from CBGB and Max's, so that included just about everyone.

The Mudd Club also had some of the best-looking women in the world hanging out there.

I know 'cause I was managing Shrapnel at the time, and I'd have our road manger, Geoff Shields, pull the band van to an empty lot nearby and have him throw me the keys, and I'd take some gorgeous creature outside to the van and we'd fuck our brains out.

It was a glorious time to be alive, but what made it so fucking interesting was not only the people but the sense of such a doomed city—that we were slowly resurrecting.

One night, after a serious bout of lovemaking in the back of the van, as we climbed back into the front seats, still putting on our clothes, talking about shit, I realized I'd forgotten how to get back to the Mudd Club, since it was unfamiliar territory, below Canal Street.

I turned on the headlights to get my bearings. My eyes adjusted to the lights to see hundreds of rats, maybe thousands of them, scurrying back and forth, some of them frozen in the headlights, and just being in awe of how far Manhattan had fallen.

Truly, this was a City of the Damned.

I thought, *If Michael Jackson could've seen such a repulsive sight as this, he never would've sung the theme song to* Ben*!* Repulsive yet fascinating.

Another night, I stood at the Mudd Club's first-floor bar and watched in horror as ex–Studio 54 co-owner, Steve Rubell, and Roy Cohn, Senator Joseph McCarthy's lead prosecutor in "The Atomic Spies Trial" of Julius and Ethel Rosenberg, arrived. The Rosenbergs were both fried, figuratively and physically, first by Roy Cohn in their trial and later in the electric chair at Sing Sing Prison.

To make it even more horrifying and hopeless, both Steve Rubell and Roy Cohn were dying of AIDS. They were both unnaturally skinny and gaunt, wandering very slowly in an empty corner of the club, deep in heavy conversation.

Though I didn't know it at the time, Roy Cohn was not only mentoring Studio 54 co-owner Steve Rubell, Cohn was also mentoring real estate mogul Donald Trump, who everyone in New York City hated with a passion; as always, it took the rest of the world a long time to catch up.

Still, I was fascinated by Roy Cohn's evil soul, though the Venona report verified that Julius Rosenberg was a Soviet spy. I was also fascinated with Cold War espionage, not because of James Bond, who was fun but cheesy, but because Jeff Goldberg and I were addicted to this seven-part BBC program, *Tinker Tailor Soldier Spy*, starring Alec Guinness, who was defining what perfection was in front of our eyes. It felt like we were on acid as we watched in delight, not having a clue of what the fuck was going on, but mesmerized by the dialogue.

Watching *Tinker Tailor* was simultaneously incredibly tedious and utterly fascinating, though I was still completely in the dark. Also, I did not have a clue who John le Carré was, the author of *Tinker Tailor* as well as *The Honourable Schoolboy* and *Smiley's People,* which comprised the "Karla trilogy"—George Smiley's nemesis in Soviet intelligence was known only as "Karla."

I was utterly amazed that the books captured the dreariness of London and Europe so authentically. Like Gene Hackman captured the degradation of New York City in *The French Connection.*

Of course *Tinker Tailor* was based on the infamous Kim Philby spy scandal in the late 1950s and early '60s, when it was discovered Philby had been spying for the Russians since the late 1930s. So, of course, I had to read every book on Kim Philby, which led me down a path to the Cambridge Five spy ring, that included Guy Burgess, Donald Maclean, Anthony Blunt, John Cairncross, and, of course, Kim Philby.

The entire Cold War tableau was ripe for my pickings!

And *Tinker Tailor* represented to me the idea of perfection, like a stunning Ramones set at CBGB in 1978. It represented to me what all of us writers and photographers and actors and musicians try to achieve, and if we're lucky, some of us get close, but seldom do any of us hit the nail on the head.

That is what all of us aspire to, whether we admit it or not.

And it's exhilarating when you get close!

Abso-fucking-lutely!

But I digress. As apocalyptically doomed as the Mudd Club was, it was also hysterically funny in the early days of 1978 or 1979, as someone was always shoving powder up my nose as I sucked on a beer and smoked a cigarette.

One night Adam Roth from the Jim Carroll Band, who played one of the great punk songs, "People Who Died," night after night, and I were rolling around on the Mudd Club floor, laughing hysterically. I forget now what was so funny.

During many of those drunken nights, I sometimes broke down in frenzies of hysterics. I'm sure it was the booze and the drugs, but I also imagine it was the fact that every night was rife with possibility that staggered the mind.

Adam Roth pointed to the crowd that gathered above us and said, "Look, there's David Bowie!"

I looked up from the floor, remembering my Suicide test pressing, and saw the Space Oddity, and he was even better looking than his photos. *Fuck!*

"That's the motherfucker who stole my Suicide record!" I said from the floor, looking up at the beautiful rock star. "He's a fucking cocksucker!"

"Literally," Adam added, and we went back to pointing at Bowie and laughing manically. What can I say, we were assholes, but we had a lot of fun.

Another night a fat, drunken, older woman grabbed my black leather jacket as she sat sprawled out on a couch. She was dressed in a large black leather motorcycle jacket of her own, her shirt open a few buttons too far, exposing the top of her bra and her cleavage, and she was stoned out of her mind.

I slapped her hand off my leather jacket. It was one of those stupid "Don't-ever-touch-my-black-leather-jacket" moments that many of us, male and female, indulged in. Dumb.

As soon as I pulled my hand away, there was a guy in my ear, saying, "Don't you know who that is, that's Anita Pallenberg, the Queen of rock 'n' roll!"

"If that's the queen, then I want off this bus," I replied, thinking, *I don't ever want to end up like her, a stone-cold junkie and drunk who lost the respect of everyone who saw her.*

Anita looked that *bad.*

"I think she likes you, Legs," the guy in my ear was whispering, "you should go home with her, I'd betcha you'd meet Keith Richards . . ."

"Get the fuck away from me," I snarled, pushing him away from me.

Besides, there were just too many anorexic Jewish girls looking to be with a genuine bad boy, a part I was destined to play, though I was more a drunken fuckup than a bad boy.

The only problem with going to the Mudd Club was I always, without fail, ended up coming out of Steve Mass's house at noon the next day.

I'd have lost the sunglasses I'd stolen from the girl the night before, and I'd hafta call Carol Overby to pay my cab fare to her apartment on 107th Street. A twenty- or thirty-dollar cab ride. And make up some story about why I was out all night, praying that she could give me a Valium to take off the shakes I endured for the entire 130 blocks from Steve Mass's place to Carol's.

"Wanna go for a drink?" I asked Norman Mailer when he took a break from the boxing ring at the 14th Street Y. It was one of those mornings, well, afternoons really, when I realized I'd really fucked up. I'd been out all night at the Mudd Club with a skinny Jewish girl with large breasts, drinking, doing coke, and getting my dick sucked, when I remembered I already had a girlfriend.

"No," Norman said. "Not now . . ."

I didn't want to show my displeasure, but I was so hung over that if I didn't get a drink or a Valium soon, I was in for full-on delirium tremens. My nervous system was so shot even my synapses were hunchbacked. Norman was brooding about something, went to a pay phone and made a call, so I couldn't tell if he was annoyed at me for asking. We were outside the gym, on 14th Street, in the bright March sunlight that betrayed how cold it was. After I remembered I had a girlfriend, I called Carol to apologize and

Me and Norman Mailer drinking at his home in Brooklyn Heights.

Photo by Victor Bockris

she was pissed. I thought it was over, forgetting that it was never over with me, that I always got away with murder.

Norman got off the phone and came back over to where I was ready to puke into a street-corner garbage can. He was wearing that impish grin of his, which bathed you in all the warmth and comfort of his celebrity. "So Legs, how the hell are you?"

"Bad," I answered, "really bad, I fucked up with Carol . . ."

Norman put his arm around me and walked me down 14th Street. I babbled how I'd been out all night with another woman and now thought it was all over between Carol and me. Norman listened patiently and then said, "Well, it's like I wrote in *The Naked and the Dead* . . ."

"I never read that one," I confessed sheepishly.

"You will, you will," Norman reassured me. "But in it, there's two guys in a foxhole in the South Pacific, and one guy has just gotten a Dear John letter from his girlfriend, and he's pissing and moaning about it, and the other guy says to him, 'Come on Joe, in a month you'll be the king of the Manila whorehouses . . .'

"And the guy with the Dear John letter says, 'Yeah, I know, but what about tonight?'"

It was pretty funny, and I knew exactly how the guy felt. Only Norman had the power to drag me out of my alcoholic self-obsessions, and even better, he said the magic words, "Let's get that drink . . ."

I was so happy I could've kissed him. We walked inside the dark bar, taking refuge from the sunlight, and I took a seat on a stool while Norman stood talking to me. I ordered a beer; Norman had a scotch. He was wearing his brown safari shirt and a ski jacket; I was in my standard black leather jacket, black jeans, pointy Beatle boots, and the sunglasses I had stolen from the girl from last night. But I didn't need them: The bar was dark and seedy enough, just the way I liked it.

"You're gonna be rich when I put you in the play," Norman boasted as he sipped his drink and rubbed his stomach. "You can get Carol back with the money I'm gonna pay you, more money than you've ever seen."

Norman was one of the most generous guys I'd ever met, but he was on some kick about producing a play on Marilyn Monroe based on his book *Of Women and Their Elegance*, starring his daughter Kate Mailer, who would be terrific as the lead. I mean, Kate was as stunning as Marilyn Monroe, the best impersonation I'd ever seen—more like she was channeling Marilyn than impersonating her.

Of Women and Their Elegance was Norman's fictional biography of Monroe, so maybe Kate had received the inside track from her father. Norman wanted me to play some sociopath who sweeps Marilyn off her feet and takes her away on a motorcycle—and I knew it would never happen. That was the official reason he let me hang out with him, but I think it was because I made him laugh. Just that morning, when I saw him, I'd said, "Wow Norman, you've lost a lot of weight, you look great! Oh shit, you don't have cancer or anything, do ya?"

Norman thought that was the funniest thing he'd ever heard, and he kept repeating, "You don't have cancer or anything, do ya?" like it was a punch line. I gulped down the beer and ordered another one. Norman ordered another scotch and paid for the round. Like I said, he was generous. So generous, that I was feeling twinges of guilt about going to Provincetown two summers ago to fuck his ex-wife—not that I did, but that was my intention. I just hoped Norman never found out about it and kept the beers coming . . .

Norman and I first met because he'd read Mark Jacobson's 1978 *Village Voice* story "Teenage Hipster in the Modern World." It was a long treatise on the excess and abandon of a surly, drunken, groupie-fucking delinquent: me.

Jacobson compared me to Ray Milland's character from *X: The Man with the X-Ray Eyes*, a sci-fi flick in which our hero's ability to see through anything leads to madness and a gruesome fate. In the end, Milland plucks his eyes out rather than see anything more, in Jacobson's mind a chilling analogy to my dissolute downtown life.

"Talking to Legs," Jacobson wrote in "Teenage Hipster," "has always given me the ghostly feeling of being with someone who knows too much for his own good. In Legs' case, it is knowing too much about the true horror of his generation. That, as it turns out, is a road to madness."

The *Voice* piece detailed my guide to being "cool in an uncool time" by celebrating everything that everyone else thought sucked: "Legs rallied against his smug '60s-loving elders. 'What do you love?' he demanded. 'Pot, long guitar solos, battling the government, wearing bright colors, being mellow? Well, I hate all that. All that sucks and is uncool.'

"'And what do you hate?' Legs went on. 'Television, burgers, drinking, violent behavior? Well, I love all that. I declare these things to be mine. I appoint liking *Green Acres* and McDonald's to be cool. I love America too. I love everything about modern America, the long freeways, the pizza joints on every corner, and the amazing pop culture. Any country that produced Eddie Haskell has to be cool.'

"Legs' coolness cosmology was, of course, total reaction," Jacobson continued. "By deciding the Modern World was his Godhead, Legs decreed that, in order to be cool, one had to be hip to how to live in such a contemporary landscape."

But there's hip, and then there's hip. As Jacobson explained the origins of *PUNK* magazine and the burgeoning punk rock scene at CBGB, he took exception to the fact that there were no African Americans involved in constructing this Brave New World. It contradicted everything that Jacobson knew about being hip: "Punk, a seemingly legitimate New York City bohemian hipster scene, appeared to fly in the face of most everything set down in the most famous manifesto that sought to separate the hip sensibility from the square, Norman Mailer's epochal essay, 'The White Negro: Superficial Reflections on the Hipster.'"

But I rejected this idea as outdated and racist. It stunk of that old idea of Blacks being closer to the earth because they came from the jungle. By the mid-'70s, the White Negro was obsolete. Written in 1957 for *Dissent* magazine, "The White Negro" failed to predict that once certain Civil Rights goals were finally achieved and the superficial barriers were broken, many African Americans rushed to join the middle class, bringing with them similar mediocre amusements as whites: disco music, polyester leisure suits, the TV show *Good Times* featuring Jimmie "Dy-no-mite" Walker, and doing stupid token McDonald's commercials. Hey, we all got to pay the rent.

By the time Norman found me, I already knew it was over at *PUNK*. We published so erratically and always had trouble paying the printer. By 1978 or 1979, I could see that we weren't going to be in business much longer. We'd lost whatever momentum we'd gained when no one knew when a new issue was going to come out—so *PUNK* was dying a slow, painful death. I liked all the free booze, cigarettes, and women, but I also wanted to be taken seriously as a writer.

Coincidentally, Norman was having similar problems. As I discovered years later, Norman was searching for an entirely new audience with the 1979 publication of his Pulitzer Prize–winning "nonfiction novel" *The*

Executioner's Song, the critically acclaimed book covering the execution of double murderer Gary Gilmore, the first person to be executed in the United States since the Supreme Court reinstated the death penalty in 1976.

I was floored by *The Executioner's Song*. I remember thinking, *Wow, this is fucking good. This is really fucking good, and if I could ever write a book like this . . .*

It was so accessible and so enthralling. Norman's other writing was a little intellectually dense compared to this, but I really loved him for being able to make *The Executioner's Song* so simple about these fucked-up people in Utah. He just nailed them, just captured that entire white-trash Romeo and Juliet romance that was Gary Gilmore's and Nicole Barrett Baker's story.

Norman Mailer wrote the heterosexual version of *In Cold Blood*. Nicole and Gary's was like every fucked-up relationship most of us have been in, only we didn't go out and shoot two Mormons in the head, like Gary did, while fucking Nicole's younger sister, because Nicole broke up with him.

Back in school they wanted me to read *The Scarlet Letter* and *Last of the Mohicans*, okay books, but a little bit boring. You've got to tell a good story—*The Executioner's Song* tells such a great story; it has so many voices in it, even though it's just Norman writing it, because he'd gotten all this great source material from Larry Schiller. It was all there. It wasn't missing anything.

I was introduced to Norman by Martha Thomases, who'd work for him, typing and transcribing parts of *The Executioner's Song*. Martha also worked for *PUNK*.

The summit was hosted by Martha and her future husband, John Tybell, in their small, rent-stabilized apartment in Manhattan's SoHo district. They probably served dinner. Probably John Tybell's lasagna.

Norman was already there when I arrived at the Thompson Street apartment; I needed a few minutes to catch my breath and stave off a headache in the dark coatroom.

When I was introduced, I said, "I've never read anything you've written, and you've never read anything I've written, so we're even." He loved that. And then I said, "Did you have any fun in World War II?"

He loved that, too, and he just went off, riffing for the first of many times on *The Naked and the Dead*: "No, goddammit, I thought I'd be the King of the Paris whorehouses and instead I'm in the fucking South Pacific doing nothing in a fucking foxhole!"

My friend from high school Tom Hearn was sitting next to Norman and didn't have much to say, except when Tommy mentioned Muhammad Ali, and Norman came alive telling him all the great stories he told in *When We Were Kings*, the fantastic documentary of the "Rumble in the Jungle," about Ali in Zaire fighting George Foreman.

It's one of the greatest fucking fights ever, where Ali let Foreman pummel him on the ropes and punch himself out until he was exhausted, and Ali came off the ropes and knocked Foreman out in the eighth round, regaining the championship taken from him seven years earlier for his refusal to be drafted into the United States Army during the Vietnam War: "No Viet Cong ever called me nigger!"

Even more impressive to Tommy was that Norman pulled out a joint, lit it up, and passed it to my high school friend while we finished dinner.

That night, I asked Norman to come to CBGB to see the Ramones play "A Benefit for Policemen's Bulletproof Vests," an NYPD fundraiser.

The fundraiser was partially a big fuck-you to the militant political correctness of forces like the *Village Voice*, which later that month would publish Lester Bangs's divisive disemboweling of the New York punk scene, "The White Noise Supremacists." At the time, you couldn't do anything in art and music unless you were a Marxist, and we were very much fighting that idea. So I proposed the Policemen's Bulletproof Vests benefit to shove it in their face. And people were really upset by the Ramones playing that show.

But we weren't just being provocative: The benefit represented a genuine empathy for the police, who were operating on a shoestring budget for a fucked-up city that four years earlier tried and failed to declare itself bankrupt. The police were very cool in that time. This was before the Tompkins

Square riots when they got all those cops who were suburban schmegegges from Long Island who hated New York City to come in and beat the shit out of everyone in Tompkins Square Park. At the time of the benefit, the cops in New York were underpaid, they were good, and they were putting in their time to get their retirement. They didn't bust you unless you really gave them a reason.

The benefit raised around $4,000, which, given CBGB's official capacity of a little over three hundred, was no small feat. Sure, it was over the fire code that night, but it was always over the fire code. Danny Fields and Linda Stein asked me if I'd have a big novelty check made up. I got drunk and forgot about it.

Earlier that night I was with Victor Bockris up at Arturo Vega's place on 2nd Street, where Joey Ramone lived and the Ramones would gather before a gig. We all walked over to CBGB, and then I grabbed Victor and said, "Come out front with me." Norman pulled up in a cab with his wife, Norris Church.

Norman and Norris's arrival caused a sensation in CBGB. Everyone wanted to sit next to Norman. Linda Stein, the ex-wife of record company mogul Seymour Stein and co-manager of the Ramones, was saying, "*I wanna sit next to Norman! I wanna sit next to Norman!*"

It was a real circus getting Norman and Norris to a table up front so they could see the show. Norman being Norman, he jumped on top of the table to watch the Ramones, teetering on the brink like a sailor on the salty deck of a ship against a howling storm of three chords of fury. In the middle of a song, "Here Today, Gone Tomorrow," maybe, he turned and shouted, "Heroic!"

Later, Norman said to me in an interview in *High Times*, "For me, seeing the Ramones felt like I was an old car and I was being taken out for a ride at 100 miles an hour and I kind of liked it because I was really getting rid of a lot of rust. I don't know if I'd like it night after night and I'm not sure it isn't absolutely killing. You got to be super human to play that stuff night after night and not have your senses absolutely wiped out by it.

But that it has a powerful impact and not just something going on I got to admit. I liked it more than I thought I would."

After the show, the party moved back to Arturo Vega's loft, as it often did. I felt like that night that Norman could hang with anybody. Just from talking to him, you got the sense that he wasn't full of himself and was interested in other stuff. He worked the party like a politician, pressing the flesh with the Ramones' roadies, thugs from Queens; you know, drug dealers and shit. But Norman went around and talked to everyone in the room, which really impressed me.

Joey Ramone, drinking and exhausted from playing two sets that night, was less impressed. He was getting drunk, and he was just wiped out and being silly, saying things like, "Oh, Norman, go write a fucking bible!"

The line was from Lou Reed's double album, *Take No Prisoners*, where Lou spent one side testing out his stand-up comedy. Of course Norman didn't hear Joey, but the lead singer thought the line was hysterical. Joey did that when he found a word or sentence that he liked; he would just repeat it over and over again. Like, "Bulbous," or "Happy, happy, happy," or "Norman, go write a fucking bible!"

At the end of the night, I found myself locked in an eerily prescient conversation with Norman. He said, "Legs, don't fuck up like I did . . ."

We were in Arturo's bedroom, and Norman repeated himself: "Don't fuck up like I did."

I said, "What do you mean?" I kept asking. And he kept slurring, "You're the guy! You're the guy!"

But I didn't want to be the guy, I hated all that Hemingway macho shit, and besides I weighed a hundred pounds soaking wet. We were so drunk we were huddled together on some chairs or on the bed, kind of swaying because the room was starting to spin. Norman finally said, "You have to interview me, you have to interview me tomorrow!" I thought he was joking, or too drunk to remember the next morning, or probably both.

The next day, Norman's office called Martha Thomases and said, "Where's Legs?"

I thought, *I didn't think Norman wanted to really have me interview him, I thought he was just saying that to be nice . . .* But I got it together and made it out to Norman's nautically themed Brooklyn Heights home the following day.

I was really hung over, and Norman wanted me to climb around in his big apartment. He had all these catwalks to get to the third floor, and I was like, "No, fuck that, no! I need a drink!"

The interview covered a lot of territory, including Norman's thoughts on the Ramones, his distaste for television ("I think the American disease is TV"), existential paranoia, and regret.

My Norman Mailer interview appeared in the September 1979 issue of *High Times*, who were offering me more money. Giving it to *PUNK* magazine, it just seemed like it would never get published.

Soon, I became a pretty regular fixture in the Mailer household, hanging out with Norman's sons and watching *Gilligan's Island* reruns. According to Mary V. Dearborn's book *Mailer: A Biography*, I made a real impression on Mailer's sons. And I also started turning up at Mailer's parties.

The guests at a party in April 1980 included Woody Allen, Shelley Winters, Kurt Vonnegut, Arturo Vega, Glen Buxton from Alice Cooper, as well as former light heavyweight champion of the world José Torres. The music was provided by Shrapnel. There was also an extraordinary gentleman dressed in an ascot, Harold Conrad. Described by my friend Mark Jacobson in a December 1991 *Esquire* profile titled "The Coolest Guy in the Room," Harold was a "newspaperman, a superflack-fixer, who arranged for the Beatles to be photographed in the ring with Cassius Clay, among hundreds of other life changing events, a true custodian of a bygone age."

Woody Allen hid in the bathroom all night, and people kept knocking on the door because they had to pee or do coke or whatever, but Woody wouldn't open the door. Finally, he opened the door a little and peeked out, and Arturo Vega opened the bathroom door all the way and said to Woody, "Boy, you really are shy, aren't you?" Then Arturo closed the bathroom door on him, in disgust.

Around that time I had been living at the Boho Club, an old vaudeville rehearsal loft on 14th Street, with Tom Baker, an actor, writer, and all-around raconteur who was twenty years my senior. Tom had had a long association with Norman, having performed in Mailer's theater production of *The Deer Park*, based on his book of the same name. I had met Tom at another one of Norman's parties and afterwards put him to shame at One-Uni, Mickey Ruskin's latest hipster bar. The actual name of One-Uni was Chinese Chance, but since it was located at One University Place and had that printed on its awning, that's what we all called it. Anyway, a whole bunch of us were all sitting in a booth inside One-Uni and Tom was reading the *Village Voice* review about his 1970 movie *Bongo Wolf's Revenge*, a documentary about some Hollywood weirdo who thought he was a werewolf, which for whatever reason was written up by Jack Newfield over a decade later. I grabbed the review out of his hands and started reading it out loud.

"Tom Baker, that notorious pedophile, debuted his kiddie-porn, *Binky Wolf's A-hole*, about a notorious squirrel who sodomizes baby chipmunks at church picnics . . . Baker said, 'This is an important cinematic achievement on par with *Citizen Kane* and *Viva Las Vegas*.'"

I had everyone in hysterics, including Baker, who didn't mind being the target of my drunken tirade. When I finished, I went to the bathroom and got a blow job from one of the hot waitresses, before spending the night with another hot woman I'd met in our booth. It was a different time, thank God!

A month later I was living with Baker at the Boho Club, and slept on the stage, next to an old black-and-white TV that all the touts from the OTB across the street would gather round on Saturday afternoon, when they'd televise the horse race from Belmont. The Boho Club was owned by Bob Brady, an acting teacher at NYU who looked exactly like Mark Twain, who I was never sure if he liked me or not. Tom was a great friend though; he would buy me my Valium on 14th Street every morning, well, afternoon actually, since I couldn't keep down my "beer-for-breakfast," which Tom always had to ward off the shakes. So Tom would buy me a coffee yogurt to go along with my morning "V" and spoon-feed me while waiting for the benzodiazepine to kick in.

"Come on Legs, ya gotta eat," Tom would say. "Open up, here comes the airplane flying into the hangar, vvvrrrrroooom, hurry up and open up, it's coming in for a landing . . ."

"Tell me about the time you were busted with Jim Morrison for hijacking an airplane," I would plead, never getting tired of hearing the story. It was true; Tom was good friends with Morrison, he even fucked Pamela, Jim's soul mate, before he met the rock star. Jim forgave him, much to the displeasure of the rest of the band and management, who blamed a lot of Morrison's drunken antics on Baker. I guess the two of them egged each other on, to the point of utter chaos and destruction. The incident on the plane happened after Jim had been arrested in Miami for exposing himself at the Dinner Key Auditorium and was waiting to come to trial. Since he couldn't tour because of the arrest, Morrison decided to buy a bunch of Rolling Stones tickets and hand them out to the fans as they entered the concert in Arizona. It was an innocent enough plan, but he took Baker with him on the flight to Phoenix, and they got drunk and caused such a scene that the FBI was there to arrest them for "interfering with a flight in progress," the skyjacking law, when they left the plane.

They never got to see the Stones. Instead they went to jail and later canoodled with the two stewardesses who testified against them at their "skyjacking" trial. That was my favorite part of the story, and by the time Baker got to telling it, the Valium was washing over my body, and I was back again, ready to face another night of endless possibilities.

It was Baker's idea to go to Provincetown; he had hooked up with Joseph B., the heir to a tinned tuna fortune, and worked out some scam involving Norman Mailer, who kept a summer home at the end of Cape Cod. I wasn't really sure why we were going, but before we left, I needed two things: more Valium and a woman. The woman was the easy part: Samantha, another skinny Jewish girl, agreed to go with me. The Valium was harder to get. I bought my drugs in 14th Street's Union Square Park, at the time a decrepit stretch of badlands where Broadway crossed Fifth Avenue, empty except for the drug dealers lurking in the shadows. The cops had just swept through the park and rounded up all the amateur pharmacists, a monthly occurrence, and for a day or two afterwards, there were never any drugs available in the park.

I was out in Union Square Park for an hour or so, searching for a dealer, but he didn't have the yellow five-milligram tablets with the *V* in the middle, just the blue ten-milligram ones, which were a bit more dangerous to mix with alcohol. I could only afford twenty pills. And then the four of us, Baker, Joseph B., Samantha, and I, drove to P-town.

I was reading A. E. Hotchner's *Papa Hemingway* on the drive to the Cape; I was deeply involved in my Hemingway obsession all young male writers of a certain age indulge in. As was my habit, instead of reading books by Hemingway, I was reading all the books about Hemingway, since I always preferred nonfiction to fiction. Hemingway's novels were okay, but what hooked me were the Nick Adams stories and *A Moveable Feast*.

"Hey, there's a picture in here of Beverly Bentley with Hemingway," I said, finally pulling myself out of the book as the car crossed the border of Connecticut into Massachusetts.

"Wasn't she married to Norman?"

"Yeah, and apparently she's gonna turn up in his next novel," Baker cracked from behind the wheel. He had an encyclopedic memory for arcane knowledge, speculation, and gossip, the real scoop on people.

"I don't like novels," I mumbled.

"Legs, you wanker," sneered Baker, starting a tirade on my literary education, before I quickly stopped him.

"Just shut up and tell me about Beverly . . ."

"She's a brunette, and this guy says, 'I thought you were a blonde?' And she says, 'My pussy hair was bright gold in high school, until I went out and scorched it with the football team.' Ha, ha, ha!"

"Wow," I said. Samantha and Joseph were laughing, but I was

preoccupied with the picture of Beverly partying with Hemingway. It was the realization that there was a living human being who was a direct link to both Ernest Hemingway and Norman Mailer. I'm sure Norman was well aware of the Hemingway connection when he hooked up with Beverly, and it made me wonder if I could capture and possess her—have her—I might be the next big thing . . .

It was an idea that lodged inside my brain as we crossed over the Bourne Bridge onto Cape Cod. Twenty milligrams of Valium and a six-pack of Bud helped keep it there.

Beverly Bentley met Norman Mailer at P.J. Clarke's in 1963, and she became his fourth wife later that year. The problem with Beverly was alcoholism and a failed acting career, and Norman may have played a role in both. Beverly was the only wife of Norman's that he wouldn't talk to after they broke up, a nasty run that wasn't truly over until 1980 when their divorce went through. She was being championed in *People* magazine as the woman who fought back against Norman. I didn't know anything about all that at the time; I only knew I wanted to fuck her. And, I thought, this was my chance.

The water was still and dark, except for gentle swells that rippled across the surface and surged onto the beach. The waves broke with the constant shushing of a running faucet, lending a calming, white-noise echo to the bay. Even though the moon was full, shadows covered our bare bodies as we all sloshed into the water and started to swim.

I had the bottle of wine and corkscrew in one hand, and swam behind Beverly and Baker, trying to keep up. They had just reached the floating dock when the bottle slipped out of my hand and quickly sank to the bottom. It was about eight or nine feet deep, so I thought it would be no problem to dive to the bottom to retrieve it. Five tries later, I still came up empty-handed and I looked over at the dock to see Baker climb on top of Beverly and begin to penetrate her desperation.

"Hey, I dropped the bottle of . . ." I called from the water, but there was no response. I treaded water, watching the two bodies writhe on the dock, under the full moon. I swam to shore, cursing Baker the whole way. I should have been cursing myself, as I already had one girl and wanted another: the story of my life.

I don't remember the drive back to New York City, only that Samantha had been crying a lot in Provincetown, so I was probably pissed and wanted to get on to the next woman before her tears dried. I hated when girls cried, though I never changed the things in myself that made them cry in the first place. It would mean a fundamental change in my entire being, so why bother?

Carol Overby was Tom Baker's girlfriend before she was mine. I first met her at the Boho Club when she came down to make it with Baker on the stage where we slept. I pretended to be asleep and watched her undress by the light of the black-and-white television set, and it was one of the sexiest moments of my life.

Carol was absolutely gorgeous, tall and thin, small breasts like a model, with the longest blonde hair I'd ever seen. She really was absolutely stunning, and I wanted her, but I knew it would never happen. Or so I thought.

Then Baker went to Los Angeles for a month, to "marry some rich girl," or so he said, and Carol had Samantha and me over for dinner. I ended up making out with Carol's roommate, Pamela, but Carol made me go home with the date I'd arrived with. Carol had impeccable manners, though the next night I was over at her apartment again, finishing what I had started: fucking her roommate.

I was there for a couple of days, drinking and fucking Pamela, when the inevitable happened and I ran out of Valium and had a bad case of the D.T.'s. Pamela split, leaving me alone with Carol to deal with my unattractive condition. Carol got me a Valium and we lay on the bed and talked for hours.

And that's how we connected. Whenever we were out with Baker, Carol and I were always huddled at some table in the corner, talking for hours.

Once, we were in a bar, and while Carol and I were discussing literature, Baker was negotiating with some guy to buy a switchblade.

She was the one woman with whom I shared my desires to be a writer, probably because I knew she was unobtainable; she was out of my league, and therefore not a threat, so I could actually be honest with her.

Hangovers always made me incredibly horny, and as we talked, lying side by side on the bed that time, I could feel myself getting more and more engorged as I stared at her—the most beautiful woman I'd ever seen. We finally kissed, then tore each other's clothes off, and got down to it.

We kept our growing romance a secret, so for a time I was making it with both Carol and Pamela—I would be kissing the roommate at a restaurant and playing footsie with Carol under the table. It was a very sexual time, until Pamela's husband returned, and they left the apartment, leaving me and Carol alone to enjoy ourselves.

The only problem was how to tell Baker that I had hooked up with one of his main squeezes. It wasn't as if he was in love with Carol, but he had marked her as his own, and so it was. I had intruded on his property, which was forbidden. Now I had to pay the consequences. I called Tom in California and tried to explain what happened, but Baker wasn't having any of it; his ego was already badly bruised by rejection of the rich girl, and now I'd usurped Carol. Baker laughed on the phone and kept saying, "Tommy Udo laughs when he kills . . ."

Baker was making reference to the giggling, sociopathic killer Richard Widmark played in the 1947 film noir classic *Kiss of Death*. Widmark's performance, for which he was nominated for an Academy Award, is highlighted by a chilling scene where he pushes a little old lady in a wheelchair down a flight of stairs to her death. Baker had starred with Richard Widmark in the film *Rollercoaster*, and we were talking about Widmark one day, drinking beer on a stoop, outside an art gallery on the Upper East Side, when Baker said, "Tommy Udo laughs when he kills," when who walked by—but Richard Widmark!

Widmark was running to an appointment and called out, "Hey,

Tommy, how ya doing?" Baker stopped him and introduced me, before letting him get on his way. Ever since that moment, Baker used the catchphrase, "Tommy Udo laughs when he kills," to emphasize a serious point.

Now he was saying it to me. I knew Baker would never hurt me, but I'd deeply hurt his pride. When he returned to New York, he would call me at Carol's, drunk and pissed off, and snicker into the phone, "Tommy Udo laughs when he kills!" It got boring real quick, and I finally forced a face-to-face meeting in the men's room at the 92nd Street YMCA while Norman was doing a reading of *Tough Guys Don't Dance* in the auditorium. We missed Norman's recitation. I was carrying a full six-pack of Bud in the ripped pockets of my black leather jacket; Baker was brandishing a butter knife. When we laid eyes on each other we broke out laughing while Baker helped himself to my beers.

I asked him what he had been up to, and Baker said he had just done a speaking engagement after showing the Andy Warhol film, *I, a Man*, co-starring Valerie Solanas, the woman who shot Andy multiple times in 1968. Baker had screened the film at Sarah Lawrence College, thinking it was the right spot to pick up a rich girl, but he went home with a gorgeous girl even poorer than himself. After our summit in the men's room, Baker went back to his usual insults for me and dropped the Tommy Udo line.

Our friendship didn't really suffer from my betrayal of Baker, although Carol was never invited to hang out with us. I left her at home, since I was now living with her, while Baker and I made our nightly rounds to the clubs, art galleries, and openings. One night we walked in on John Waters, who was premiering one of his films and was stressed out about it and having a bad night. Waters took one look at us and howled, "*Oh no, not you two, that's all I need tonight!*"

Another night we went to see Chet Baker, the famous junkie jazz singer and musician; we got drunk and melancholic and went back to the Boho Club singing "My Buddy." A few nights later, Baker told me that the Boho Club was having a special visitor that night and that I should be on my best behavior. He was uptight and nervous, an unusual condition for him.

Finally our guest appeared, but Baker took him first into the seedy kitchen off the hallway and didn't come out for a long time. I was getting impatient, wondering what the hell was going on, when Baker emerged from the kitchen and said, "So, Legs, wanna meet Chet Baker?"

I followed him into the kitchen where Chet Baker had his jeans and underwear pushed down around his knees, while he cupped his scrotum with one hand, and held a syringe with the other hand, looking for a vein on his uppermost thighs.

"Ohhh Chet man, what the fuck are you doing? Come on, that ain't cool," Baker scolded the legendary jazz man, who looked up for a second, then quickly went back to his search. Tom nodded for me to leave the kitchen, while he huddled in conference with Chet, trying to offer him some advice. I watched bad TV on the stage waiting for the "all-clear" signal that never came. Instead I heard the door slam shut; Baker locked the four locks, and then came back to the stage, saying, "Well, that wasn't any fun! Fucking Chet, he really knows how to add sand to the sandwich, doesn't he?"

I never liked heroin. Or junkies. Tom knew that. In fact, the reason I had moved into the Boho Club with Baker was that I had found a set of works in the linen closet of my girlfriend Shelly, who I was living with on 72nd Street, right next to the Dakota. I knew it was over the minute I saw the needle—because there is no reasoning with junkies.

So when Baker suggested we visit "Joe the Junkie," his dealer on Clinton Street, after he received some birthday money from his parents, I said, "Fuck that shit, you don't need it, let's go out and get drunk instead . . ."

"You're no fun, Legs," Baker whined, but he could tell I was serious, and we went to the Lion's Head, a writers' bar in the West Village, instead. It was right next to the famous Stonewall Inn, where gay liberation had erupted in 1969, when the police hassled a bunch of drag queens, and they went ballistic and kicked the cop's asses. I thought that was the end of the heroin discussion, but a day later, Bob Brady called me with the news.

"Legs, Tom's dead," Bob told me over the phone. "I came home and found him lying on the floor of the stage . . ."

My world crashed and burned. Tom had gone to see Joe the Junkie the next night and shot up a speedball—a mixture of cocaine and heroin. He had overdosed, causing his heart to fail. Baker had such a big heart I thought it would never expire. He was sprawled out where he had collapsed, his thick, vibrant body now cold and lifeless. I sat sobbing on the stage with Tom Baker for five hours until the paramedics finally came to bag him up and take him away.

Like I said, heroin always wins.

The first time I shot dope was Dilaudid with Glen Buxton, the former guitar player in the original Alice Cooper band, and one of Alice's closest buddies. It must have killed Alice to fire Glen for being such an incurable junkie. It must've killed Alice to get rid of the entire band when his alcoholism took over and he woke up from his blackout and found himself on *Hollywood Squares*.

Dilaudid is a synthetic form of heroin, equally as potent as smack. Glen skin-popped me in the ass, the place with the most meat on my body and the most painless spot, since I was terrified of mainlining. I hate needles.

Immediately all the lights suddenly transformed into dull fluorescents. Time dripped by. I was back in Yale New Haven Hospital. It didn't matter that I was sitting next to Glen as we screamed down Fifth Avenue in his Pontiac Trans Am with a V top headed to the Mudd Club from West 72nd Street, I wasn't there.

I was in the operating room. Masked, white-coated doctors and nurses surrounded the operating table, preparing for surgery—on me.

I could taste the painkillers and sedatives they pumped through the IV. The operating room smelled of sterile gauze. I wished for an out-of-body experience, but none ever came.

The fluorescents burst into blinding intensity, and I was unconscious, even though we were downstairs sitting at the bar at the Mudd Club and I was nursing a beer, but I couldn't get drunk. I couldn't feel that warm glow of alcohol.

Suddenly the fluorescence exploded into a thermonuclear brain freeze, and I was fifteen years old and lying on the operating table in Yale New Haven Hospital. And I could feel them sawing through my right femur—and felt the snap of Dr. Margolis taking the two inches of bone out and tossing it into a small tray a nurse was holding in front of him.

I can feel that snap of the bone being cut out even now as I write this.

A horrid memory from the "corrective surgery" of my youth.

I woke up after that surgery and had a small tube running from my leg into a stainless-steel bucket that was slowly filling with pus.

"We have to let the wound drain," a nurse told me, and I couldn't even look at it. But how can you not look at something that is attached to you?

My roommate in the hospital was an idiot who got drunk and was hit by a train.

I mean, who gets hit by a train? Couldn't he see it coming? I mean, *a fucking train?!!*

Even I wasn't that stupid! His face looked like a Picasso painting, with too many right angles, caused by a deep crater on his forehead from where the train hit him. Only instead of a wound, the crater was squared off, like someone had rearranged his face with a buzz saw. A multiple-dimensional Picasso portrait.

Suddenly all the guys at the Mudd Club had caved-in foreheads. All the girls looked like the perky, blonde physical therapist who beckoned me to get out of bed and stand up.

"We're going to get up and walk today," she told me, and I thought, *What's this "we" bullshit?* I told her I wasn't strong enough. She didn't listen. Nobody ever fucking listened to me. They still don't.

Instead she handed me a glass of grape juice after she wheeled me into the physical therapy room where the parallel bars were waiting for me to attempt my walk.

I guess she thought the grape juice was like spinach in a Popeye cartoon, and I'd swallow it down and leap up and miraculously walk.

Instead I tried to stand on my own, threw up the grape juice, and fainted.

Anyone with a pair of eyes could see I wasn't ready. I weighed about eighty-nine pounds, had a gaping wound in my right thigh and my right hip, and black-and-blue bruises on my arms from all the IVs, besides my eyes being pinned from the morphine injections four times a day.

The Dilaudid made me feel the same way, crippled and helpless, and to make matters worse, I couldn't even feel the alcohol I was drinking.

"What's the matter with you?" Glen asked me, and he had a squared-off dent in his forehead too. "My leg, my leg," I mumbled in that typical junkie stammer, and he just shrugged and went back to stealing money off the bar. I didn't possess the vocabulary to describe the experience, nor did I want one. "Hemihyperplasia" is the technical word for being born lopsided; the right side of my body was two inches longer than the left.

"I'm asymmetric!" I'd shout to myself. "I'm lopsided, living in a lopsided world!"

That was the only thing that made sense.

I met William S. Burroughs sometime in 1976, brought to his bunker on the Lower East Side by Victor Bockris, Billie Bartlett, and Jeff Goldberg. Burroughs gave me one of his hats, green felt with a little feather sticking out of it. I lost the hat later that night.

I went from meeting Burroughs to hanging out with Debbie Harry and Chris Stein from Blondie. I was drunk and showing off, leapfrogging parking meters, and right in front of Phebe's Tavern on the corner of East 4th and Bowery I missed the last one and dove head first onto the sidewalk in full view of everyone in the place.

Whenever I saw Burroughs after that he would always tell me to say hi to Norman Mailer. They ran in different circles—Burroughs was a gay

William Burroughs and me target shooting at the Stone House,
Lawrence, Kansas, October 30, 1990. I missed the target.
Photo by Jim Tynan

junkie, and Norman a macho celebrity—but they respected each other. And it was because of Norman's praise that *Naked Lunch* was even published in the United States. And he stuck up for Burroughs again, testifying when *Naked Lunch* was on trial in Boston when the book was banned in 1965. The court ruled that the novel was obscene and upheld the ban, but a year later Burroughs's publisher, Grove, appealed the decision and the Massachusetts Supreme Court overturned the ruling. A dissenting judge called *Naked Lunch* "literary sewage," maybe the best blurb a book has ever gotten, you know?

Sometimes when I was over at the bunker, William and I had some awkward moments.

"You like sports?" William S. Burroughs asked sometime in the late '70s, staring down at me like Peter Graves in *Airplane* when he asks the little boy on his knee if he likes gladiator movies.

"Nah, you?" I muttered.

"Not particularly," Burroughs snorted, "though I must say, I do like guns. But of course, I don't have any here. Against the law, you know . . ."

And then he snickered, showing some teeth through those pale, thin lips, and I felt like I was sharing a laugh with the Grim Reaper himself. We were sitting across from one another at the dinner table inside the bunker, an old YMCA locker room on the Bowery that poet John Giorno had converted into a loft and that Burroughs called home. It was a hulking, white, windowless, concrete slab of a space that reeked of naked men being functional. Perfect.

Victor Bockris, who I'd managed to become friends with after he broke up with Billie Bartlett, and Burroughs's personal adjutant, James Grauerholz, were in the other room going over manuscripts. So it was just me and William, both of us so drunk and stoned that we were trying to keep from nodding out as we exchanged pleasantries. Two guys with no use for small talk, small talking.

"I do have some things of interest, though," Burroughs said, rising from his chair, looking quite brittle and teetering from the effects of potent chemicals. I felt like I should've grabbed him before he fell, but once on his feet, Burroughs righted himself, strode across the room, and returned with a Bowie knife and a blowgun.

"Cool, a blowgun," I managed, as he handed it to me along with a steel dart. Burroughs unsheathed the knife for himself, which turned out to be not a knife but a small sword.

"Chris Stein gave this to me," he said, referring to the Blondie lead guitarist. "An excellent piece of workmanship!" And then he started to slash the imaginary bears coming at him.

I put the dart in the blowgun and stood up beside him. Staggering a bit. And just as I raised it to my lips, a little gray mouse—a real mouse—scurried out from underneath a cupboard and ran across our killing field.

"GET HIM, LEGS! GET HIM!!!" Burroughs yelled as he clutched the sword overhead. ***"GET HIM!"***

WHHAPPP!!!

I missed by ten years; the dart bounced off the wall, nowhere near the crevice the mouse disappeared into. Burroughs looked at me with disgust.

"The object was to hit the mouse, not the goddamn wall," he hissed.

"Uh, sorry . . ."

"Well, I guess it takes some practice to hit a moving target," Burroughs mumbled, excusing my aim, though his entire six-foot frame sulked.

"What are you two doing in here?" James Grauerholz asked, reentering the room to see what the ruckus was.

"Mouse hunting," I told him.

"Having any luck?" James grinned.

"Noooo, we haven't bagged anything yet," Burroughs huffed, still upset that I'd blown such a great opportunity. His sulking seemed to say: *If only he had the blowgun, instead of the knife, we'd have a trophy mouse to show for our efforts.*

James went back in the other room to finish up with Victor, and Burroughs sat back down at the dinner table. I quietly took my seat across from him, and we both stared at the table.

"Plenty of vodka left," Burroughs sighed, being polite, though it was obvious he was bored with me.

"Great, can I get you a refill?" I asked, trying to make it up to him.

"No," he huffed, "I'm doing just fine, thank you."

A few decades before we met, in his quest to map the outer limits, Burroughs searched for the mysterious drug yage, which he had heard came from the jungles of South America.

"It's an interesting drug, yage," Burroughs told me as he lit another Player's, exhaling a long blast of smoke that drifted close to him, bathing him in a ghostly shroud. "It's a blue drug; you take it only at night. Every medicine man has his own recipe. It was quite an experience. The first time I had a bad trip. I took too much."

Writing to Allen Ginsberg in 1953, Burroughs detailed what happened when he finally located the mythical drug in the jungles of Colombia.

"I sat there waiting for results and almost immediately had the impulse to say, 'That wasn't enough, I need more.'"

Burroughs wrote of a nightmarish experience as the drug quickly moved through his body, causing intense delirium, hallucinations, paranoia, and nausea.

"I was saying over and over, 'All I want is out of here.'"

Drawing on his Player's, Burroughs stated matter-of-factly, "The stuff is quite toxic. If I hadn't puked my guts out, I would have been dead."

Burroughs found yage the most powerful mind-bending drug he had ever taken, and after his experiences with it and the accidental shooting of his wife, he felt he had gone beyond the limits; the seeds of *Naked Lunch* were sown, and it was time to write it down.

Upon returning to New York, Burroughs learned that Ace Books had decided to publish his first effort, a *You Can't Win*–styled manuscript of his continuing exploits as a heroin addict; the book was titled *Junkie*, and written under the pseudonym William Lee so as not to embarrass his family, who was still supporting him with a monthly stipend of two hundred dollars.

Taking up again with Ginsberg, Burroughs decided, much to the anguish of Ginsberg, that they were going to become lovers. At first Ginsberg accommodated Burroughs, loving him as a mentor and close friend, and not wanting to hurt Burroughs's already severely damaged feelings. But Burroughs's obsession and neediness were too much for Allen, and he finally exploded, rejecting Burroughs, who fled to Tangier and resumed his routine of scoring junk and paying boys for sex.

"Could you have written *Naked Lunch* on junk?" I asked him as we sat there smoking cigarettes.

"No, I don't think so. I was coming off junk."

"Was that the main reason you stopped—to write the book?"

"No. Not really." Burroughs thought about it hard and long. "No. I had gotten to the point where I had a fairly heavy habit, and I had to stop."

It was a two-year-long process of cure and relapse involving sleep cures in Morocco and apomorphine treatments in London before Burroughs finally finished *Naked Lunch* in Tangier. Not long after, in February 1957, Jack Kerouac visited Burroughs, bringing with him the exciting news that Allen Ginsberg was becoming the rage with disenchanted college students across America through readings of his poem "Howl," and Kerouac himself had signed a deal with Viking to publish a novel on one of his crazy cross-country road trips with Neal Cassady, to be titled *On the Road*.

It was all coming together. Hip had been born through the desperation of this wacky trinity of William Burroughs, Jack Kerouac, and Allen Ginsberg, and the world was waiting to embrace it. But unlike *On the Road*, published in late 1957, when it soared up the bestseller list, making Jack Kerouac a hipster celebrity, *Naked Lunch* took nine years to find a publisher brave enough to put it out. And if *On the Road* was a celebration of the new existential hero and his quest for God, *Naked Lunch* was a descent into hell and a hard fuck in the ass by the Devil himself.

I'd been working freelance for around five years after leaving *PUNK*, and I got a call out of the blue from Glenn O'Brien from *SPIN* magazine. Glenn was part of Warhol's Factory scene and had been a writer and editor for magazines like *Interview*, *Rolling Stone*, and *Playboy*. He claimed he was the model in his underpants in the inner sleeve of the Rolling Stones' 1971 album *Sticky Fingers*, and who am I to argue?

SPIN was founded by Bob Guccione, Jr. with a loan from his father, the founder of *Penthouse*, and later *Omni*. *SPIN*'s headquarters were one floor below *Penthouse* in an office building at 1965 Broadway that isn't there anymore, replaced by a luxury condo building called the Grand Millennium. New York City will do that to you.

Glenn asked me to come in for a formal interview, and when the elevator doors opened, all I saw were these huge pictures of girls with enormous tits. It was the most vulgar thing I've ever seen, and I'm no stranger to vulgarity. The doorman looked at me and thought, *This is a guy who'll appreciate enormous tits,* and had sent me up to the *Penthouse* offices, and the receptionist immediately sent me back down to *SPIN*. Even though I was probably destined to live in limbo between the two, *SPIN* is where I was meant to be that day.

I was aware of *SPIN*; I'd seen their June 1985 cover with Talking Heads in front of a bright-yellow background. But I hated rock writing, you know? So I knew about *SPIN* but wasn't reading it.

Glenn asked me to pitch some ideas, and I have no idea what I came up with. I guess it didn't matter, because the formal interview was just a formality.

"You're an asshole, Legs," Glenn said. "But you can write."

Glenn introduced me around, and I think I met Bobby, the junior Guccione too.

I knew from reading *SPIN* that Henry Rollins was my biggest competitor because he was a fun writer, with a great voice and a sign that there was at least something happening of value there. Plus I was creatively inspired by the competition. It was like the bands at CBGB: The Ramones, Talking Heads, Blondie, the Dead Boys, they were all pushing each other to make better music to keep up. Henry Rollins wasn't a foil; I just wanted to be better than him.

It's amazing to me how many real-life *This Is Spinal Tap* moments I've had. I always wonder, *Did that really happen, or was I so fucked up that I just imagined it?* You know, tramping around a backstage construction area in Seattle with INXS, searching for the stage door for an hour before giving up. They eventually wound up onstage, and so did I, playing tambourine during their encore.

Then there was the time I saw a groupie's face melt after finding out the opening band she'd just gangbanged wasn't the headliner, Danzig. And my personal favorite, when the Ramones demanded that me and the staff at *PUNK* magazine cross out, by hand, all references to them as a punk band in a cover story. They just didn't think the term was "accurate."

I'm also reminded that some of the dumbest heavy metal moments provided the most profound experiences of my life. I had one of those bizarrely significant escapades with Ozzy Osbourne in Nuremberg, Germany, in the same stadium where Leni Riefenstahl had made her Nazi propaganda film, *Triumph of the Will.*

I was traveling with Scorpions, a huge heavy metal phenomenon of the '80s. They were so internationally famous that I had to wonder if the whole world had gone batshit crazy. Not that Scorpions sucked. Far from it; they were a decent band with some great songs, and they put on a fantastic show. But it was the ratio of fame to talent that was a bit disproportionate, if not utterly ridiculous.

Still, Scorpions were good guys. Then again, they had their roadies strip my clothes off and strap me into a harness, sending me sailing high above the band—naked—in front of 50,000 commie kids in Budapest, Hungary. Maybe I deserved it.

It was in the last years of my drinking, when my life was an utter train wreck. The chaos followed me to Eastern Europe, on tour with Scorpions. First, I caused the press junket to miss our flight because I was having too much fun in the airport bar. Then I offended everyone at the reception at the German embassy in Budapest, though I was so drunk I don't remember why.

And then I called a girl back in New York City who I was having an affair with and passed out on the phone, leaving me with a $700 phone bill the following morning.

The first night in Budapest, I caused a real barroom brawl—complete with Russian soldiers battling it out with Hungarian draftees—smashing everything in the joint, from the big barroom mirror to the tables and chairs. I hid under a table, giggling madly.

That was a lot of fun, actually. It was almost like being in a cowboy movie when the local ranchers meet up with the cattle rustlers and kick the shit out of each other. Fun until two KGB agents found me hiding, dragged me outside, stuck me in a little car, and drove me to what I thought was going to be prison. Since I was so fucked up, and already living in one movie, I just switched the channel to some spy flick and growled, "You goddamn commie bastards, you'll never get anything out of me except my name, my New York City library-card number, and my blood-alcohol level!"

They ignored me.

But instead of a place of torture, they dropped me off at some Roman ruins that'd been transformed into a swanky tourist spa and restaurant booked for a meet-and-greet dinner with Scorpions. I was more horrified than if they'd taken me to jail, thinking, *Fucking Disneyland? Lenin's dream of a workers' state now holds all the charm of a waterslide park? Is the entire world turning into fucking Cheez Whiz?*

Budapest was only eight hundred miles from the Chernobyl nuclear power plant in Ukraine, which had just melted down in April of 1986, sending clouds of Cesium-137 wafting over the Hungarian countryside. As such, I thought it best if I didn't eat the lamb, beef, or chicken. Instead, I ordered the frogs' legs. When my plate arrived it looked like the frogs had been cut in half, their little hips still attached—so alcohol told my brain to shove a frog up my nose. It really looked like the frog had jumped up there. Scorpions thought it was mildly amusing, except for the drummer's girlfriend, who began vomiting at the sight.

The party broke up pretty quickly after that, and that's why they strung me up naked over the stage the next night. I was swung bare-assed over the band. It was humiliating. But even after all of that, as I watched the rest of the Scorpions' show from the side of the stage, I couldn't help thinking that communism wouldn't stand a chance against the power of rock 'n' roll. I thought, *If this is what communism looks like, it's over.* And four years later, it was.

On the short flight from Budapest back to the west, I was feeling a bit like the boy who gets caught jerking off to really depraved porn: disgraced.

Everyone on the plane was giggling at me. Thank God we were getting out from behind the Iron Curtain, where Scorpions were rejoining the 1986 Monsters of Rock tour.

Our first date back was in the charming little city of Nuremberg, Germany. I quickly joined the roadies and guitar techs in the hotel bar to resume drinking and restore my confidence, since I'd realized that the way to maintain my alcoholism was to blow through the stop signs. I knew that if I paused for a second, I was in for some horrible withdrawal symptoms. The obvious conclusion was to just keep going and pretend Budapest hadn't happened.

I was sitting in the Nuremberg hotel bar with all the other drunks when Ozzy Osbourne made his first grand entrance. He was dressed in some extravagant bright suit with scarves, gloves, top hat, and other weird shit. It looked like he was about to take the stage in front of thousands of people. We all just laughed. There were no women in the bar or record company people and therefore no one there to impress except for the seven or eight of us lowly drunken rock 'n' roll functionaries shaking off last night's hangover.

When Ozzy didn't get the reaction he desired, he disappeared back into the lobby and reappeared about ten minutes later, having changed into an even more elaborate costume. What the fuck was he doing? We just laughed even harder and went back to our drinking. It was pretty pathetic really: Ozzy's desperate attempt to get a reaction from a bunch of losers like us, and us laughing at such a gross display of drug-induced insanity.

We really got into it as Ozzy disappeared again, only to reappear another ten minutes later, having changed his clothes again. It was ugly. He made about six or seven entrances into the bar for our amusement, before he finally ran out of gas. The whole time we were screaming at him, asking him how many dicks he had to suck to get his shoes or whether or not he could stuff a bit more down the front to draw more attention to his crotch.

Maybe it was his pre-show warm-up, or he did it out of sheer boredom, but I wasn't expecting much from the Prince of Darkness that night at the show knowing how wasted he'd been that afternoon.

It wasn't until I arrived at the Zeppelinfeld, where the concert was being held, that I realized I'd seen the place in hundreds of documentaries on World War II. It's the famous stadium that Albert Speer had built for Hitler with the giant concrete swastika on top of it that always explodes in that dramatic film footage that starts every Nazi documentary.

I was a bit shocked that I was so familiar with this place, since I'd never been there or even knew we were going. None of the road crew had any interest in history, and to them it was just another venue. But I knew what this place was and what it stood for: Hitler's rise to power.

Without Ernst Röhm's million-man army of National Socialists called the SA, Hitler wouldn't have had the base of support essential to his early successes and probably would've become just another angry guy shaking his fist at the sky, muttering about the "injustices" of the world. Instead, Röhm carried Hitler into power as the Reich chancellor in 1935, with Hitler disbanding the German Republic and transforming it into a fascist dictatorship. Once securely in power, Hitler no longer needed his old pal Röhm, and on the week of June 30 to July 2, 1934, had Röhm murdered along with thousands of other SA members in what became known as "The Night of the Long Knives."

In order to unify any hurt feelings over his liquidation of Ernst Röhm and the SA, Hitler held a rally at the next Nazi Congress in the Nuremberg Zeppelinfeld, where 700,000 Nazis swore their personal allegiance to Adolf Hitler. The film of this event was titled *Triumph of the Will* and became the most stunning piece of propaganda ever produced.

"When Hitler finally appeared on the balcony for a moment," William L. Shirer wrote of the Nuremberg rally in *Berlin Diary*, "[The people] reminded me of the crazed expressions I once saw in the back country of Louisiana on the faces of some Holy Rollers . . . they looked up at him as if he were a Messiah, their faces transformed into something positively inhuman."

I sat watching the Monsters of Rock concert from Hitler's box seat, right in the middle of the stadium. The giant steps where Hitler and all the Nazi high functionaries stood during the rally had become the bleachers for the concert—everything had been reversed. And I was reminded of the Shirer quote, as the fans looked equally insane, possessed, and inhuman. Maybe it was all that cheap wine, bad dope, glue fumes, black leather, and denim, but the most disturbing thing about them was that a lot of them had the Confederate flag stitched, stapled, or painted on their jackets as an homage to American rock 'n' roll. This was pretty much the most evil symbol the fans could have used, since the swastika was banned in Germany and most of Eastern Europe at the end of WWII. I'd never seen the Confederate flag used so unironically.

Just as the crowd was building to testosterone frenzy, Ozzy took to the stage. Somehow the Blizzard of Oz, the craziest fucker in rock 'n' roll, the man who'd been doing bizarre costume changes just a few hours ago, faced this savage beast of a crowd and began to sing. And not just any heavy metal song, but the most appropriate song ever to be played in this fucking cesspool of evil: "War Pigs."

And then everyone in the audience began to sing along with him:

"Death and hatred to mankind / Poisoning their brainwashed minds—OH LORD YEAH!"

Never had I been so moved by a metal song or so grateful for Ozzy's fucking brass balls as I'd been that night, sitting in Hitler's box seat, dazed by this confluence of history and pop culture. God bless Ozzy!

Even though I was an occasional coke user, I never bought it, I only let my friends shove it up my nose. For the money, coke seemed like a waste. Fun, if someone was giving it to you, but not a necessity. Free-basing coke had been in vogue since the late '70s, but I was uninterested in the high because it involved a chemistry set. Too much work for too little reward.

So I had no idea about crack cocaine, but I was about to get a lesson that lived with me for the rest of my life.

"You never go out for a drink with me," I whined to Carol in her gorgeous 107th Street apartment. Harlem didn't really start until you crossed 110th Street, but it was a cool neighborhood.

When I moved in with Carol in 1980, the streets were crowded with musicians with

their saxes slung over their shoulders, coming and going from the West End Bar, the hottest hipster jazz club in Manhattan. It's the joint where Kerouac, Ginsberg, and Lucien Carr hung out, talking about writing over beers.

It was a hip neighborhood, but I had no idea that crack cocaine was first introduced to New York City, in 1985, at 105th Street and Central Park, and swept the Upper West Side like an avalanche.

"Really," I told Carol. "You never go out with me!"

"That's 'cause I have to get up at 7:30, and I have to work in the morning," Carol said in that true passive-aggressive voice—the one where I really wasn't sure if she was being sarcastic or genuine.

"Oh come on, you never go out with me anymore, just one drink . . ." I pleaded.

"You've never had just one drink . . ." she answered.

"Stop being such a stinker!"

And I laid into her, until she finally relented, and I found a nice dive bar on 105th Street and Amsterdam Avenue. The place was your typical Manhattan dive: long, dark bar, a pool table in the very back, and empty tables across from the bar.

There was no one in there except me, Carol, the bartender, his girlfriend, and another guy who were all involved in a serious game of Eight Ball.

Carol and I were sitting at the head of the bar, by the front door. Actually, there were two front doors, the front door to the bar, and a screen door that looked like you could just push it to open, but in reality, you had to pull it open. Very confusing.

"So how was your day?" Carol asked.

"They fucking took *The Rockford Files* reruns off and replaced them with reruns of *Little House on the Prairie*," I complained. "There really is no God!"

"Such a pity," Carol quipped. At least she hadn't lost her sense of humor.

Just then another guy entered the bar. He was wearing a black hooded sweatshirt, so I couldn't see his face, and he fast-walked down the length of the bar to the pool table.

There was a commotion in the back that I ignored, and I continued whining about *Little House*, when I noticed Carol, the bartender, and the girl had disappeared.

"What the fuck?!"

Then I saw the hooded sweatshirt guy struggling with the pool player guy, fighting their way up to me at the end of the bar. Then I saw the gun in the hand of the hooded guy, and the pool player guy swatting it away frantically. They were getting closer.

And the closer they got to me, the slower the action became, until it all finally flickered in slow motion. My eyes were fixed on the gun. Hooded guy pointed the gun at the pool player, who managed to swat it away.

But when they got to me, hooded guy stepped back so pool player couldn't slap the gun away. He pulled the trigger twice—and it must've been a twenty-two 'cause it sounded like a cap pistol.

As hooded guy turned to leave, the gun was pointed right at me. Maybe he wasn't finished?

I dove to the floor, my ass pointed toward the gun. I thought that would be my least vulnerable body part to get shot at, since the rest of me was skin and bones.

When I looked up, hooded guy was punching the screen door to get it open, before he finally figured out you had to pull it, and he was out the door and gone.

At that point Carol popped up from behind the bar, where she'd crawled, and said in a very proper, even tone: "Someone call 9-1-1!"

And disappeared again.

I stood up, transfixed, watching the pool player have the exact same fight with the screen door that the gunman had fought with, just seconds before. When he finally got it open, he collapsed, half inside the bar, half outside.

I crawled over to him and lifted his T-shirt, and there were two small-caliber bullet holes in his chest, with just a trickle of blood. A bad sign, as he was suffering massive interior hemorrhaging. I started giving him mouth to mouth resuscitation.

"That's what killed him!" all my funny friends have commented, so don't bother.

The cops didn't wait for an ambulance but threw him in the back seat of their cruiser and sped him up the street to Mount Sinai Morningside Hospital, where he died on the operating table. It was immediately a homicide.

The detectives loved Carol. I mean, she was the perfect witness right? She was a sober,

Intelligent, and gorgeous eyewitness to a murder, though I don't think she saw him pull the trigger.

She was on the floor by then. I was the only idiot dumb enough to be swiveling on my bar stool as the two guys played "keep away" until pool player lost. For good. It's no wonder Carol left me a few years later; she could've been killed.

The best thing I ever did was stop drinking. It didn't feel like that at first, and it was a lot of work and a lot of desperation. But I was ready. I'd actually started losing the desire to drink when I was in detox several years earlier, but I kept drinking. I finally took it seriously when I realized I had to learn how to be sober from other people. Stick with the winners, you know?

After Carol kicked me out, I crashed for a couple of weeks with my friend Jeff Goldberg and his wife at their place on Fifth Avenue, and then I stayed with Duncan Hannah for a few weeks.

I started going to meetings of the Sober Sailors Society all over New York City. I was drawn in by the program's steps, including the fictitious 13th Step: Go for coffee and fuck a sexy girl.

That step did help keep me sober, but only if the girl was really into me, and I, her.

It didn't matter where the Sober Sailors Society meetings were, it was a matter of when. There was a big one in SoHo every Friday night, and that was kind of my regular meeting. But I met my co-skipper Gary Kott at a meeting on the Upper West Side.

Gary knew who I was. He saw me, and everything I was talking about, he had already done. He'd fucked every girl I'd fucked. We understood each other. And he was cool. He wasn't an asshole.

He was writing and producing *The Cosby Show* when we met, and I used to call him when he was in the booth or on set. I think I was one of the only people who'd get through to him there.

"Gary, you got a call from Legs . . ."

We always had really good talks, and we liked talking to each other. I'd call him every day, and if he had the time we'd hang out. But he was always busy, especially during production.

When he was working, he was working all the time. He had this great loft on 17th Street, and a phone in the shower. Sometimes I'd hear the water running while we shot the shit.

Before Gary and I became close, Carol would call him and say, "Legs is out drinking," and Gary would just say, "Well, he'll call me when he's ready." He was done chasing people down.

And that's why it worked. He wasn't going to scold me. It was more like, "Okay, then what?"

That's why I struggled to quit. "Then what?" I was afraid if I stopped drinking, I wouldn't be able to write. And later, when I got sober, when I had to do longer pieces, I realized that I became a much better writer. But to get there, I also had to let myself not be a better writer.

I was hired to write a back-page piece for *Omni* magazine, which had to be funny. And it was a miserable fucking slog. So I called Gary and said, "You know if I had two beers, I would be really funny, and I'm just not being funny with this one."

And he said, "Well then go have the two beers."

I said, "Okay, I get it, so what do I do?"

I didn't want the beers anymore, but I was still blocked. And Gary told me to let myself off the hook.

"Legs, you're gonna write a mediocre piece. And you're gonna take the money and pay your rent. And that's the end of it."

And that flipped a switch. I wrote a mediocre piece—using my real first name, Roderick—and I took the money and paid my rent. And that was the end of it.

Gary was lousy at telling me what I wanted to hear, but he was really good at telling me what I needed to hear, even early on. Not long after I got sober, he told me to go apologize to Guccione, Jr., which I *really* didn't want to do. And it was humiliating.

"Have you stopped drinking?" Bobby asked.

"Yes, I've stopped drinking."

"Are you going to meetings?"

"Yes, I'm going to meetings."

And it worked. Though, I dunno, maybe as penance I was rehired to do the record reviews, which, you know, I'd rather have my cock run over by the L train. But I was allowed to be candid, so if I thought an album was a piece of shit, I'd say so. And if it was something I couldn't even be bothered to listen to in the first place I'd just assign it to someone else.

I'd wanted to tell Bobby Guccione, Jr. to go fuck himself, but I needed the job, and I was newly sober so I was trying to be good. But I realized the only way I was going to be able to keep going was to take any assignment that wasn't about music. Because I was sick of rock stars and their attitude.

I was already tackling whatever stories nobody else wanted.

After I got sober, I was made a senior editor at *SPIN*, and I was still doing anything I could to avoid writing about music, since I was convinced that nothing could be better than what was coming out of CBGB: the Ramones,

Patti Smith, the Dictators, the Dead Boys, Suicide, Johnny Thunders and the Heartbreakers, or Richard Hell and the Voidoids, etc., etc., none of which were true commercial entities at the time.

During the 1980s *SPIN* was shaking up the music industry by promoting itself as being an alternative to *Rolling Stone* magazine, although the cover stories that sold *SPIN* were Madonna (six covers), Jon Bon Jovi (two covers), and Kurt Cobain and Nirvana (six covers). Not exactly groundbreaking music, with the exception of Kurt, who quickly became *SPIN*'s cover boy before and after his suicide in 1994, until it ceased publication of print issues and went digital in 2012.

Since I hated writing about music, I took any assignment that had to do with anything other than lame rock 'n' roll bands that were so prevalent in the '80s, which usually meant covering wars, drug trafficking, or UFOs. Anything but music!

My first overseas assignment was to cover the war in Northern Ireland in 1988 with ace photographer Jim Tynan, who'd been to Belfast a few times before, as well as El Salvador and the Philippines, all hot spots during the '80s. But the trip to Belfast came with a catch: After spending a month or so covering "the Troubles," as the war in Northern Ireland was nicknamed, I was to go to London to interview Sinéad O'Connor, a new singer that I knew absolutely nothing about.

Sinéad was signed to Chrysalis Records at the time, and since they were picking up all my airfares, I thought the least I could do was spend an hour or so interviewing their next big thing.

My assignment for Belfast came directly from Bob Guccione, Jr., who said, "Go check it out and write what you witness." That was it. Luckily, as I said, Jim Tynan had been to Belfast a few times before and knew the ropes, and he found us a house to stay in up on the Falls Road with a lower-middle-class Irish Catholic family that wore the Troubles close to their skin like underwear.

There was no escaping the horror of these people's lives; the British soldiers used to count the number of milk bottles delivered in the morning

The Joyriders of Belfast

Photo by Jim Tynan

to see who was having visitors for the weekend. There were pictures of a pretty college-aged woman around the house, and when I asked who she was, the parents said, "Our daughter, she's serving life in prison for killing a policeman."

All the houses on the Falls Road were like my mother's. They had the same plastic flowers, so it felt like home in a way. And you could tell within a day of being in Belfast who was Catholic and Irish. Because everybody who was Protestant looked English, and everybody who was Irish looked like my relatives, you know. I felt comfortable there immediately.

The technology the British employed to keep the Catholics oppressed was staggering. Tynan and I took to going to the housing project where the Troubles first began in 1969 and hung out with the "hoods" and "joyriders," preteen delinquents who used to steal cars most nights. "Divis Flats" was more like a concrete concentration camp than a slum. Though they could barely see over the steering wheels, the joyriders would run the

British checkpoints, ram the car through shop windows, loot the places, then drive around until morning, when they'd set the cars on fire.

Tynan got fantastic shots of the kids dancing on burning cars. It seemed to us to be a pretty good indication of how the Troubles had devolved into pure anarchy.

While we were waiting to make friends with the "hoods" in Divis Flats, British helicopters would remain overhead, fixed in the sky for hours, observing us, and I'd wonder how much money they were wasting checking us out, instead of fixing up Divis Flats.

It was a seemingly endless, moronic war, and one I was happy to leave after a month and a half to fly to London to interview Sinéad O'Connor.

Her first album, *The Lion and the Cobra*, had just been released, though I hadn't bothered to listen to it until I arrived in London to stay at writer Barry Miles's apartment, where he suggested we put Sinéad's tape on the stereo. We were both unimpressed. It may have been that I was emotionally exhausted from my time in Belfast and hadn't switched gears yet, but I didn't fall in love with the record until I met Sinéad.

We met a day or so later at the Chrysalis Records office in downtown London that was filled with multiethnic, stunning-looking receptionists, but when Sinéad walked into the office, she blew them all away. She was wearing an unfashionable Elmer Fudd hat with flaps over the ears and when she took it off, I couldn't believe how stunning she looked. She was absolutely bald and absolutely drop-dead gorgeous. Her lack of hair only seemed to emphasize her beauty. It was undeniable, and throughout the interview Sinéad kept asking me what I was staring at, to which I answered, "You . . ."

After the interview Sinéad invited me to hang out with her, and we talked about the Catholic Church in Ireland, the pope, a spiritualist church she was a member of, and the United States. Sinéad was smart, extremely articulate, funny, and the most gorgeous creature I'd ever seen.

I thought Sinéad was extremely normal, especially compared to my other friends: Joey and Dee Dee Ramone, and Nancy Spungen and Sable Starr, to name a few.

Since I'd just come from covering the war in Northern Ireland for the past month, that was also a large part of the conversation, but I had to catch a flight back to New York in the morning to make my deadline, and we agreed to continue our conversation over the phone.

She was the first person I called when I got back home, and Sinéad was upset that she was scheduled to do a remote live CBS or NBC interview from London the next morning, and she was furious that the powers that be insisted she take a car to the interview instead of the Tube that she preferred. There was an innocence about her, as well as a very strong will and bravery she possessed that the world would soon come to know—and condemn, even though she was usually correct. Sinéad's big problem was that she thought people were smarter than they were.

I had to leave New York almost immediately to cover the war in El Salvador on returning home. I was working with Jim Tynan again, and we were supposed to come in together but wound up booked on separate flights.

The minute I got there, I was terrified. I don't know why, because there wasn't really anything to be terrified of. There wasn't any fighting going on. There was only one province that was guerrilla controlled, which we planned to visit. But as I was going through customs, there were guys with machine guns everywhere. It was a weird welcome.

From the customs line I saw Jim in an office, arguing with somebody who was really angry. And Jim had a temper, you know? He was Irish. And things seemed to be going very badly in that office.

But then he came out and he was smiling ear to ear.

"Legs, Legs!"

I was trying to pretend I didn't know him. But he finally made his way over to me.

"Legs, Legs! They wanted to give us two weeks, but I got us eight weeks!"

And I thought, *Eight weeks? Fuck you!*

We wound up staying for around a month.

I wrote a lot about history, though I originally meant to contrast the upcoming presidential election in El Salvador to the US presidential election between George Bush and Michael Dukakis. It was kind of a shitty article, but I had kind of a shitty time.

I was never a fan of flying, but fear of flying, actual visceral terror in the air, that happened in El Salvador. On our flight to the guerilla-controlled province, our small plane hit a series of violent updrafts and downdrafts while flying over seven volcanoes, pitching and diving and flipping over. I was sure I was gonna die. I hadn't been sober long enough to deal with this shit.

In Belfast, Jim and I had gone to meetings of the Sober Sailors Society, which was everywhere. Well, everywhere but anywhere I was in El Salvador. But while we were there, we ran into an ABC newsman Jim was friends with, and they were wrapping up because the war was finally winding down. And the guy said, "Hey, Jim, you're not drinking."

And Jim told him he'd gotten sober, and the guy from ABC said, "I am too."

I'd actually met Jim at a meeting, and he gave me an invite to his photography show. I thought it was really great and bought one of his photographs. I told him to come up to *SPIN*, that maybe they'd hire him, and they did.

So we had a meeting in El Salvador, with just the three of us, me, Jim Tynan, and the guy from ABC News, and it was fine. I was in my first year of sobriety, so it meant a lot to be able to do that with fellow Sober Sailors. But Belfast was fun. El Salvador wasn't fun.

We went to see Alfredo "Freddy" Cristiani, who was running for president of El Salvador and doing a speaking tour. And while we were there, a guy who was involved in the 1980 assassinations of Archbishop Óscar Romero and the four Catholic nuns came in and threw a hand grenade into the auditorium.

Fortunately, everybody had already left, and I was having lunch with some journalists, real journalists, when I heard the explosion. But that was the worst of it. El Salvador may not have been much fun, but it wasn't frightening. The fighting was mostly over, and in 1989 Cristiani won the presidency.

When I returned home after six weeks in El Salvador, Sinéad O'Connor immediately flew in from London. But her timing wasn't great. After I told her how much I was looking forward to seeing her, I remembered that I'd set up sort of a salon with some friends to come to my apartment and read what they'd been writing.

The timing wasn't great not just because I'd told Sinéad to stop by, but also because my friends were all women, women I'd been fucking. And some of them didn't know about the others, and it was one of the most uncomfortable evenings of my life.

And then it got worse: Sinéad showed up, picked up on the tension, and completely enjoyed watching me squirm.

"It serves you right for being such a slag and a weasel, lying to all those nice girls so you can get in their knickers," she laughed. "Womanizing scum, you're going to burn in Hell."

"It's not like that . . . I . . . ummm . . . Well, you know, Sinéad, I am single. And I'd been with someone for seven years, and . . ."

"And broke the poor girl's heart with your filthy, dirty ways. It's no wonder she left you for someone else."

I was already falling in love with Sinéad O'Connor, and she was already falling in love with New York City.

We were both exhausted. Sinéad had just flown in from London and was jet-lagged. I'd just flown in from covering the war in El Salvador and was shattered. What we both needed was a good night's sleep, but instead we were having lunch at some trendy, yuppie restaurant called "America" on 18th Street with my agent, Susan Lee Cohen, who was delighted to meet Sinéad.

Susan was the only happy one at our table, as both Sinéad and I were ready to collapse. We both ordered Fluffernutters and barely had the strength to get them up to our mouths, but Susan was beaming as the yuppies from the surrounding tables stared at Sinéad's bald head, as she wasn't yet that well known in America. *The Lion and the Cobra* had only been released a year earlier and Sinéad was just gathering the attention she deserved.

Later, when we got back to my studio apartment on St. Mark's Place, Sinéad told me that when she left the table to go to the ladies' room, John F. Kennedy, Jr. handed her a piece of paper and pencil and asked for her phone number. The arrogance of John-John earned the wrath of Sinéad, and she broke his pencil and told him to "Fuck off!"

I was flattered that Sinéad picked me over Kennedy, knowing that every girl in Manhattan would've given John-John her left ankle tattoo in favor of a date with him. Such is the power of "guppy love," as Susan told me we reminded her of.

I gave Sinéad the keys to my place while I went to work at *SPIN*, so she could explore Manhattan on her own. She was happy but kept bugging me to take her to Harlem to get "tram lines" carved in her head.

I had no idea what she was talking about but took her to a barbershop on 125th Street anyway. The barbers and friends who hung out in the shop were smirking and rolling their eyes, since not one of them could understand what she was saying through her thick Irish brogue, so I had to act as interpreter. Sinéad was so small the barber had to put the child's seat on the barber chair so she could be even with him. The barber held up his hair clippers and looked at me and shrugged, and I had to ask her what exactly she meant by "tram lines."

Apparently Sinéad meant "train tracks," those hair designs that appeared as shaved lines in short hair during the 1980s. She pointed on her head to where she wanted her "tram lines," and the barber obliged, I paid, and Sinéad left happier than I'd ever seen her.

I'd make bubble baths for Sinéad in my tiny apartment's tinier bathroom, and when the tub filled up with bubbles and she climbed in, I'd scoop the soap suds up in my hand and start sculpting different hair styles on top of her bald head.

"What are you doing?" she'd ask, and I'd say, "Seeing what you'd look like with hair . . ."

"You don't like the way I look?" she pouted.

"I love the way you look!" I answered.

"Then why are you doing that?"

"Because I was wondering if hair would detract from your natural beauty . . ."

"Well?" she asked.

"I don't think anything could," I said, "but I like you better without it! Your face is perfect!"

Sinéad smiled that smile that could melt an iceberg and we continued our dalliance until *SPIN* came out with the cover story a few months later. It didn't end because of a fight. It just ended.

In fact, the only argument Sinéad and I ever had, and it really wasn't an argument but a disagreement, was one morning when I woke up at Sinéad's place in London and we wanted to get some breakfast. I suggested we feast on cheeseburgers and Sinéad was appalled at the idea: "*Legs, you can't have a cheeseburger for breakfast!*"

I was aware of how unappetizing English food is and snapped, "Of course I can have a cheeseburger, who says I can't?"

"I do," she answered. "It just isn't done!"

Here was the world's most famous nonconformist telling me I couldn't have a cheeseburger for breakfast and I was pissed. "Who says it isn't done?"

It might have been different if she was a vegetarian and was for animal rights, but it wasn't that, it was more of a case of being too déclassé, too lower class, too trashy. But I didn't care and told her, "I can have whatever the fuck I want to eat, you don't have to have one, but I'm dying for one!"

So she sat across the booth at the Wimpy burgers, glaring at me, while I gobbled down my cheeseburger, and I knew right then and there that our relationship wasn't meant to last. And it didn't.

After we broke up, Sinéad and I remained friends, even when the difficulties started during America's first Gulf War when Sinéad refused to let some New Jersey patriots play the national anthem at some outdoor stadium before her performance. I stood up for her in the press and said, "What band or singer wants to listen to the national anthem before they go onstage? When was the last time you heard someone sing the Star-Spangled Banner before a rock 'n' roll show? It's a ludicrous idea!"

Instead, Sinéad became a late-night comedian's favorite punch line and Frank Sinatra threatened to kick her ass. She was misrepresented in the mainstream press as anti-American, when she just didn't want to be told how to do her act. The second affront she committed was worse, far worse, and completely unnecessary—tearing up a photo of the pope on *Saturday Night Live*. Why someone in Sinéad's entourage did not explain to her that the pope in America was thought of as just a nice old guy, not taken too seriously, instead of the fascist dictator he was in Ireland, is a mystery to me.

Friends would ask me about her problem with the pope and I'd try to explain that the pope meant something completely different in Ireland, just ask the surviving members of "the Magdalene Girls," who were Ireland's deepest shame—unmarried women who were raped by priests, doctors, or teachers, etc., and were committed by the patriarchy to "Magdalene Laundries" or "Magdalene Asylums," where from the eighteenth century to 2013, the shamed women were warehoused by Catholic religious institutions. In 1993, after 155 bodies were discovered in an unmarked grave at one of the "Magdalene Laundries," an investigation was launched, and in 2013, a formal state apology was issued, and a £50 million compensation scheme for survivors was set up by the Irish government.

Sinéad was right to stand up against the Catholic Church since she had been committed to one of the "Magdalene Laundries" for five years for shoplifting and being incorrigible and had witnessed the horrors firsthand.

But no one listens, and once people hate you for being different, the truth no longer matters. It doesn't matter that Sinéad was right about Catholicism in Ireland, right about the "Magdalene Girls," right about the "Me Too Movement," before it even had a name, right about abortion, right about racism in rap and hip-hop being unacknowledged by the music industry, and right about the Grammy Award members being slaves to fame and fortune and cowards for not speaking out on America's ills, but that was the '80s and '90s. Nowadays it's pure fascism.

What broke my heart was when I saw Kris Kristofferson take her in his arms when she was booed off the stage during a Bob Dylan tribute concert at Madison Square Garden two weeks after the *Saturday Night Live* pope scandal, but I couldn't hear what he whispered in her ear: "Don't let the bastards get you down!"

Eventually it wasn't the bastards that destroyed her, but when her second son, Shane, escaped from a hospital after being put on a suicide watch, and killed himself on January 7, 2022. The pain was just too much for Sinéad. She'd had enough.

Shortly after we split up, Sinéad released a video of her cover version of Prince's song "Nothing Compares 2 U," and suddenly she was everywhere—on TV sets around the world.

Sinéad had become one of the first superstars of the 1990s, even though that was not her intention. As she explains in *Nothing Compares*, the 2022 documentary about her life, "There was no therapy when I was growing up, so the reason I got into music was therapy, which is why it was such a shock to become a pop star, it's not what I wanted. I just wanted to scream."

"Nothing Compares 2 U" was a smash, causing the album *I Do Not Want What I Haven't Got* to sell over seven million copies and top worldwide charts. In its stark video, Sinéad sings in front of a dark background. It was shot in a single devastating take, and by the end a tear rolls down her cheek.

It's incredibly moving, so much so that people began asking me if she was singing about me, especially after my name turned up in the album's liner notes. I said no, but no one believed me, but I didn't care 'cause I was getting girls like crazy.

Eventually I had to say, "It's a cover of a Prince song you morons!"

Not long after I got sober, Bob Keating, another editor at *SPIN*, came up with a story idea based loosely on journalist John Howard Griffin's lurid 1961 book *Black Like Me*. Griffin's book was an account of the author's harrowing journey through the racially segregated Deep South disguised as a Black man. My version would also involve a journalist going undercover, but in this case I'd transform from a Lower East Side lowlife into a generic, well-heeled young urban professional: *Yuppie Like Me*.

To make me over, like a gay John Wayne riding out of the sunset, came Jonathan Marder, the publicist who'd arrange for my airfare and hotels in exchange for a mention of one of his clients, which I usually forgot to do.

We'd never met, we only talked on the phone, until one night when I was just about to fuck this gorgeous redhead in my new studio apartment on 6th Street, above an Indian restaurant on that entire block of Indian restaurants. Just as the redhead was seductively taking off her clothes and climbing into bed, the door buzzed.

Who the fuck could that be? All my friends had abandoned me, not that I blamed them, so I had no idea who could be buzzing my door. Probably a wrong dinner delivery, just ignore it, and they'll go away. But the buzzer kept buzzing. I went to the intercom and turns out it was the voice of that guy who got me my airfare and hotels, Jonathan Marder.

He came up the stairs singing the *Patty Duke Show* theme song, "*But Patty's only seen the sights / A girl can see from Brooklyn Heights! What a crazy pair!*"

When he got to the top of the stairs, I saw he was dressed in a suit and tie and brown expensive loafers with tassels on top. I wanted to slam and lock the door, but Jonathan persisted, spreading out his arms to give me a big hug and singing, "*But they're cousins . . .*"

He danced his way right into my apartment and immediately chatted up the redhead, who was naked under the sheet, on the mattress, on the floor, reaching for a cigarette.

She was laughing hysterically.

"And nobody ever said you'd last on your own," he giggled with the girl. "And here you are a month later with the most stunning beauty in your bed! Why, remains a mystery, of course, but this is cause for a celebration!"

"Uh, Jonathan, I had other plans if you get my drift . . ." I gave him *the look.*

"Oh, nonsense." He winked at the girl. "What you need is a good night on the town!"

"He can't go," the girl giggled. "He's got to get up early and start his new life as a yuppie!" She exploded in laughter.

Jonathan's eyes gawked at me, before he joined her on the mattress, rolling in hysterics.

"Oh you have to let me help!" Jonathan begged, tears of laughter still in his eyes. "It would make me feel so good, knowing I gave something back to the world!"

"Tell him your name!" she choked out in between belly laughs.

"*Fuck off!*"

"What is it?" Jonathan pleaded, still laughing.

"*Fuck off!*"

"Maybe a book deal . . ." he sang.

"Okay, for a book deal—Roderick . . ."

I don't know if I was more embarrassed at the howls of laughter coming from Jonathan and the redhead rolling round the mattress, holding their sides to keep from bursting, or when Mrs. Coward called for attendance the first day in first grade. Either way, I hated the name. I was not a Roderick.

Still, Jonathan thought Roderick was the perfect yuppie name and was sure of getting people interested in a book and a movie deal. And incredibly, he and my agent Susan Lee Cohen got me a book deal.

That's what Jonathan did, he offered your dream on a silver platter. He delivered the cash, after a series of strategies had been figured out, so he could mold public opinion.

How he started out in the public relations business was by scamming the media outlets of the tri-state metropolitan area. Jonathan once rented the Central Park lake and filled it with dry ice. Then he floated a canoe with twelve bodybuilders dressed like cavemen rowing Elvira in a skimpy Vampira outfit. The boat emerged through the thick mist, Elvira's arrival being filmed by all the local TV channels airing that weekend. The same weekend her crappy movie was opening.

Timing is everything.

It was the perfect gimmick, and Jonathan knew from gimmicks. All the local TV shows would showcase his cheesy events, like when he had Freddy Krueger slide down a grand opera staircase, flying on a thin wire, for the film *The Phantom of the Opera*. That first weekend was packed, before word on the street leaked that it was a shitty flick.

But it wasn't about the fucking movie, it was about that first weekend's box office cash receipts! If Jonathan could create enough buzz around *Basket Case 2*, or *The Lair of the White Worm*, or *Elvira: Mistress of the Dark* so they could do boffo opening-weekend box-office numbers—$10 million! $20 million! $30 million!—then Jonathan won!

If you're making a movie for one or two million bucks, a huge opening weekend is fantastic business. More business, richer clients.

Jonathan was understated gay, always wore a suit and tie, and had studied at Bard, the notorious drug college in Upstate New York. Somehow we became fast friends. Jonathan and I were like Neil Simon's *The Odd Couple* times a thousand. We shared a love of history, though his knowledge of old-world European history was much better than mine, while my knowledge of the American-Soviet Cold War was far superior.

It was at Bard College where Jonathan gained my respect as a true schemer. The scam went like this: Jonathan and his Bard buddies were bored and out of drugs, so Jonathan convinced his father he'd gotten some dorm slut pregnant and needed money to pay for an abortion.

His dad proudly wired him the money and Jonathan spent the windfall on an acid party for his friends and had a great time. And his father could have more great years deluding himself that his son wasn't gay!

Jonathan also had a wicked sense of humor, but when he dragged me to Brooks Brothers to purchase new clothes for my yuppie undercover character, I was not laughing.

Apparently Jonathan had taken this "Roderick McNeil" concept a bit too seriously.

The saleslady was in her mid-fifties, dressed in a suit, with graying hair, and eyes that danced over us, trying to figure us out. Jonathan was in his standard eight-hundred-dollar suit, color-coordinated shirt and tie, and the shoes with the tassels. My assistant Daphne was in her best Minnie Mouse outfit: baggy pants and sneakers, polka-dot blouse, and huge ribbon in her hair. And I was wearing what I always wore: black T-shirt, skinny black jeans, and a pair of black Beatle boots.

"Can I help you?" the saleslady asked, really wanting to call the security guard.

"Oh, can you?" Jonathan enthused. "That would be wonderful. This gentleman here needs a new outfit; he was mugged and all his clothes were stolen, a horrible ordeal, but one he's recovering from nicely, thank you very much. But he's still a little drowsy, so I'll direct you. Just don't pay any attention to anything he says, because he's still not himself. I think we'll start with some of those striped shirts over there . . ."

So it was to Jonathan I went with the difficult job of transforming me into a cultured and civilized human being. Now that I had a book deal, I was willing to pay him anything.

"Are you kidding? I can't take any money from this; this is a once-in-a-lifetime dream! It's as if God is giving me the chance to pay him back for all the wonderful things he's done. And just think I'd be doing the world a huge favor transforming you into an acceptable human being! A Nobel Prize! They'll write on my grave: 'Here Lies the Man Who Made Legs McNeil . . .'"

"Boring," I offered.

"Now that kind of attitude isn't going to help; you have to think of this project as a new adventure, a fantastic experience to see how the other half lives . . ."

"Where do we start?" I asked.

"Brooks Brothers," he snapped back.

"Wow, it doesn't get any more exciting than that!" I quipped. "How much is this going to cost me?"

"Five grand," he said without blinking.

"What a fucking waste."

It felt even more so when we got to Brooks Brothers and I saw the clothes Jonathan was picking out, white crewneck sweaters; varied striped button-down, handwoven, Indian oxford shirts; short-sleeve madras and batik button-down shirts; cotton chambray shirts; and pleated, pre-washed, heavyweight cotton twill trousers. Stacks of clothes. I almost had an allergic reaction just looking at them.

As we were counting up all the loot, I saw the saleslady whispering and Jonathan giggling.

"What was that all about?" I asked.

"She wanted to know what country you were from," Jonathan laughed. "She thought that you must be a foreigner because you'd never been to Brooks Brothers before. She couldn't conceive of anyone living in New York and not shopping at Brooks Brothers."

"Jonathan, were you one of those kids who had to wear these?" I said, pointing to a pair of bright, white shorts hanging off the rack in the boys' department.

I could just picture Jonathan as a tortured, scrawny little kid with a distinguished nose being strapped down by big, burly maids, evil domestic servants with arms like Popeye, stripping off his dungaree cutoffs, only to be replaced by white Bermuda shorts. It was a horrible vision, but one Jonathan wouldn't let me enjoy.

"Of course I wore those; it was wonderful, *I was the best dressed kid in Westchester!*"

"You mean you liked wearing white Bermuda shorts?" I was stunned. I'd never met anyone who ever copped to that fact. "You're such a homo!"

He looked over at Daphne and shook his head. "We couldn't all be little monsters, Legs. Some of us enjoyed being clean . . ."

"Yeah, Jonathan, but you're gay," I argued. "You could pull this off. I can't believe there were actually little heterosexual kids who enjoyed wearing white Bermuda shorts."

"I guess some of us just grew up with a more cosmopolitan view of the world," he snapped back. "You white-trash kids were raised with such a narrow mindset, a narrow mindset and bad teeth. Why your parents never discovered orthodonture, I'll never understand. In this day and age, there's no excuse for kids having bad teeth, none at all. Did you floss today?"

"Can I help you?" a salesman asked as he approached us.

"Oh, yes, please," Jonathan smiled. "My client here needs some suits; he just arrived in New York after a harrowing experience off St. Barts; his sailboat was commandeered by drug dealers and he was set adrift for three days. They got everything but *thank God* he was unharmed."

The salesman, a round guy in his fifties with an unpleasant smile, looked over at me skeptically.

"They had machine guns," I tried to explain.

The salesman didn't buy it; his eyes could tell that I wasn't up on duty and honor.

"Most unfortunate," the salesman said. "Now, what suit did you have in mind?"

Twenty minutes later I was standing in a fitting room while the salesman was going over me with a measuring tape. Then he sent me into the little cubicle to change.

"Oh, you look so handsome! You really don't look like yourself at all!" Daphne squealed.

"Whoever thought it would work? You really do look fantastic!" Jonathan chimed in. "It was rough going there for a while, but I guess I really am a miracle worker."

"I should probably thank you for all your help, Jonathan," I muttered, thoroughly humiliated, "but somehow I don't feel too grateful. In fact, I feel kind of empty. Are you sure the pants are supposed to be this baggy? I feel like I could fit another four pairs of legs in here."

"They haven't altered it yet," Jonathan explained, "but they will be a lot looser than those tight black jeans you've been wearing. Daphne, you stay here until the suits are ready, I have to go back to the office, then a screening and dinner. We'll meet up at nine at Legs's house. Tonight we move into the next phase of operations, *THE SHARE PARTY*."

"What's a share party?" Daphne asked.

I stuck my hand up, "Me, me, me, call on me!!!"

"Roderick?"

I repeated what he'd driven into my head just to show him I had been listening: "A share party is a unique Manhattan experience wherein people from similar careers and interests get together at someone's apartment for a party to see if they would be compatible sharing a house in the Hamptons for the summer."

"Very good," Jonathan nodded.

"Oh, it sounds dreadful," Daphne scrunched up her face.

"The worst—talk about your yuppie scum," Jonathan giggled to her. "But then *we* did not sign a legal document saying that we would live a life undercover to get the dirt on these people. It's not *our* job; we just have to prepare him."

"I don't know if I'm ready," I squawked.

"Legs, don't you get it," Jonathan grabbed me by the shoulders and stared right at me, "it really doesn't matter what you think, the machinery has been set in motion. The switch has been pulled. You've got a publishing agent, a film agent, a lawyer, a publisher and editor, me, Daphne, another apartment, a house in the Hamptons, a car . . ."

"A car, what kind of car do I get?" I asked, finally excited. "A BMW? A Mercedes?"

"No, Roderick isn't that trendy," Jonathan rationalized.

"So what do I get?" I asked again.

"A Chrysler LeBaron convertible," Jonathan stated. "It's a mini-lease. You pick it up from Avis on Wednesday."

"A Chrysler!" I cried.

"Roderick is a very big fan of Lee Iacocca's," Jonathan continued justifying his spending my money. Overnight he had become an expert about what Roderick liked and didn't like, and it was nauseating to watch.

"He would be! What else does Roderick like that you haven't told me?" I asked. "That he likes to be tied up by prison guards and made to take it up the ass?"

"Testy, testy, aren't we?" Jonathan, the expert, giggled. He really was a sadist, enjoying every second of making me squirm. "No, he's not there yet—Roderick would probably want to sleep with all the girls Legs sleeps with, but is too afraid, so he'll settle for someone with half a brain, that he looks good with. Someone that won't embarrass him."

"Geez, what a snob," I cracked.

"Yes, now you're getting it," Jonathan lectured, "and you better get to know Roderick fast because you're going to be spending a lot of time with him."

"Yeah, but who the fuck is this guy?" I asked him, a little too seriously. "You know, at least when I was drinking I had an identity, I was that 'drunken guy.' It wasn't much, but at least I knew who I was. When I stopped, I was terrified that I wasn't anybody anymore. It's only been six months, I feel like I'm just getting to know this sober guy, and now I have to become someone else . . ."

"I know it's hard," Jonathan condescended, the obsequious bastard, "but everybody's job is hard."

Then he was gone, leaving me weighed down in bags and boxes, trying to hail a cab at rush hour.

I headed out to the chic end of Long Island in my rented Chrysler LeBaron convertible; the electrical system didn't work. Fuck Lee Iacocca!

Leaning into my trip to El Salvador, I told people I was a commodities trader advising coffee-growing concerns, but I knew nothing about commodity trading. I don't know if anyone believed me, but nobody ever said anything.

I had a much more difficult time integrating myself into the yuppie lifestyle because I fucking hated the people. My Sober Sailors Society co-captain Gary Kott had a house in Southampton, and every time I stopped by for a dose of sanity, he'd just laugh and buy me another stripy Paul Smith tie. Not fucking helpful, Gary.

I was supposed to stay the entire summer, but I only lasted a month. And even that was a stretch. I was already uncomfortable around all those money-obsessed yuppie assholes, and being newly sober only made it worse. It was so bad I didn't even fuck this woman who was really into me, and that was out of character for me; it was just too creepy, I couldn't do it.

Two days after the "Yuppie Like Me" *SPIN* story hit the stands, the check from Penguin cleared, and thanks to Jonathan and my agent, Susan Lee Cohen, they'd done the impossible and gotten me a $50,000 book deal. That's when the film agent called me.

"Hello?"

"Hello, Legs, this is Terry Lovejoy, the film agent . . ."

The voice resounded with clout, like it was used to getting just that far, "the film agent . . ." before all the doors of the Kingdom opened. Only I didn't recognize it.

"Nice work if you can get it," I said, "but, uh, whose film agent?"

"*Your* film agent." He laughed to tell me he got my joke, but I wasn't kidding.

"I didn't know I had one."

He kept on laughing.

"So, when are you going to have some pages for me to read?"

"I just got the check," I tried to explain, but he wasn't listening.

"Hey, congratulations, the coast is showing a lot of interest in this project, and the sooner we can show 'em something to read, the faster we can—"

"Coast?" I was confused. "What fucking coast? What the fuck are you talking about?"

"'What fucking coast?' I like that," he spoke without any irony. "You're not being the yuppie now, are you? Who are you, Legs or Roderick?"

"Listen, I'm kind of busy here." I tried to hurry him up. "I'm on deadline. What is it that I can do for you?"

"I was talking to one of the producers," Terry continued, "and we were thinking . . ."

"Hey," I said, "could I just screw the book and wait for the movie like everyone else?"

He was laughing again, but I wasn't. I hated this whole idea.

"You're being Legs now, aren't you?" he asked, still without any irony. "That's funny, screw the book and wait for the movie . . . Anyway, we were thinking what would really help the project work is a love story. It would be great if you could fall in love with a yuppie girl to show the human side of yuppies . . ."

"Listen," I asked him, "how much money are we talking about here?"

"If we option the property or sell it outright?" he asked me.

"Sell it outright," I answered, not knowing what the hell I was talking about. But why not go for the gold?

"Six hundred, seven hundred thousand dollars," Terry answered. That was an awful lot of cabbage. I had written pornography for *Swank* magazine, so I knew how to write a great love scene; a lot of thrusting, throbbing, wet, hot, quivering, flesh folds of love.

"To fall in love?" I told him. "Something I do for free all the time? Sure, no problem. If it's a love story you want, it's a love story you'll get."

"One other thing," he threw out.

"Anything, just ask," I said, already spending that dough in my head.

"Could you get engaged?" he asked.

"To be married?" I asked.

"Think you could pull it off?" he prodded.

"How much money are we talking about?"

In the early '90s, after I'd left *SPIN* for good, John Holmstrom pitched the idea of my becoming editor-in-chief of a failing magazine that was being rebranded as *Nerve*. And *Nerve* was a fucking disaster.

High Times had this magazine called *Reflex*, and basically *Nerve* was taking over *Reflex* and changing it and seeing if it could sell. *Reflex* was very well written, but they weren't sure what they wanted to be. They covered alternative music and culture, but also a lot of sci-fi, and it was being managed in a very sci-fi way. So they'd have musicians on the cover, but inside it'd be something written by Philip K. Dick.

I was also still writing for *High Times*, like an interview with Jerry Garcia about saving the planet and preserving the rainforest; *SPIN* didn't want it, but *High Times* did. Jerry and I talked about amphibians, which didn't come up in most rock star interviews. Still, I was embarrassed.

Reflex was part of the *High Times* empire, and Holmstrom was involved. Our relationship hadn't ended with *PUNK*. Holmstrom and I had worked together when I was with *SPIN*; he did the graphics for the story about me and Richard Hell going down the Mississippi. We wrote a Ramones story together, which the Ramones hated. It was just like the good ol' days.

But with *Nerve*, I begged him to draw some cartoons, and he refused. I didn't understand why, but Holmstrom always had a knack for predicting the future. Maybe he knew *Nerve* was doomed from the start.

I did a newspaper interview trying to sell the idea of *Nerve* as a tonic for how rock 'n' roll had become corporate, comparing Madonna to IBM and Prince to General Motors, and saying our magazine would appeal to Generation X readers who didn't want to be treated as demographics. I can't remember if I actually believed that, but nobody else did.

We didn't have the best writers, but there was occasionally some good stuff in there. We got Lenny Kaye to write for us, and Jim Tynan did a great interview with Ice-T when he was still more like an outlaw than a cop on *Law & Order: Special Victims Unit*.

Our timing didn't help either. The internet was becoming popular and everybody was going to shorter pieces. People weren't reading longer pieces like what I wanted in *Nerve*, and they certainly weren't buying them. Everything was suddenly bite-size. I completely misunderstood my audience. They just didn't want to read anything we were putting out.

Nerve was essentially a rock 'n' roll magazine, and I realized that a rock 'n' roll magazine was like pornography. It didn't matter what was inside, the cover had to be great. Of course that's what *Reflex* had already been doing: They'd have Jane's Addiction or Ice Cube on the cover, but there'd be interviews with Terry Southern or R. Crumb inside.

I also lost $50,000 with *Nerve* because I wanted to hire an art director and they made me cover it out of pocket. That contract lasted twice as long as the magazine.

From the very first issue of *Nerve* we just sold poorly, and sales were like a snowball in reverse. It was depressing. And the business of writing and being an editor-in-chief really fucking bothered me. I had to focus on so much mundane shit that I just wasn't interested in.

After that sixth issue folded, I'm surprised it lasted that long.

Nerve was a hideous misadventure, I lost a lot of money, and nobody cared. I had so many hits at *SPIN*, and suddenly I was a miserable failure. I was glad to be done with *Nerve*, but everything else sucked. I was just unhappy with what I was doing. I was artistically adrift. I wanted to work on something where I'd really be able to take my time instead of cranking out material on a monthly deadline. And that's when I came up with the idea for *Please Kill Me*, though I was using the working title of *Chinese Rocks*.

I first met Gillian McCain through our mutual friend, the late writer and poet Maggie Estep. People in New York are always introducing people to one another to see if they'll get along, or fall in love, or become the next great partnership. It's one of the city's favorite unspoken hobbies.

Maggie brought Gillian over to my tiny apartment on St. Mark's Place one night, telling us both beforehand we *had* to meet. And she was right, we instantly got along, so well that I asked Gillian out that night.

When I walked her to the street, a cab pulled up to drop off a fare, and as she was getting in I said, "Do you want to go out sometime?"

And the lady who'd just gotten out of the cab turned to Gillian and said, "If you go out with him, you're crazy!"

That's also one of the city's favorite unspoken hobbies, giving unsolicited opinions to total strangers. But luckily, Gillian didn't listen. But we only dated for about a month before we realized our relationship was about more than sex, and she became my best friend.

As Gillian told Marc Maron on his *WTF* podcast in 2015, "It's something you need to get out of the way."

Which is what we did. We slept together until the day we looked at one another and said, "This is too weird." It seemed a tad incestuous, not a turn-on for me.

Sex with Gillian was too familiar. Gillian was too nice. She was always laughing at me. I mean, she called me "Bunny," and of course I did the same. So we stopped sleeping with each other and I slept with all her friends instead. It destroyed all her long-term girlfriend relationships, but we remained each other's first phone call in the morning.

Gillian and I loved *Edie: An American Biography*, the definitive oral history about Warhol superstar Edie Sedgwick by Jean Stein with George Plimpton. I'd published excerpts from interviews plenty of times, but this was different. A good oral history is a collage of interviews with different people to tell the whole story. *Edie: An American Biography* blew our minds.

Around this time, Dee Dee Ramone approached me about working on his biography, and I said, "Why don't we do it as an oral history?" And Dee Dee and his agent didn't know what that was. I couldn't believe it, but nobody really knew what that was. *Edie* was published in the early '80s, and this was now the '90s, and nobody but me and Gillian and maybe some people in publishing knew about it. I first heard about it because Norman Mailer had said, "This is the book we've all been waiting for."

What really started *Please Kill Me* was my interviewing Danny Fields for the Dee Dee book in March 1993, historically speaking the worst possible month to shlep across Manhattan from my place to his.

Dubbed "the Storm of the Century," a nor'easter buried the Eastern Seaboard in snow on March 12, 1993. It seemed like there were snowstorms every couple of days that March, enough that the city was only plowing the uptown and downtown streets, leaving everyone on the crosstown streets to fend for themselves.

So I'd have to trudge through the filthy, dog-piss-dotted snow with my tape bag once a week, Tuesdays or Wednesdays, I forget which. And I'd pay Danny $200 or $300, turn on the tape recorder, and he would just talk for a couple of hours. I'd say, "Tell me about Max's Kansas City," and he'd tell these incredible stories.

I would get the Danny interviews transcribed, and Gillian would read them and she'd be laughing hysterically. Danny knew everyone and had fantastic stories, but he was also so funny.

Gillian and I would read our favorite parts and laugh until we ached. So I asked her if she wanted to do the book with me, because I knew it would be a lot of fun. And then she turned to me and said, "This is so much bigger than Dee Dee; we should do the whole New York punk scene."

Dee Dee was hanging out with Johnny Thunders, and Richard Hell, and everyone in Blondie, and all these different people, and through the interviews with Danny Fields we were just getting a much broader story. If not for those interviews, *Please Kill Me* might never have happened. Eventually we dedicated the book to him.

For his gorgeous taste in music, his generous intellect, and his killer sense of humor, this book is dedicated to Danny Fields, forever the coolest guy in the room.

Talking to Danny, I knew there were certain beats I'd have to hit, like Iggy Pop going to Chicago to be a drummer in Black blues bands and coming back to Ann Arbor to form the Stooges. And I knew I had to incorporate that stuff. I didn't know what the whole story was yet. I was finding it out as I went along.

Once we realized what we wanted the book to be, Gillian and I knew we had to talk to everybody. And everybody wanted to talk to us. Well, almost everybody. Not Patti Smith, which was disappointing. I spent years wondering why she didn't want to talk to us for *Please Kill Me* when everybody else did, and I finally figured it out fifteen years later when I read her memoir, *Just Kids,* about her love affair with the late artist Robert Mapplethorpe, the gayest guy in New York City who loved shooting S&M pictures and fucking Black guys.

And I realized that Patti hadn't talked to me for *Please Kill Me* because she wanted to reinvent herself again. She didn't want to be part of this story. She's very shrewd and she knows her audience. *Just Kids* was written for all the women who went to art school and wanted to become artists, but instead they got married and had kids and got a regular job. Reading *Just Kids*, they could dip into a bohemian life they longed for before fate pulled them into the morass of the suburbs.

Just Kids was a bestseller and won the National Book Award for Nonfiction, which to me just seemed preposterous. It's very well written and a very romantic picture of New York City, but it wasn't true. It was a fantasy story. I mean, sure she loved Robert Mapplethorpe very dearly, but was the book nonfiction or mythology? And maybe it wouldn't have worked out the way it did if she'd given us a truthful account for *Please Kill Me*.

Jim Carroll certainly had it figured out. I interviewed him for *Please Kill Me* at my studio apartment on June 16, 1995, and he talked about moving into the loft Patti and Mapplethorpe shared on 23rd Street.

Robert was still trying to convince himself that he was at least bisexual, but he pretty much knew that he was gay, and there was no turning back . . . Patti didn't speak about Robert as a boyfriend . . . She made it sound like they were like brother and sister, you know?

Patti Smith was a rare interview we didn't get, though John Cale also said no, and maybe a few others too. But I bought a Patti interview from Victor Bockris, and John Cale from Mary Harron. And we got permission to use other interviews with people like Nico, Jerry Nolan, and Nancy Spungen because they were either unavailable or dead.

Otherwise, our timing was perfect. When we started working on *Please Kill Me*, everybody had kind of forgotten about punk. And because I'd just come off this horrible failure with *Nerve*, I don't think anybody ever thought *Please Kill Me* would come out, so why not tell me their most depraved stories?

We probably interviewed around two hundred people, some for long sessions. Richard Hell we talked to over and over again. Ron Asheton from the Stooges did around ten hours, Scotty Asheton about five hours. And I'd also interviewed Kathy Asheton, their younger sister. So by the time we got to Iggy Pop, I was ready.

And I said, "Okay, Jim . . ." Iggy's real name is Jim Osterberg. "Okay, Jim, it's 1967, and you go to see the Doors at the Yost Field House on the University of Michigan campus in Ann Arbor, you're with Ronnie and Scotty Asheton, and they don't get in because they don't have their University of Michigan student IDs, 'cause they never went there, but you still have yours from when you went there for three months. So you show your student ID and you walk in to see the Doors. Tell me what happened when you saw Jim Morrison . . ."

Iggy said, "He looked incredible. I remember thinking, Hedy Lamarr in *Samson and Delilah*, because his hair was Hollywood-coiffed ringlets, and it was blue-black, greased and shiny. It was some good hair, I'll tell you."

He talked about how much the Doors couldn't fucking play and they sucked that night, which by all accounts they really did. And Jim was singing in this Betty Boop voice. The kids nearly rioted, which Iggy appreciated.

Iggy and me listening to his *Raw Power* remixes.

Photo © Bob Gruen/www.bobgruen.com

"That's when I thought, 'Look how awful they are, and they've got the number one single in the country! If this guy can do it, I can do it. And I gotta do it now. I can't wait any longer.'"

I thought that was brilliant. And I think we got it because we'd done our homework. We'd already spoken to Ron and Scott Asheton, and their sister Kathy. We'd have interviewed the other original Stooge, Dave Alexander, but he'd already died in 1975. And I'd interviewed John Sinclair and Wayne Kramer from the MC5 by then too. We knew a lot before we talked to Iggy.

And Danny Fields had been the Doors' PR guy, and later managed the Stooges, and it all started coming together. When *Please Kill Me* came out, some people were surprised that we'd included the Doors, and the Velvet Underground, the Stooges, and the New York Dolls, but I didn't care. It was what the story was. It made sense to me.

But we should have trademarked that connection, because every documentary that came out about punk followed the formula for *Please Kill Me*.

A lot of people who've read *Please Kill Me* don't realize the book begins with a question from Lou Reed:

"Rock 'n' roll is so great, people should start dying for it. You don't understand. The music gave you back your beat so you could dream. A whole generation running with a Fender bass . . . The people just have to die for the music. People are dying for everything else, so why not the music? Die for it. Isn't it pretty? Wouldn't you die for something pretty?"

It seemed like the perfect way to begin a book called *Please Kill Me,* you know? I thought that would be a worthwhile question to pose, especially since the basis of all philosophies is: "To be or not to be?" I mean, why go on? Is life too shitty to continue? The history of punk is sort of an answer to Lou's classic question.

THIRTEEN

Long before we got a book deal for *Please Kill Me*, Gillian and I started putting the early chapters together, and I met up at a diner with Gary Kott, my co-skipper in the Sober Sailors Society, so I could show him what I was working on. I was really proud of it, and I guess I was looking for affirmation.

As I sat across from him absently poking at my egg salad sandwich, Gary read the pages. And he was absolutely stone-faced the whole way through, and when he finished he took off his glasses and rubbed his eyes, and then he let out a deep sigh. And he put his glasses back on and looked at me, and said, "Legs, you weren't victims, *you were the perpetrators!*"

Fuck! He was absolutely goddamn right! I felt so stupid. It's such an obvious statement of fact. *We were the artistic perpetrators!*

As it sunk in, I became furious. I wasn't angry with Gary; I was mad that he was right and I hadn't seen it myself. And I didn't talk to him again for close to three years, until after we finished the book.

Gillian and I worked as a team on *Please Kill Me*, though it wasn't always easy. Very early on, I gave Gillian an assignment to cut the Dead Boys chapter, and she came back and it was a mess. So instead, I'd rough out the chapters, and we'd read them out loud to each other, instantly recognizing the weaknesses and strengths of the chapter, and we'd edit it together.

It was just much easier to do it that way. And when Gillian really dug her heels in with more than a suggestion, I listened to her.

She usually had a definite idea.

For example, there was a part where Duncan Hannah goes to the Deauville Film Festival.

Gillian said, "This has got to be in there!" And I thought it had nothing to do with anything, but she kept hammering away at me. And I realized she was right.

Before everything went to shit in the book, it had to reach a point where everyone realized their rock 'n' roll fantasy. Richard Lloyd takes a limousine with Anita Pallenberg to cop dope. It's not the dream of making it big, because almost nobody did. It's the rock 'n' roll wish fulfillment everyone had to realize before the roller coaster drops back to ugly reality.

And after that section, everything goes to shit.

Gillian and I really worked well together, and she made important suggestions on a lot of things. Gillian would make damn sure the voices were all purely authentic, as well as copyediting the entire manuscript.

Gillian was also necessary in our discussions about that structure, as well as keeping track of when someone was talking about a certain time; Gillian made sure that time and event went exactly into that specific chapter in the book.

Gillian was also responsible for the title of the book. We had gone to San Diego to interview Terry Ork, the first manager of Television, as well as being the man behind the counter at Cinemabilia, perhaps the greatest movie bookstore that ever existed. He was also the producer and owner of Ork Records, which released Richard Hell's best version of "Blank Generation," among dozens of other musicians' fantastic singles.

When we met him in a hotel in San Diego, Terry was six days out of federal prison for fraud and, believe it or not, came with handwritten notes. Terry's interview was one of the highlights of the McNeil-McCain collaborations.

Gillian and I were riding back to Los Angeles from San Diego on the Amtrak, and Gillian said, "I've got the title for the book . . ."

We'd spent a fair amount of time talking to Terry about Television rehearsing in his loft and a lot of time talking about how Richard Hell, Tom Verlaine, and Richard Lloyd interacted. And of course Hell's "Please Kill Me" T-shirt came up in conversation, and how Hell was too much of a coward to wear it, instead forcing it upon Richard Lloyd.

"That's the title of the book, *Please Kill Me*," she said and I wanted to strangle her right then and there. I mean it was so obvious! Apparently it was more obvious to her than me, and it was the perfect title. I was furious, just like I'd been when Gary claimed, "You weren't the victims, you were the perpetrators." She figured it out before I did. It just pissed me off.

But we were laughing a lot. Gillian was a lot of fun to work with at that time. We'd play air guitar to the Stooges' "No Fun" back-to-back, and then she'd roll around laughing so hard it would make me laugh even harder. Once our two horselaughs became one, there was no stopping us!

After the misfire with Gary Kott, the only people who saw what we were working on were Gillian and me, and our great assistant and main transcriber Dawn Manners. I didn't want anyone else's opinion. I didn't care. I just wanted this to be what I wanted it to be, and I didn't want to hear from anyone about it anymore.

I knew it was good, but I just wanted to get it out of my fucking life. When you work on a book, you live in it, especially in a studio apartment constantly filled with three people sitting at computers transcribing interviews. It was a big fucking nuisance.

I wanted all that work to mean something, but I didn't have much hope for success, because I'd just gone through some really shitty years after my first real flop with *Nerve*. Knopf made an offer, which I was really happy about, but it was only $20,000; Grove offered $30,000 for both the hardcover and paperback. And when Penguin saw the book they bought the paperback rights from Grove for $80,000, and I was thrilled about that. Penguin's orange spine is just so iconic.

When I write something, I always write it for one person in mind, and with *Please Kill Me,* I had Gary Kott's voice in my head telling me we weren't the victims, we were the perpetrators—the pirates, hustlers, scoundrels, and whores, the scourge of the Bowery.

When I got galleys back from Grove, I had Dawn take the first copy to Gary Kott. I wanted, maybe needed him to be the first outside of Grove to read it.

"It's really good, Legs."

That was all I needed to hear. *Success!*

Gillian said she had a nervous breakdown when we finished the book. Which I didn't really understand, because I was doing all of the physical edits. She'd come in later and clarify an idea I was trying to make or tie together different sections I was having difficulty with, besides the grammar and spelling, but the work wasn't anything to have a breakdown over. It was probably me sending her to Cafe Mogador so I could have sex breaks with my girlfriend that sent Gillian over the top.

I think even Gillian would have to agree with me when I say, "When you're really nailing it, when you're truly in the flow, it's not you writing the book . . ."

It's like what William Burroughs said to me a hundred years ago: "Norman Mailer said I might be possessed by genius," William told me. "Well, *that's* the point. You don't possess it. You aren't a genius, but you're lucky when you're possessed by it. The more you're thinking about your individuality, or your *me*, the less you're going to be contacting anything of the slightest bit of interest.

"You become the tool," Burroughs continued, "exactly. Henry Miller said, 'Who writes the great books? Not we who have our names on the covers.' The writer is simply someone who has an antenna of which he tunes into certain currents. Of times, when he is lucky. A medium, as it were."

That's what Gillian and I'd become, mediums to let the story flow through us. We were just human conduits the stories poured through and were lucky enough to possess a perverse sense of humor and a loving empathy for the outcast. Thank God Gillian and I shared the same sense of humor! We felt truly blessed to have channeled *Please Kill Me,* and

Gillian told me, "I would've been so jealous if my name wasn't on this book!"

No need to worry, I couldn't have done it without you.

People were calling me all the time asking for *Please Kill Me*. I'd get on the phone at nine o'clock in the morning, and I wouldn't get off until five in the afternoon. Being asked for copies of the book became like a regular job. It was a nightmare.

Anyway, I think most of the galleys Grove printed were stolen right away, which was a pretty good sign. And then the reviews started coming in and everything was glowing. The short-lived *New York Observer* sent a former journalism student to interview me for a front-page story that read: ***"Legs McNeil Still Hates Everybody Including You."*** Not true! Only a few of you!

People loved *Please Kill Me*. To celebrate, Gillian's father, Harrison McCain, came to town and took forty of us out to dinner, including my mom, who kept saying, "Oh, he's such a nice man."

My mom had a crush on Harrison McCain, and since Gillian had lost her mother a year before we started working on the book together, I said, "Mom, if you marry Mr. McCain, I'll forgive you for everything!"

"What do you have to forgive me for?" my mother asked, puzzled.

"Just marry Mr. McCain!"

Everyone had a great time at that dinner and the next day at the book launch, held at the Gershwin Hotel. Gillian and I arrived two hours late to the Gershwin because after spending the day in a hair salon, she looked like Shirley Temple and had to redo her hair herself.

By the time we arrived at the Gershwin, all the beer had already been drunk. Not that I was drinking anymore, but I noticed it was going to be the kind of night where the booze just evaporates.

Later, I passed a hotel room with the door open, and inside I saw my mother with her shoes off and her feet up on the table, drinking beer and telling about ten girls humiliating stories about my childhood. Thanks, Mom!

During the chaos of the *PKM* publishing party, Gillian's father,

Harrison McCain, tapped me on the shoulder and said, "Legs, can I speak to you for a minute?"

Oh shit! Now I'm in for it!

Mr. McCain was the self-made founder of a multi-national corporation that grossed billions of dollars a year. Not a pushover by any means.

I knew this night was too good to be true!

"Can we take it outside?" Mr. McCain asked in a voice that was impossible to read. Harrison McCain is not a guy you want to fuck with. He reminds me of Norman Mailer, with the same commanding intensity and authority. The kind of guy who's not afraid to show you his displeasure.

Fuck! I spent too much money! Damn, I was too myopic in my zeal to get this book done! And now I'm gonna pay for it!

I'm an expert on how to get out of a crowded room fast, but this time I felt like I was marching to a firing squad. We pushed through the crowd, and once we were free of people outside the Gershwin Hotel, I turned to face Mr. McCain.

He was reaching out to shake my hand, saying, "I just want to say thank you for teaching my daughter how to do this . . ."

I was speechless!

"My pleasure," was about all I could manage, thinking, *What class this guy's got!* Gillian had told me stories where he'd stood up to the really, really big boys, like Presidents and Prime Ministers. And Mr. McCain was truly proud of Gillian, as was I.

"And I want to thank you for looking out for her," he added, "and continuing to . . ."

"Of course, of course," I stuttered, shocked that a parent could be that supportive of their kid. *I wanted one!*

I wanted to say, "Hey, just marry my mom and we'll call it even," but for once I didn't ruin the moment, and accepted his gratitude as graciously as I could.

A few years later, after I moved to Los Angeles to work on my porn book, Mr. McCain took to calling me after a few cocktails and always began the conversation with the same line, "Hey, Legs, looks like the serial killers haven't gotten you yet . . . ."

And then he laughed uproariously. God Bless Harrison McCain!

Please Kill Me was so successful, or maybe notorious, that I started hearing about it from everywhere. I remember walking home with someone after a meeting of the Sober Sailors Society, and the guy was saying, "Was *Please Kill Me* this big 'Fuck you!' to everyone?"

And I looked at him aghast, and I said, "No, I loved everybody in the book! I loved interviewing them; I loved hearing their stories, and I loved sharing them, you know?"

But he didn't believe me.

I mean, Cheetah Chrome throwing guinea pigs out the window, and the cops come in and he's wearing really tight spandex pants, and a cop says, "Put on some pants!"

Cheetah yells back, "I *am* wearing pants!"

Hilarious. Everything that made me and Gillian laugh when we were the only ones reading it. It wasn't a fuck you; it was a love letter.

Years later, sometime in the late '90s after *Please Kill Me* was published, I was home in my studio apartment on St. Mark's Place, and the doorbell rang. I don't know how he'd found me, but I opened the door and there he was, Tom Katz.

"Where have you been?" I asked. I was kidding, sort of. We hadn't seen one another for more than fifteen years!

"You did a really good job," Tom said. It was the second-best compliment I received for *Please Kill Me* after Gary Kott.

I asked Tom if he wanted to talk to Holmstrom, and he said, "No! Holmstrom's crazy!"

It was a really nice reunion, and then he was gone again.

Former President Bill Clinton receiving a signed copy of *PKM*. Inside I wrote, "You might not want to show this to your wife . . ."
Photo © Bob Gruen/www.bobgruen.com

The notoriety of *Please Kill Me* didn't stop for a long time. I'd go into bookstores, or to buy DVDs in the downtown shops that aren't there anymore, and people would be staring at me.

I'd been out of town when the *Please Kill Me* paperback came out a month earlier in the summer of 1997, and since it was "laundry day," I was wearing a sweatshirt and baggy pants when I went into a bookstore with the girl I was dating, and there was a stack of *Please Kill Me* paperbacks, and people were grabbing them and buying them up before my eyes.

I said to one couple, "Hey, I co-wrote that. Would you like me to sign it?"

And the girl I was with said, "Oh, he just says that to everybody!"

I was dressed like, well, not like Legs McNeil, Resident Punk, so they believed her, and people would reel away in horror. And my girlfriend of the moment would just laugh hysterically.

In the middle of all this chaos, I found myself in a large board of directors meeting room facing all the scariest male and female executives at Pepsi-Cola's headquarters in Purchase, New York. It was them against me. Corporations never fight fair.

"Can you make the book more 'snappy'?" asked a woman I could never see myself touching, let alone fucking; not because she wasn't sexy, but her skin looked like plastic. So did her face. Even her eyes.

"What exactly do you mean by 'snappy'?" I asked. "Like peppy? Like on speed? Like crystal meth? Or kinda crackling? Like 'snap, crackle, pop'? Like breakfast cereal crackling or crows cackling? But if they're crows cackling, ya gotta bring in the whole Edgar Allan Poe thing, and I don't know if Pepsi wants to be associated with an opium addict and husband to child brides."

I had no idea how I got here, and I'd become my worst enemy: a yuppie.

It all started with a guy named Benito Villa, who worked for an exclusive book design and packaging firm. A very rich people's publishing company. Benito said he wanted to hire me to write Pepsi-Cola's one-hundredth-anniversary book, to be sold in supermarkets across the country.

I told him, "No way, José."

Benito kept calling back offering more and more money.

Finally it would've been stupid to say no.

Let Benito tell you what happened, he has a better memory than me:

"When graphic designer Bill Bonnell and I sold the Pepsi marketing people on our way of honoring the Pepsi-Cola centennial in one hundred stories, we were asked for someone 'cool,'" Benito Villa wrote for a now-defunct website.

"I knew of Legs McNeil through downtown friends who were in the film and music video scene. Legs had just finished *Please Kill Me,* and his ability to compose a salable oral history was attractive to my Pepsi marketing clients and made business sense to them—I just never told anyone that Legs's next book was going to be an oral history of the porn film industry.

"The Pepsi people wanted to meet Legs and have him meet their boss before giving the final 'go-ahead.' So I drove Legs from Manhattan up to where Pepsi-Cola marketing was then based. Here I've got a shaggy-haired, cigarette-smoking gangster/savant—who I don't know—wearing leather pants and a white T-shirt, and I'm due to walk into a Pepsi-Cola corporate headquarters that then was more prim, buttoned-down, blue-suit-white-shirt-striped-tie than even IBM or Chase Manhattan Bank. Sporting a checked caramel Barneys suit, dark-coffee wingtips, a white button-down Brooks Brothers shirt, and a red Jerry Garcia tie, I'm thinking I'm doomed. I'm not getting this deal done.

"Luckily, the boss, the guy who would bless or kill the book project, was an urbane, laid-back chief marketing officer named Brian Swette. Any awkwardness between Legs and Swette disappeared when Swette revealed he had been based in Central America during the Iran-Contra affair; Legs having covered the war in El Salvador, asked a couple of questions about that gig and got Swette talking about his hanging out of a helicopter during a sudden liftoff to avoid ground fire between rival generals—a story Swette said we couldn't use, but something that brought he and Legs together like a pair of schoolboys set to pull off a prank."

It felt that way with Brian Swette—that we were two delinquents who'd accidentally been given the keys to the Kingdom.

I was being driven from the East Village to Purchase in a stretch limo twice a week, and I was going to write the book for Pepsi's one-hundredth-birthday celebration, titled *Pop Culture: 100 Stories from Pepsi-Cola's First 100 Years,* available at supermarket checkout counters across the country.

I must say, limos are fun to fuck in. Just drop by her place, have the driver escort her into the car, put up the divider, and just drive around the city aimlessly, making love until the cows come home.

I was about to become a national author. A corporate shill, even though I loved writing this book and I loved the fantastic stories we uncovered!

As Benito wrote about my behavior, *"'I can't be talking to corporate stiffs; I need real people,'* Legs snarled out loud on the car back to the city. 'The corporate people are going to be like rock stars before a tour—saying, 'the band's together, playing better than ever'—or baseball players before a season—saying, 'the team looks good; I've got a good arm, this is gonna be our year.' *We can't have any of that crap in there; no one will care.*'"

The best part of working for Pepsi was that Brian Swette let me run my own shop. I constructed a narrative of three or four actual Pepsi stories from each decade and era of the last one hundred years, from the turn of the century to World War I, to the Jazz Age, proceeding all the way to the then present: 1997.

The perks weren't bad either. Brian had become notorious at Pepsi for renting an entire island in Hawaii and converting an inactive volcano as the stage for the world's best rock 'n' roll group, the Rolling Stones, to play a show for the thousands of executives invited to the private one-hundredth-anniversary party. It took some doing and millions of dollars to pull that one off.

So I felt kinda safe with Brian, especially when he sent a limo to pick me up and take me to meet him at Giants Stadium to watch the Stones on their *Bridges to Babylon* tour.

We had fourteenth-row center seats. We were right in front of Jann Wenner and Yoko Ono, who were smoking the strongest pot I ever inhaled. That's when I finally truly got Yoko. She was dancing like a banshee, just rocking the fuck out, and I realized, *Oh, she's just an artist who happens to be a rock chick. I know you!*

Benito tells the rest of the story: "Though the book was completed, it has never been released. When Swette was fired after his 1998 Super Bowl campaign fell flat with the Pepsi bottlers, many of his projects were 'killed' after the new marketing chief came in; *Pop Culture* was one of those projects that was made to 'go away.'"

Brian Swette's mosquito-drinking "Brown Sugar" Super Bowl commercial wasn't bad; it was just kinda weird, kinda zany weird. But you know how corporations are; the minute you color outside the lines, you're history.

So me and *Pop Culture* were history. It was a book I'd come to love because it revealed all the racism, sexism, exploitation, and other bold inconsistencies of the American Dream, as well as all the fun stories, like the Beatles communicating with the outside world through a portable Pepsi transistor radio because they were such prisoners of fame when they arrived in New York in 1964. Stories that told a true account of the America of the past one hundred years.

Exiting Pepsi only made me want to get out to LA sooner than later and begin on my masterpiece, *The Other Hollywood: The Uncensored Oral History of the Porn Film Industry.*

I didn't want to be known as the guy who wrote *Please Kill Me*. Too late now, but I felt I had written the punk book, and I didn't want to talk about it anymore. Iggy Pop invited me to hear his remixes of *Raw Power*, and it was a nightmare. Twenty years earlier, I'd have loved that. But I didn't want anything to do with it anymore. Besides, Iggy's remixes sucked.

At the same time, I was an unindicted co-conspirator in the *SPIN* sexual harassment suit, which my agent thought might air on Court TV. I'd always wanted to be an unindicted co-conspirator and be on Court TV, though maybe not for something like this.

The sexual harassment suit bothered me because I thought we *should* be talking about sex, you know? So I wanted to do a book about the porn industry, because of my involvement with *Blow Dry*; I'd known these people and liked a lot of them. And I fell in love with one of the girls, who was very, very nice, a lovely woman. I wanted to get the hell out of New York, go to Los Angeles, live in the San Fernando Valley, and do the porn book, *The Other Hollywood*. Which I eventually did—and is another book in itself.

But I wasn't ever finished with *Please Kill Me*. Gillian and I got a movie deal with Universal Studios, and they were paying us $50,000 every eighteen months to develop a script. Well, I was developing a script, but I couldn't write it. And Gillian just wasn't having a good time.

Please Kill Me should not have been a ninety-minute movie. It was just a nightmare trying to cut the book down to that length. But that was just how Hollywood thought in the '90s. Today, it might be pitched as a ten-episode TV series for HBO Max, or even the Disney Channel. Instead it was like a sprawling epic being forced into a TikTok clip.

As much as I hated working on the *Please Kill Me* script, I also didn't enjoy either of the book tours. They were a nightmare. After my experience in El Salvador, I was done flying, so I was driving from city to city to promote the book. Gillian and I were exhausted, and I think on the second tour, for the paperback, we just stayed at the Chateau Marmont in Los Angeles for three months.

I had no confidence in *Please Kill Me* at first. I don't mean the book itself, because I worked really hard and the material was so good. But I didn't think anyone would buy it. I mean, it's not like anybody bought the Ramones or Iggy Pop, Television, or the Dead Boys the first time around. Nobody bought *The Legend of Nick Detroit*. So why would they care now?

Of course, it did sell, approximately two and a half million copies worldwide, and continues to, and *Please Kill Me* has sold more records than any music book in history. Even today, kids are reading it for the first time and then going looking for Ramones albums, or Suicide's self-titled first album, or *The Dictators Go Girl Crazy!*, or *L.A.M.F.* by the Heartbreakers, or *Young, Loud and Snotty* by the Dead Boys. It's crazy that some record company never came along and put out a soundtrack for *Please Kill Me.*

It's not too late, assholes!

What was also really annoying was that people started telling me and Gillian stories from the book like we didn't already fucking know them.

It was very weird. I'd see Gillian cornered by a bunch of nerds in glasses held together by Band-Aids, drooling over her, telling her stories from the book. Later I'd say, "What the fuck was that? Just say 'Excuse me, I'll be right back,' and then don't come back . . ."

Gillian seemed lost in the confusion of fame and publicity. Especially when she was elbowed out of a Canadian MTV film interview 'cause the jealous interviewer wanted a shot of me without her.

After that Gillian said, "Fuck this," and I realized maybe she was too fragile for the ugly occupation of fame. For the first couple of decades, I made sure her name and my name were the same size on every poster, advertisement, or marquee where we were reading, signing, or promoting. By about the third decade of Gillian being misrepresented in the press, I was already immersed in the world of American pornography and had forgotten all about *Please Kill Me.*

Unfortunately, Gillian had not—and who could blame her? I wouldn't want to be a co-writer on a book and never have my authorship acknowledged. I did my best to make sure she got the credit she deserved. But it's never enough, is it?

"Where's your new book?" a small voice asked behind me.

I was standing outside Fallout Records in the Capitol Hill section of Seattle, smoking a cigarette and checking out the gathering crowd. I turned around and she was just adorable: black beret, black hair, exotic almond eyes, and a mouth fixed in a permanent half-pout/half-grin configuration, suggesting that her teenage braces might have come off just a bit early. If that wasn't girlish enough; she didn't wear a stitch of makeup.

She looked like a mix between a Parisian schoolgirl and a Baader-Meinhof terrorist. Some kind of stunning, juvenile delinquent getaway driver, but she was in her late 20s. I just stared back at her, struck by how beautiful she was. Beautiful and disinterested in me. Her eyes kept darting away; she wouldn't even look me in the eye.

But she was also expecting an answer. There was a determined way about her, as she sucked on her Old Gold Filter 100; an impatience that begged, "Just tell me where to buy your new book, so I can get it, go home, and read it." Her question rang entirely functional, void of any invitation.

Just my luck.

"Who are you?" I asked, not wanting to let her get away. I had to slow it down, knowing if I gave her an easy answer, she'd take it and leave. There was something extremely fleeting about her; elusive, ephemeral, impermanent, brief.

"Shannon," she said, looking at me straight in the eye for the first time. They were killer, her eyes.

"Shannon what?" I asked.

"Shannon McNamara."

Her name fit the Irish Catholic bad schoolgirl fantasy standing in front of me: smoking in the girls' lav, drinking rum in the cemetery under a full moon, French-kissing behind the Dairy Queen, breaking windows and running from the cops, hysterical laughter, going to second base in the field behind the church parking lot, ID bracelets, passing luv notes in study hall, detention, trouble, marry me.

I was still staring.

"Great name," was about all I could manage.

"So where's your new book?" she asked again, referring to *The Other Hollywood*—the porn book that I'd been working on for four years.

"It's not finished yet," I told her, "but I'm gonna read a chapter from it today, about John Holmes and the Wonderland Avenue murders . . ."

Shannon was suddenly very interested; I'd hit a nerve, but I doubted it was the porn angle. Most girls aren't that interested in pornography. And though Shannon was quite sexy, she dressed to cover it; black leather jacket, long-sleeve dark-blue cardigan sweater shrouding any cleavage from her black T-shirt, black pants with racing stripes, and black-and-white creepers.

After four years of interviewing porn stars, I could tell there was nothing remotely "stripper" or "sex worker" about her. She even folded her arms over her breasts so I couldn't tell how big they were. She flaunted nothing.

On the other hand, I also found, most girls aren't interested in murder, so I doubted it was that. I couldn't figure out what grabbed her.

"Yeah," I told her, "I'm really liking the porn book, I mean, porn itself is kind of boring, but the story of the porn industry is really interesting," giving her my standard defensive pitch about the book, instead of the real reason: to hang out with people who fuck, so I could figure out why I had sex with all those girls—so I could finally understand what sex is really about. But that was my secret.

"What were the Wonderland Avenue murders?" she asked, completely indifferent to my lame justifications. So it was the murders that got her. Okay. I felt like I was on surer ground.

"The Wonderland Avenue murders were the basis of the film *Boogie Nights*. Remember when they go and rob the rich coke dealer and his Chinese houseboy keeps lighting off firecrackers?"

"Oh yeah, Alfred Molina in his Speedo underwear, listening to mix-tapes," Shannon grinned, and when she did, her whole face beamed. Talk about cute.

"Well, the part played by Mark Wahlberg, the main character, Dirk Diggler, was loosely based on John Holmes, the real-life porn star," I started to say, but it was no use, she got the giggles.

She couldn't stop laughing. She was trying to listen, but I could see it was hard to compete with the image of Alfred Molina in Speedo underwear dancing to Rick Springfield's "Jessie's Girl."

There was a sizeable crowd milling outside the bookstore, and I was interrupted by various fans asking me to sign their books, while Shannon talked to no one. She was comfortable being by herself, maybe too comfortable, like she'd always been on her own.

Even though she told me she lived just a few blocks away, she didn't know a soul at the reading. No, "Hi, hey, how ya doing?" No, "Sorry, I've been meaning to call you." No recognition of anyone.

She just stood a few feet away from me, smoking, aloof, waiting to resume our scattered conversation. When we did, I was stunned by her confession.

"I saw you read in New York, at the Continental, with Wayne Kramer, when the paperback came out . . ."

"Really?" I asked in disbelief, because surely I would have remembered her.

"You signed a book for me, downstairs, by the bathrooms; I asked if you knew where Johnny Thunders was buried and you said, 'There's Walter Lure and Joey Ramone, let's go ask them . . .'"

"I remember you!" I told her. It was true; I did remember her.

"You do not," she contradicted me.

When she snuck up behind me by the bathrooms, downstairs at the Continental, she vanished before I had a chance to talk to her. I was so bummed out; I walked the three blocks to my apartment on St. Mark's Place in Manhattan's East Village and went to bed. Three hundred fans to choose from—and this one tantalizing specter swiped the moment and disappeared into the night.

"I turned around and you were gone; how come you ran away?" I asked.

"Because when I asked where Johnny Thunders was buried, you said, 'There's Joey Ramone and Walter Lure, let's ask them . . .' And I didn't want to bother them," she laughed, nervous and embarrassed. "I didn't want to come across like some stupid ***fan***."

The way she said it made it sound like the worst thing in the world.

"You know, I was so bummed that night, after you ran away, I left and went home, *alone*," I tried to convince her.

"You did not," she sneered, hard and dismissive.

"I did too!"

She made a face, disgusted that I'd try to get one over on her. She looked straight at me with eyes that said, *Don't try to bullshit me.* ***Ever.***

I was finally telling the truth, and she didn't believe a word I was saying.

Since there was nothing I could say that would convince her otherwise, I dropped it, even though it was all true.

"I remember Gillian was wearing these killer black leather pants," she giggled, "and I was *so* jealous."

"Well, why didn't you just hit her over the head with a rock and take them?" I asked. She laughed, and for a moment, she looked straight at me, and I could see she was scrutinizing me.

Her eyes saw everything. They darted, stopped, stared, absorbed, remembered, and then moved on. When they bothered to linger, she was casing me, sizing me up, waiting for me to say something stupid or disappointing, or worse, boring, so she could move on. It's the same thing I do, and it was very curious to be on the receiving end of it for a change.

But she was better at it than me; I have a tendency to stare. I'm obvious. She was so smooth; her face never betrayed all the calculations tallying up behind those big beautiful brown eyes. In fact, her entire face was disciplined in *not reacting;* she possessed a sophisticated coolness that only true sociopaths are born with—and mere mortals only learn to master after navigating the most savage nightmares.

The rest of the punk fans gathering outside Fallout Records and Books looked like innocent children in comparison.

Then it clicked; of course, Shannon was a predator, just like me. Nothing escaped her. She evaluated all threats, competition, ulterior motives, opportunities, and advantages in an instant, with flawless detachment, not one inch of her divulging her expertise.

Just those darting eyes—Shannon McNamara—they didn't look Irish. Maybe Italian? Or Jewish? Or Asian? Or Mexican? Or Native American? What exotic mix went into the pot that cooked up this beauty? Where did she come from? What was her story? Who was this girl?

But before I could find out, she was running away again. My back was to her, I was signing another book for some kid, and when I turned around, I saw her skipping away.

"Where are you going?" I called to her.

"To get a Coke, you want one?" she said.

"No thanks, are you coming back?"

"Yeah," she answered, but I didn't believe her.

"I won't start reading until you get back," I called after her, but she was off, down the hill to buy her Coca-Cola. I stood outside the store, shaking hands, signing books, trying to be friendly and stalling for a time.

The tiny place was packed. Gillian was inside, cornered by a gang of fans, making small talk—her worst nightmare. She kept looking out the window at me, with eyes that begged for us to start. Tim Hayes, the owner of Fallout, kept coming out and politely asking me if we could start.

"One more cigarette," I kept telling him, staring down Capitol Hill, waiting for Shannon to return.

She didn't.

More kids showed up. More books to sign. I asked them to spell their names so I wouldn't ruin their copies. After all, they bought them, and I can't spell for shit. "John, is that J-O-N or J-O-H-N?" I kept looking for Shannon, but didn't see her, and then I couldn't put it off anymore, it was time to start.

I walked inside and there she was, standing in the crowd, waiting for the reading to begin, like she was just anybody. I didn't know how she got past me.

"I was standing outside waiting for you, why didn't you tell me you were back?" I asked a bit too urgently. The punk girls crowded in the doorway turned and stared at her, wondering why she deserved my attention.

Shannon stared back at me, blank; numbed by this sudden blast of attention. She looked like she just got caught; ambushed on the street by a crazy homeless man who spewed his bi-polar rage at her.

"I was ***waiting*** for you," I told her again, knowing Gillian and I had to drive to Oregon immediately after the reading. This was Wednesday night. I had to be in Guerneville, California, at noon on Friday, to resume filming the TV show based on my porn book. Then on to San Francisco Friday night, film there for two days, and then drive back to Los Angeles on Sunday. Then get on the train to Miami on Sunday night. Then drive to Washington, DC. Then Denver, and then home . . .

And Gillian had to catch a flight out of San Francisco Saturday morning to be at a wedding in Denver at noon. So there wasn't much time to make a connection with Shannon.

"Stick around afterwards, I want to talk to you, okay?" I asked her, dodging and weaving through expectant faces, trying to maintain eye contact with her as Tim Hayes made a path for Gillian and me through the crowd to the back of the store. The room was too small and there were too many people, and I was afraid if I lost sight of her, Shannon would disappear again.

"You'll stick around? Okay?" I called through the crowd. What I really felt like doing was taking her by the hand, leading her to the back of the room with us, and telling her, "Okay, just stand there until we finish with this. Don't go anywhere . . ."

Instead Shannon just stood nervously by the doorway. Not flattered, embarrassed.

"*OKAY?*" I yelled to her again, separated by bodies pushing toward the back, where the PA was set up.

"Okay," she nodded.

After a quick introduction by Tim Hayes, and a nice round of applause, I was speaking in front of the room—and noticed my hands were shaking. I could see the galley proof pages wiggling in my hands. I grabbed my wrist with the other hand to stop it; when that didn't work, I just put my hands behind my back.

That was a bit odd. Gillian and I had read every night for the past week and my hands never shook. It's not like you have to memorize lines or get into character.

Reading out loud is kind of fun, actually. Just read two short chapters from the book for half an hour, answer questions for half an hour, sign books, and talk to the kids for an hour outside the bookstore. Then go back to the hotel, get up, drive to the next city, and do it all over again.

I usually don't care about readings; I rarely go see other authors read because most literary types are as boring as fuck. But I don't mind doing readings—probably because Gillian used to work at the St. Mark's Poetry Project and presented hundreds of poets and writers, three nights a week, and is a natural in front of a crowd. She's also a natural at reading out loud, especially our book. But tonight I cared how this reading went.

It mattered because I wanted Shannon to like me. I wanted to impress her. I wanted her to think I was a cool guy. I was embarrassed by how much it mattered to me what Shannon thought, and that only made my hands shake worse.

Luckily Gillian started the reading off—we alternated between the different voices of our oral history—and once I heard her, I started to laugh; she read so skillfully that the crowd was usually in hysterics within minutes, with me laughing along with them. So the reading went okay. During the question-and-answer period, I was actually funny. I kept looking at Shannon to see if she was laughing. She was. I felt less nervous.

I kept thinking, *Well, she did come to see me read in New York. I mean, maybe she might be interested, I mean, why would she come see me read again? I'd never go see somebody read twice. But then, I'd never go see them read once. I mean, maybe she's aloof because she doesn't want to come off like some fan? But then, maybe she was just walking by and didn't have anything else to do? I mean, how much is there to do in Seattle?*

I found Shannon right after we were done, and she seemed a bit more comfortable with me.

The only problem was, when we walked over to the Crescent Lounge across the street, six or seven girls followed us over. Ordinarily, the girls afterwards seemed like a payoff for the reading, but tonight they were intrusive. I just wanted to be alone with Shannon. And stare at her. I really liked staring at her.

The Crescent Lounge was a hole-in-the-wall drag-queen karaoke bar and punk club, the kind of place where overweight Goth girls drool over their cute, gay boyfriends. Sexually doomed couples sit at tables in the corners, the girls talking endlessly about how they feel unfulfilled, while the gay guys keep glancing at the crowded bar, checking out the other guys.

When we sat down at the table, all ten of us, the manager came over to tell us what a fan he was of our book. Gillian excused herself and sat at another table with an old friend from Seattle, leaving me to deal with the fans. Some of the girls had their faces covered in glitter, making it seem more like a children's birthday party than a bar scene. The girls asked me to pose with them, handing their disposable cameras to the waitress to snap our pictures. "Put your arm around me." They read aloud the inscriptions Gillian and I scribbled in their books. I always wrote the same thing, ***"Thanks for a wonderful night! You were the best! Love and kisses, Legs."***

I was thoroughly mortified by my own obsequiousness, but Shannon was nice, she pretended not to notice any of these ugly little price tags that come with notoriety. And she saved me by saying something interesting.

"I've been to see Ann Rule read a couple of times, she's really nice," she offered, referring to the bestselling crime writer who once worked with Ted Bundy at a Seattle suicide-prevention hotline. Ann Rule's first book, *The Stranger Beside Me,* is her personal story of how she was friends with Bundy when he was an unknown law student, and, at the same time she was writing articles for detective magazines about a series of grisly unsolved murders around Seattle.

The book is a classic in the true crime genre because Rule discovers through the course of the book that the savage monster responsible for Seattle's multiple murders is actually her mild-mannered friend, Ted Bundy. This is why it's everyone's "first book of serial killers," and ***the*** primer for a wicked psychopath obsession.

"You ***know*** Ann Rule?" I asked, impressed.

"No, not really, I mean, I've called her on the phone, she's listed, and I talked to her about Jennifer, and she was really nice."

"Who's Jennifer?" I asked.

"She was my best friend who was murdered by a serial killer," Shannon told me without a hint of emotion.

"Your best friend was murdered by a serial killer?" I asked, not knowing what to say, but the obvious, so I said it: "Jesus, I'm so sorry . . ."

"She started smoking crack, and became a prostitute, and she moved to this really bad section of town. I kept trying to find her. Then, last year they found her skeletal remains at a dump site."

"I'm so sorry," I said again, meaning it. I didn't know what else to say.

"I still talk to Jennifer's mom," Shannon continued. "She's really nice. We went together to the trial of the guy who did it. A Pakistani guy. They never got him for Jennifer's murder, just some others. But we knew it was him because he used box cutters. And they found a bunch of them when they found her bones. Plus there was an eyewitness who saw him fighting with Jennifer on the street the night she disappeared."

"I'm really sorry," I said for the third time, still shocked.

"I'm kinda better from it now."

"Is it what got you into crime?" I asked, thinking I'd discovered a real insight into her.

She laughed. "No, you'd think it would be, but I was always into it, probably growing up with Ted Bundy and the Green River Killer in Seattle." She kept giggling, growing more embarrassed.

"What's so funny?"

She hesitated to tell me, then let it out.

"I've gone on field trips to all of Ted Bundy's dump sites, you know, where he dumped the bodies . . ."

"Really, would you take me there?" I asked, almost pleading.

"Sure, if you ever come back to Seattle . . ."

"I'd like that," I told her.

We glanced at each other timidly. It was one of those awkward, gentle moments: perfectly still, endless, and dizzy. If only I could have leaned into her, smelled her hair.

"Hey, do you know who Bob Keppel is?" Shannon asked, breaking the moment.

"Isn't he the FBI serial-killer profiler who writes all those books?" I asked.

"No, that's Robert Ressler," she corrected me. "Keppel was the homicide detective on the Bundy Task Force, who later worked on the Green River Killer Task Force."

"I don't think I know about him," I confessed.

"He teaches a seminar on serial killers here in Seattle; I've taken it twice, and I'm gonna take it again in November. He's really, really good."

She could see I was both envious and impressed; she gloated just a touch as she sucked on her Old Gold 100.

"Okay, if you're so smart," I asked her, "if you're such an expert on Ted Bundy, what was the name of the girl that Ted murdered, the one he was eventually executed for?"

Shannon stared across the table, remembering. She went blank. What I didn't know is that Shannon was accessing her photographic memory. I never knew anyone who had a true photographic memory, and to access it, her eyes went blank as if reading a teleprompter inside her head.

"Kimberly Leach, twelve years old, Lake City, Florida?" she asked, but it need not have been a question.

I was stunned. Nobody ever gets that one right. This girl really knew her stuff.

I couldn't help it, I leaned into her and whispered, "Do you want to come to LA and be with me?"

Now she looked even worse, like I'd just slugged her. Completely vulnerable, like I was holding out a golden carrot, intending to yank it away the minute she showed any interest. There was something about her that said she was used to having it all yanked away. She looked visibly pained, as if fighting off stabbing jabs of hope and dread, unable to decide which is more lethal.

"How do you know I'm not some crazed stalker?" she laughed,

recovering with a quip, but I didn't feel like giving her an easy way out. I wanted to let her know I was serious. I was tired of her doubting me.

"I *know*. I always ***know***. And so do ***you***," I told her. "You find most people disappointing, boring, and small. No one holds your attention longer than a few minutes, let alone an entire evening. You're absolutely amazed at how tedious most people are.

"You're just like me, and when you finally meet someone else, ***you know***."

She turned away, blushing. As if to make my point, the other girls at the table continued their questions about *Please Kill Me,* unaware they served as perfect exclamation points.

"*Does Iggy Pop really have a big cock?*"

"*Is Dee Dee Ramone really as crazy as he seems?*"

"*Do you think Sid really killed Nancy?*"

While I was busy answering them, Shannon sat there quietly, refusing to look at me. Finally, after a long moment, she turned to me and said, "I have to go . . ."

"You can't go," I told her.

Shit, I've blown it, I thought. *I should've just lied. Said something charming. Talk about coming on too strong.* She looked extremely uncomfortable.

"I have to go home and walk Riley, my dog," she said, getting up, buttoning her sweater, and zipping up her jacket. I had to think fast. I couldn't just let her walk out on me again.

She was adjusting her beret. *Is she ever cute.* I picked up the *Penthouse* galleys of the John Holmes article and wrote my cell phone number at the top of the page, with a note telling her she had to call me the moment she finished reading it. Tonight.

"You really want me to read it?" Shannon asked without any faith that I'd be interested in her opinion. She really didn't believe me. Not only about coming to LA, but everything I'd said.

"It's got the part with the ***murders***," I teased her, and Shannon laughed at how obvious I was, and how obvious it was she wanted to read it. Gillian and I only read the first half of the Wonderland Avenue murders story at the reading, just up to the murders. We left it a cliff-hanger, and I think the real reason Shannon agreed to go for a drink with me after the reading was to find out what happened in the story.

"Come on, ***you know*** you want to finish reading it," I needled her. She laughed, staring me straight in the eyes, and for a brief second, she looked like she liked me, delighted that I'd figured out what would make her pause.

"It probably won't be until much later," she said, taking the galleys.

Oh thank God!

"That's okay, I'll be driving all night," I answered her. "Call me as late as you want."

Shannon thought for a moment, seriously considering my offer, then agreed to it. We shook hands. She said goodbye to Gillian over at the other table, and I watched her walk out the door, desperate to follow her outside, pull her into a doorway, and kiss her.

My ex-wife, Carol Overby, bought me a nice, classy picnic basket for a housewarming present when she first visited me after I moved into my home in Valley Village, in the San Fernando Valley, in the late '90s. The picnic basket was a beautiful wicker thing, with gingham material lining the inside, that held different compartments for silverware, champagne flutes, an elaborate corkscrew, and other expensive devices that I never figured out how to use.

It really was a nice present, but one I knew I'd never use. So it sat in a corner of the den, like a tombstone to a better life never realized. It sat for years and gathered dust like a tennis racket or a pair of barbells, too valuable to discard, too cumbersome to use.

I was staring at the picnic basket when I got home from Denver and it suddenly hit me. I'll take Shannon on a picnic to the Spahn Ranch!

Yeah, Charlie Manson's old haunt on the edge of Box Canyon was the perfect place for a first-date picnic! It was such a brilliant idea that I couldn't believe I actually thought of it! And if I knew my Shannon, she'd love it! And hopefully, love me for taking her there!

I decided not to tell her; it would be a surprise. I was so nervous that she was actually coming to stay with me that I couldn't sleep the night before she arrived. I felt like the biggest weenie that ever lived, but I didn't care, because she was coming. The next morning, Neal Colgrass, my new assistant and tape transcriber, drove me to Burbank Airport to pick Shannon up because I was so nervous I was afraid I'd get into an accident.

I was chain-smoking outside the small terminal at Burbank Airport waiting for her Alaska Airlines flight from Seattle, sending Neal inside every five minutes to check on her flight status, and he was getting more than a little annoyed with me.

Then I was inside and I saw her skipping out of the gate, looking exactly like I pictured she would—black leather jacket, blue cardigan sweater, black T-shirt, pants with the one stripe on each leg, and her creepers. She looked perfect, and even more delicious than I remembered. We hugged ecstatically; gave each other a timid peck on the lips, nothing sexual, just warm and overjoyed that we were finally together again. On the short ride back to my house we gushed about everything, and I could tell that even Neal was smitten with how unique Shannon was.

"I can't believe you're really here," I kept saying over and over, beaming at her. I felt like the luckiest guy in the world, because I was.

Once inside the house, after she unpacked and settled in her room, Shannon walked into the den and stared in awe at my dead gangster photos. They were mostly old news photos of murdered mobsters taken by tabloid photographers and were exhibited under the title "New York's Greatest Hits." I was so captivated by the collection that I bought the entire exhibit. They weren't particularly valuable, except to someone like me who knew the stories behind each of the photos—like how the cops had shoved the cigar back into Carmine Galante's mouth after he'd been shot while eating lunch on an open patio at Joe and Mary's Italian-American Restaurant at 205 Knickerbocker Avenue in Bushwick, Brooklyn. I remember the 1979

New York Post cover photo of the dead Galante on the front page with some great banner headline, and now I owned the same photo.

I was so happy that I purchased the entire collection because Shannon was walking around them, studying each photograph, wanting to know every detail of each victim and the story of every murder. Finally, someone didn't walk into my house and grimace at the photos; finally someone appreciated them as much as I do. Suddenly the world was a less lonely place.

"And, of course, you must remember this one," I said, going down the line of pictures, "this is Gambino Godfather Paul Castellano, outside of Sparks Steak House on the Upper East Side . . ."

"Isn't he the one John Gotti had hit so he could take over the family?" Shannon asked as she stared at the dead Castellano, half-covered by a blanket just moments after Gotti's hit men pumped six slugs into him. I told Shannon how Sammy the Bull and John Gotti watched the assassination from a parked car across the street, as hit men dressed in white trench coats and black Russian ushanka hats opened fire on Castellano and his underboss, Thomas Bilotti, killing them as they walked out of Sparks Steak House.

"Cool," she whispered, then smiled and giggled, "I *love* your house!"

I was thrilled. We seemed to have the same aesthetic, like the dead gangster photos. I've always preferred photographs to paintings, gritty realism to artist's interpretations, and black and white to the wonderful world of color. It isn't so much the stark photos of the dead mobsters, though that's part of it, but also the stories of betrayal, greed, and revenge they evoke. Shannon and I both seemed fascinated with the victim's last thoughts; did he know they were coming for him? What was he thinking when he saw the hit man start blasting away? Was he sorry?

Did he think, *I really fucked up this time*?

Since Shannon seemed to be as caught up in the drama of each picture as I was, I realized it was the perfect time to tell her my surprise . . .

"So I thought," I told her, "if you didn't have anything else you wanted to do today, that we might go on a picnic?"

Shannon lowered her eyes to hide her disappointment. "Oh yeah, okay, sounds good . . ."

"Aren't you even gonna ask where we're going?" I grinned, delighted with my secret.

She saw she was being set up, that I'd tricked her, and she was suddenly glowing, all the lights on inside her eyes, dying to know where we were going.

"Where?" she asked in a whisper.

"Spahn Ranch!"

"OH MY GOD! CHARLIE MANSON'S SPAHN RANCH! REALLY? I'VE ALWAYS WANTED TO GO THERE! CAN WE? WHEN? DO I NEED TO BRING ANYTHING? CAN I BRING MY CAMERA? WHEN ARE WE GOING?"

She was hopping up and down, delirious with joy. She helped me gather up cans of Coke and some cold fried chicken from the fridge, and we packed it into the picnic basket like two schoolkids pretending to be adults. We were giggling and laughing and so fucking happy.

I was carrying the blanket and the picnic basket, and Shannon had the camera around her neck. I helped her down the embankment and held her hand over the bridge of two-by-fours traversing the fifty-foot creek bed that channeled a tiny trickle of water. On the other side of the moat was the pathway leading into the center of a heart-shaped rock garden—landscaped by some obsessed Manson fan. It was a rustic love letter to Charlie. Dead flowers in clay pots littered the center of the heart.

"Can you see that it's heart shaped?" I pointed out, when we were both in the center of the stone valentine.

"Who built it?" Shannon asked, visibly shaken, looking around, expecting to see Manson girls lurking behind every tree, clutching knives in their teeth. The heart-shaped rock garden provoked an authentic goose-pimple moment, and proof that the Manson Family still lives in somebody's heart.

"Some Manson freak," I answered.

"Creee-py!" Shannon giggled, thrilled that thirty years after Manson's reign, there was still some lingering insanity to be found at Spahn Ranch.

"Come on, the best is yet to come," I said, as I led her through thick briars and branches to where the creek opened into a still pool of water about five feet wide. On the other side stood the infamous Manson cave, actually a rock ledge where *LA Herald Examiner* photographer Michael Haering assembled the remaining Family members, those not in jail for the Tate-LaBianca murders, and posed them for one of the most infamous crime-scene photos of the century.

"Get inside, I want to take a picture," she said from the sandy shore of the pool, waving me across. I obliged her, hopping over the narrow part and crouching down inside the cave. Now she'd have to love me forever for bringing her here. But after she snapped a few pictures, she took the camera away from her face and announced, "*I don't think this is the right cave . . .*"

"Whattya mean this ***isn't*** the right cave?" I answered, dumbfounded. "There aren't any other caves . . ." How could she dispute such an infamous American crime-scene shrine?

"Well, I don't think this is the right cave, the real one looks much bigger in all the photographs," she told me, walking back and forth, now on higher ground, scrutinizing the cave from every angle.

"That's because they were all crouching," I explained.

"No, this cave couldn't have fit all those people." She shook her head, unconvinced.

"Do you really think I'd take you to the wrong Manson cave? What kinda guy do you think I am?" I was offended. "Geez, you're really the original doubting Thomas, aren't you? You don't believe anything."

"Maybe I have my reasons," she said, with the camera in front of her face, taking another picture.

"Like what?" I asked.

"Okay, maybe it *is* the right cave," she conceded. "We can check the books when we get home . . ."

"What are your reasons for not believing anything?" I asked, more than a little curious.

"I said it ***could*** be the cave." Shannon avoided the question entirely, smiling at me.

I was staring at her, completely captivated. She liked the way I was looking at her.

I hopped back across the shallow pool of clear water where copper newts darted beneath submerged rocks. The tree branches high up swayed in the breeze, filling the quiet with the sexy rustling of thousands of silky green leaves. Even the mosquitoes left us alone.

I couldn't stop staring at Shannon, and then it occurred to me that sometimes life doesn't suck.

As extraordinary as it may seem, sometimes the gods are too preoccupied to conspire against me. Maybe, after all this waiting, I can actually get what I want?

Sometimes, like in that moment, it felt so right; I couldn't even remember the bad. Sometimes things turned out just as I imagined they might. Sometimes it was just perfect.

This was one of those times.

"Let me take a picture of you." I reached for her camera.

"Uh-uh, I hate getting my picture taken." She pulled away. "Why do you keep staring at me?"

"'Cause you're so beautiful," I answered.

She blushed, turned away, cutting that off immediately. "Where to now?" she asked, like some kid that just hopped off the Ferris wheel and wants to run over to the roller coaster, so I took her by the hand and led us out of the trees.

It was easy to see why the Manson family ended up at Spahn Ranch; it's the exact opposite of Los Angeles. Shade trees instead of palms. A slow-trickling creek instead of a concrete riverbed. Open fields instead of manicured lawns pitted with spitting sprinklers. Stillness instead of the constant trudge of five-lane, bumper-to-bumper traffic.

"Got to get back to the land and set my soul free," Joni Mitchell sang in her 1969 song "Woodstock," and Spahn Ranch, at the northern end of the San Fernando Valley, sprawling across Box Canyon, was the hippie ideal. It's a Huck Finn oasis just outside of a *Day of the Locust* nightmare. A forty-four-acre rolling playground, perfect for frolicking. But the sun sets too quickly in Box Canyon. Shadows start to reach out and snuff patches of daylight by early afternoon.

"No one actually got murdered here, did they?" Shannon asked as we made our way up the dirt road that led to the last owner's house, abandoned on top of the hill. Even though we walked out of the woods, into the open fields and late-afternoon sun of the canyon lands, the creeping shadows eclipsed the landscape as if night was born again under every boulder and bush.

"You scared?" I asked her.

"Uh-uh."

"You sure?"

"It's a little creepy," Shannon laughed, looking back over her shoulder. She turned back at me, grinning, absolutely thrilled to be here.

"Gets dark here early," I said. "You wanna go back?"

"No," she insisted. "Not yet."

Shannon was caked in a light sweat, huffing and puffing as we walked up the hill, clear that she wasn't going to make it to the top. When we reached the first plateau, right before the road took a steep hike up to the owner's house, I spread out the Indian blanket.

"If you're hot, you can take off your sweater," I said, handing her the picnic basket. She was wearing the blue cardigan, which she hugged tighter at my suggestion.

"No, that's okay, I'm alright."

Not exactly the prelude to a wild make-out session.

Even though she was grateful to stop, she didn't look relieved. Shannon kept glancing across the fields, as if she saw figures coming from behind every bush.

"There's no one here; we're all alone," I told her.

"You didn't answer my question," she reminded me, sitting down on the blanket, grabbing the Cokes out of the picnic basket, and handing me one. A lizard scurried through a dry bush behind us, making a loud crackling noise, and instantly Shannon's neck was straining; her head turned, her eyes searching for the culprit.

"It's a lizard."

"You sure?"

"Yeah, I'm sure."

"Then answer my question."

"Which one?"

"Did the Manson Family commit any murders here?"

"Just one," I began. "Shorty Shea was murdered here, some say by the creek, where we just were," and Shannon was riveted, her big brown eyes staring at me, unflinching. She wanted to hear it all.

"Shorty was the ranch hand who worked here taking care of the horses. George Spahn, who owned the place, kept it going by giving Girl Scouts and elementary school kids horseback riding lessons, you know, class 'field trips' to Spahn Ranch."

Shannon sipped on her Coke without breaking eye contact.

"So Shorty lived here along with the Manson Family, but he *hated* Charlie. And when the Family was first arrested for stealing cars on September 15, 1969, right after the Tate-LaBianca murders, they thought Shorty had turned them in to the cops, that he was the snitch. Fortunately for Charlie and the Family, and unfortunately for Shorty, the warrant for their arrest was dated wrong so they were all released from prison within a day or two. After they got out, Charlie decided to take his revenge against Shorty and stabbed him to death. As usual, Charlie also made sure Tex Watson, Bruce Davis, and Steve 'Clem' Grogan all got their hands dirty by making each one of them stab Shorty, even though he was most likely dead already.

"Apparently they tortured Shorty before they killed him. Rumor had it that they cut off his head, chopped him into twenty pieces, and buried him in twenty different places all over the ranch."

I loved Shannon staring at me so intently, and I couldn't resist telling her.

"Do you know how gorgeous you are?"

"Don't," Shannon barked.

"What?" I asked innocently.

"Come on," she demanded, "finish the story."

"But first I want to kiss you," I informed her.

She rolled her eyes, hugged her sweater tighter, and looked away.

"You know, I've been waiting since forever to kiss you," I told her. "But, then again, maybe you don't want to kiss me?"

"I ***didn't*** say that," she pouted, both shy and bored with my sudden shift in topics.

"Then you ***do*** want to kiss me?" I probed, trying to clarify the matter in my best district attorney's voice.

"You're such an asshole." She flicked her lighter and sucked hard on an Old Gold 100. I didn't think they even made Old Gold Filters anymore.

"Okay," I sighed, "where were we?"

Shannon broke into a gigantic smile, beaming, like, *OH GOODY, MORE STORY TIME!* It was extraordinary how her mouth could instantly transform from "The Pout" into this bubbling, gushing grin; her entire face radiated, even her eyes laughed, and I didn't have any control, I'd do anything to see her filled with such joy.

"They were cutting Shorty up and burying him all over the ranch," she recapped enthusiastically.

"Okay, I'll continue, *but do you really know how gorgeous you are?*"

"Thank you," she said very formally, blushing a little, accepting the compliment so I'd get on with it.

And I did. "So, after the Tate-LaBianca murders go down, and Charlie, Tex, and the girls are put on trial and found guilty, the cops also arrest

Family members Bruce Davis and Steve Grogan, aka 'Clem,' for the murder of Shorty Shea.

"What's weird about their trial is that the cops still hadn't found Shorty's body. Without the body, they didn't have proof of a murder; they didn't have a writ of habeas corpus, which literally means 'the right to produce the body.' I don't know how the DA did it—how he tried them without a dead body—but Bruce Davis and Clem, along with Charlie and Tex, were all convicted of Shorty Shea's murder."

"Even though they never found Shorty's body?" she asked, her sense of fair play offended. "That doesn't seem right."

"Exactly." I nodded. "But it doesn't end there. You have to remember that Clem was thought to be the dumbest member of the Manson Family, a dope, a real moron. One of the Straight Satans, the motorcycle gang that used to hang out here at Spahn Ranch, told the cops, 'Clem was a certified idiot. He was an escapee from Camarillo, the state mental hospital. Whatever Charlie said, Clem would parrot it.'"

Shannon was giggling uncontrollably.

"Okay, so Clem gets put in Tracy, the state prison, where Bobby Beausoleil is also incarcerated. If you remember your Manson Family history, Bobby Beausoleil is the Family member who murdered Gary Hinman over a drug deal gone wrong. But that's another story . . ."

"Will ya tell me that one later?" Shannon asked, like a five-year-old begging for another cookie.

"For you," I said, "anything."

She beamed, and I continued. "Okay, so Bobby Beausoleil and Clem are in prison together, and Clem is complaining how they will never parole him because the parole board thinks he cut off Shorty's head. So Bobby says to him, 'Well, why don't you make a deal with the cops; show 'em where Shorty's body is buried in exchange for early parole?'

"So Clem, the certified idiot, the one everyone thought was such a dummy, makes the deal, shows them where Shorty's body is—and he wasn't tortured or dismembered. In exchange for showing them where Shorty's body was, Clem was paroled! Clem becomes the only Manson Family murderer ever to be released from prison. Everyone always says that if they release any of the girls from prison that they will just kill again, but Clem's been out for a decade and he's a fine, upstanding citizen, so that just goes to show you what the experts know . . ."

"Really?" she asked. "Where is he now?"

"Who, Clem? Last I heard he was a housepainter somewhere in the San Fernando Valley."

"You mean around your house?"

"He could be living next door, or down the block."

"Creee-py!"

"The only thing that doesn't make sense," I added, "is that according to Bruce Davis and Clem Grogan's parole hearings, they killed Shorty in the middle of the afternoon and buried him alongside one of the roads that runs through here, and that completely contradicts Barbara Hoyt's interview that she did with us. She said it was in the middle of the night, under a full moon, and that they killed him down by the creek, so somebody's lying . . ."

"Does that mean they killed someone else besides Shorty?" Shannon asked, her eyes wide.

"I don't really know," I answered. "So did you like your story?"

"Yes, thank you very much."

"So whattya wanna do now?" I asked, a little too obvious. I'd never be accused of being Mr. Subtlety.

"Are you going to kiss me?" Shannon asked, looking a little scared.

"Well, don't look too thrilled," I told her. "I mean, if it's too high a price to pay for the Shorty Shea murder story, just tell me and we can get outta here . . ."

Shannon looked wounded, frightened, unsure. I lit a cigarette and pouted. She looked off in the other direction. Neither of us spoke. I was expecting the "I-really-like-you-and-don't-want-to-hurt-you-so-let's-just-be-good-friends" spiel and I was really not up for it. This was all too perfect to end in the toilet. I wish she'd told me that on the phone; saved us both a lot of embarrassment.

"I just don't want to get hurt," she said after a long while.

"I didn't know kissing me would be so painful . . ."

She lit another cigarette, suddenly unable to look me in the eyes again. It was all going to shit, so I decided, what the hell.

"Do you know how crazy I am about you?" I told her.

Shannon snapped around, furious: ***"But don't you say that to everyone?"***

She had me there. It stopped me.

"Yeah, well, I guess I do," I confessed, "but I never meant it like I do now."

"Bullshit."

"It's true."

"Well, I just don't want to be another girl you ***fucked*** at Spahn Ranch!"

I laughed, thinking of the last girl I invited here, who was horrified at the suggestion: ***"Why would I ever want to go there?!!"*** Indignant, instead of intrigued. She was the same girl who asked me, "Why do you have pictures of dead people on your walls?"

I said to her, "Listen, baby, you really wouldn't understand . . ."

But Shannon did. Understand, that is.

"What's so funny?" she asked.

"You're the only girl I've taken here, besides Gillian, but that doesn't count because she's really like my little sister, ya know?"

"Really, you never took another girlfriend here?" Shannon asked, genuinely surprised.

"Nobody else would ever come here with me," I explained, "nobody else is into the same stuff I'm into, except you . . ."

I paused to see her reaction. Shannon was just looking at me, wondering whether to believe me or not.

"I was as crazy about you then as I am now," I told her. "I was like some nutcase, you know, when you left that night at Crescent Lounge. I just wanted to follow you out and grab you and push you in a doorway and kiss you and bury my head in your hair . . ."

"Well, why didn't you?" Shannon asked, looking right at me, suddenly fearless. Now she was daring me.

"Awww man, I can't believe you, do you know how hard you made it at the reading? You were so scared of me; you were trying to run away the whole time . . ."

"You coulda run after me . . ."

"I did, and all I've been doing is running after you, ever since I met you. I'm ***still*** running after you. Jesus, can't you give a guy a break and slow down so I can catch you? I'm old, you know."

"You're not that old."

"Really? Then do you know how much I wanna fuck you?"

"Sorta," she answered, not at all afraid; brazen almost, grinning like, *What took you so long?*

"Do you wanna be my girlfriend?" I asked. "And move in with me? And live happily ever after?"

"Yes," she said without any hesitation; all her confusion and ambiguity suddenly vanished. Shannon could be crystal clear when she wanted to.

"Do you know how much I wanna be with you?"

"Well, don't blame me," she dared, giggling, "if you can't catch me."

Then I was on top of her, kissing her, doped up on wanting to penetrate every warm, sleek moment of her. We were making out, with our hands under each other's shirts, feeling each other's skin for the first time, trying to melt into one another. As explosive as every touch was, it went beyond flesh, to something I never feel; that rare glow of wanting to ***stay***. I held her tight long after our sweat, saliva, and semen had soaked through the blanket.

I was still crisscrossing the country doing video interviews for my three-part Court TV show on the history of pornography titled *Adults Only, The Secret*

History of the Other Hollywood. Shannon was back in Seattle, working for a lawyer, or so she said. We'd just been in Manhattan, staying at Gillian's apartment on Hudson Street, when suddenly Shannon had to get back to Seattle. Her legs were all black-and-blue. She looked like someone had beat on her legs. I was appalled. I tried to talk to her about it, but she just brushed it off to moving boxes into a new office; she lied so effortlessly, like I used to do.

I would've talked to her about it more, but I was in the middle of a crisis. I was supposed to drive to Florida to interview Chuck Traynor, Linda Lovelace's ex-husband and manager, that Linda trashed in all her books. I'd never read Chuck's side of the story, but I had bounced a check on him, and he was calling on the phone to have words with me.

I apologized profusely to Chuck and said that I'd FedEx him a check that day, overnight delivery.

"Okay partner," Chuck spat, "I'll take your word for it, that it'll be here tomorrow . . ."

"You have my word," I reassured him. Chuck was not the kinda guy you wanted pissed off at you.

"You'd better," he growled and I got the message.

When her car arrived to take her to the airport, I kissed Shannon and told her to call me when she got off the plane. Then I packed for Miami. Gillian was a real supporter of the porn book and even became friends with the circle of '70s and '80s porn stars I was hanging with.

The next day I was driving down Interstate 95 to Florida, and somewhere around Baltimore, Shannon called and told me she was in excruciating leg pain, and I immediately told her to go to the emergency room. There was a flurry of phone calls to Seattle until she was admitted into the hospital.

But I couldn't find out what was wrong with her, which caused another flurry of phone calls to Seattle, this time to the doctors and nurses working Shannon's case.

Finally a female doctor called me back; by now I was in Southern Virginia.

"Shannon has been infected again with necrotizing fasciitis, more commonly known as flesh-eating bacteria," the doctor stated officiously. "And right now, we don't know how far the infection has spread."

"Is she going to make it?" I asked, praying against the worst.

"It'll be touch and go until we can stop the spread of infection."

She didn't sound hopeful. I was stunned. This couldn't be happening.

"How can a thing like this even happen?" I asked in a state of shock.

"From injecting black-tar heroin infected with necrotizing fasciitis directly into the vein," she said matter-of-factly.

I was in the middle of heavy traffic on 95. I felt like I had left my body but was still driving anyway, so I decided to get off at the first exit and check into a motel and call Gillian, who seemed to be as charmed with Shannon as I was. I filled her in on the doctor's report.

"Jim said she was high when she was here," she admitted, referring to her husband James Marshall, the noted writer.

"Why didn't anybody say anything to me?" I asked.

"You wouldn't have believed them," she said in a soft voice. And I thought about breakfast at Cafe Mogador, a few days previously, with Shannon and Pete Pavia, who was working with me on the porn book, helping me talk to cops, FBI agents, lawyers, and DAs. Pavia worked the law enforcement side of things fantastically, getting FBI agents to talk who had never given interviews before.

Pete was a master talking to the cops and the FBI. Then I'd come in and get any remaining good stuff.

At Cafe Mogador, Pete confronted Shannon right there at the table.

"Are you high now?" he asked her, looking her square in the face. Shannon was mortified. I paid the bill and got out of there as fast as I could, apologizing to Shannon all the way.

When I finally scolded Pete for his rudeness, he told me, "Okay, sorry, forget I ever said anything, just trying to save you some grief . . ."

"Well no thanks," I snapped before storming off. Of course Pete was right.

My fear of flying still in high gear, I decided to take a train to Chicago and change there for Seattle. When I got off the train in Chicago, I called Gillian from a pay phone along the platform.

"I've got bad news for you," she bawled. "Shannon's right leg has been amputated, and they don't know if she's going to survive the operation. Check into a hotel, and I'll fly out in an hour and pick you up in Chicago, and we'll both fly to Seattle."

I checked into the hotel Gillian recommended; she arrived a few hours later and had a doctor friend deliver some Valiums to the hotel so I could get on the plane.

But when we got to the airport, as we were about to check in, I got the phone call that Shannon was dead.

I collapsed.

All the people who died, died.

EPILOGUE

Grief is a motherfucker. It drowns you in agony twenty-four hours a day. It's like being wrapped in a cocoon with a swarm of wasps. The answer, more Xanax. And with my alcoholic brain, I was soon crossing the border into Mexico to buy bars of the stuff, and smuggling them back to LA.

Handfuls. I was a mess.

I fell into a wicked Xanax addiction that was fueled by a selfishness I didn't know I had in me. I needed a good kick in the pants, to bring me back to reality, and I got one, and my Xanax addiction ended in 2010.

Almost twenty years after Shannon passed, I was lucky enough to fall in love again in the same way that I was with Shannon, deeply, that brings me constant love and joy. Alexis makes me laugh. We love a lot of the same things and she's as smart as shit.

"What are you reading?" I sent the text to her over Instagram. I was poaching Duncan Hannah's friends and followers since Duncan always got the hottest babes. "What are you reading?" is the perfect way to find out if you have anything in common with someone in a noncommittal way, and certainly nothing that would indicate sexual harassment or creepiness. Besides, I'm always just curious to hear what people are reading.

"*Edie*," she said, referring to the Edie Sedgwick book by Jean Stein and

George Plimpton, that Gillian and I modeled *Please Kill Me* after. Bullseye response.

"Cool."

"Actually, I read *Edie* a few years ago," she admitted. "I'm actually reading *In My Blood: Six Generations of Madness and Desire in an American Family* by Edie's cousin, John Sedgwick, but I didn't think you'd know the title."

"Even cooler," I said, loving people who took their obsessions to the next level.

We started talking on the phone four and five times a day.

That first week of talking, she said, "You know I'm engaged to be married to this tax lawyer . . ."

"So?"

She started laughing hysterically. We have each other in hysterics constantly. We fell in love over cell phones.

The first time Alexis came to New York turned out to be great. Amy, my ex-girlfriend and close friend, picked up Alexis at Penn Station, since she was coming in on the Amtrak from Boston. I was already at a reading in Brooklyn and her train was late.

Amy said, when she picked up Alexis on the train platform, "She looked like a little fawn standing up for the first time, in a tight above-the-knee black skirt, showcasing her skinny-spindly legs and six-inch heels. I thought she looked adorable!"

Duncan Hannah and I stayed friends over the years and we'd get together for dinners every year or so, and they were always a gas. One of the last ones was after a Tosh Berman reading in Brooklyn when he read from his book *Tosh: Growing Up in Wallace Berman's World*.

Alexis walked into the reading late, wearing a black velvet Betsey Johnson off-the-shoulder, slinky dress; Dunc slid up to me and whispered, "Who's Vampira?" referring to the cult-film actress Maila Nurmi, who starred in the Ed Wood classic *Plan 9 from Outer Space*.

Duncan Hannah and me.

Photo by Dustin Pittman

Duncan always had an eye for unique and obscure beauty as his Instagram account and his portraits proved. I didn't dare tell him that I had poached Alexis from one of his followers on his Instagram page, not that I think he would have been pissed, since he was married to Megan Wilson, a fantastic editor at HarperCollins, involved in designing book covers. Megan's cool.

The dinner was at the Wythe Hotel, and the long table was filled with old friends and new ones. The star of the evening was Tosh Berman, who told tales of his influential artist father, and at one point, Duncan, who was sitting across from Tosh, held the plate of butter in his hand, too engrossed in his conversation to realize where he was passing it.

The plate of butter was orbiting Duncan, back and forth, and back and forth, making me dizzy, like some Marx Brothers bit, until I shouted, ***"Duncan! Pass the fucking butter!"***

Dunc exploded in laughter, as did most of the table.

The last time we had dinner, Dunc; his wife, Megan; my future wife, Alexis (Vampira); Dunc's friend Bingham; and I met not far from Cornwall, Connecticut, at the White Hart Inn. It was as festive as all the other dinners and, as usual, Dunc and I got into an argument. This one was over whether Holden Caulfield would've had sex with the prostitute in that famous scene in *The Catcher in the Rye*. I said he definitely would've made her. Duncan said Holden would've stuck to his principles, as he did. I said, "Bullshit, what horny fifteen-year-old wouldn't go for it—if a hooker was offering to fuck him?"

At this point, a tipsy Alexis shot, "Oh Legsy, shut up, leave Duncan alone! He has great hair!"

Even Duncan had to laugh, as he blushed profusely. Even Megan was in hysterics.

Alexis and I were married in 2020, the best decision of my life (after the one to stop drinking), and I began making films like *Pusherman: Frank Lucas & the True Story of American Gangster* and the forthcoming *Johnny in Wonderland: John Holmes & the True Story of Hollywood's Most Notorious Massacre*, which you can watch for free on Tubi. And I have a Substack page, so you can keep reading my stories.

A curious thing happened on June 11, 2022. Alexis and I were waking up in bed, and she was telling me about a dream she had that Duncan made a guest appearance in. I knew she had a mini-crush on him, but I also knew she was too ethical to act on it; besides, she liked Megan, Duncan's wife, too much.

"So what happened in the dream?" I asked.

"He was sitting on the edge of a stage, and he looked fabulous as always, but he was just glowing! And he called me over to the stage where he was sitting, and I asked him if he was busy, because there were other people around, and I didn't want to intrude, but Duncan just laughed and said, 'No, not at all. Come sit with me . . .'

"He seemed really happy. So I sat down with him and he was really stunning looking, as always, and he was his charming, funny self, as always . . .

"Have you talked to him?" she asked.

"No, not in a while." I felt guilty. "I should give him a call . . ."

Later that day we were pulling into the A'Dello Winery when Alexis looked at her phone and let out a shriek as I parked the Jeep.

"What's the matter?"

"It's Duncan," she sobbed. "He's dead . . ."

We were both shocked. Duncan looked so happy and healthy the last time I saw him.

He died of a heart attack on Saturday, June 11, 2022, while watching a pretentious French film, just to remind all of us that we'll never be as classy as him—and we won't.

"I think he came to me," Alexis said after processing the shocking news. "I think he came to say goodbye, but what impressed me was how happy he looked . . ."

I knew the dream was real because I was the first one she told that morning, and there was no way we could've known that Duncan was already deceased. The news didn't hit the internet until later that afternoon. It was one of the weirdest psychic events I've ever witnessed.

Alexis is not in the habit of telling me her dreams, but her Duncan one was so powerful, she kept referring to it, all day, until we pulled into A'Dello Winery and she learned the dreadful news.

We're all here for such a very short time.

ACKNOWLEDGMENTS

To: Tom Hearn, Ann Hearn, Grady Hearn, Pat Hearn, Margret Hearn, Claudia Hearn, and, of course, no Hearn Family is complete without a David Huntley! Hi Dave!

Lots of love and kisses to Carol Overby.

And special thanks to Kristina Berg.

Also to my assistants and fellow collaborators Gillian McCain, Danny Fields, Burt Kearns, James Marshall, Mark Jacobson, Mike Randall, Michael Daly, Peter Pavia, Tom Piazza, Peter Alsen, Gisela Freisinger (sorry about the apartment), the late Bill Brown, the late Bill and Virginia Kelly, the late Bob Brown, the late Duncan Hannah, Keith McQuirk, Nils Grivilious, Mary Greening, Jonathan Paley, Price Abbott, the late Don Gilbert, Bill Bonnell, Barbara Koppelman, Brian Sweetie, Patti Adcroft, Bob Gucionne Jr., Nina Guccionne, Rudy Langlais, John Leland, Joe Levy, Mim Udovitch, Blair Winston, Stacey Asip, Glenn O'Brien, Mary Harron, Roberta Bayley, the late Hilly Krystal, the late Karen Krystal, Lisa Krystal, Merv, Bob and Elizabeth Gruen, David Godlis, Bobbie Grossman, Billy Altman, the late Marcia Resnick, the late Terry Ork, Gerard Malanga, Victor Bockris, Jeff Goldberg, Bobbie Bristol, Stewart Meyer, John Lindsay, Barry Miles, the late Walter Stedding, Steve Mass, the late Otis Brown, the late Kathy Acker, the late Susan Sontag, Chris Makos, Vincent Fremont, the late Andy Warhol, the late Ronnie Cutrone, the late Joe Stevens, the late James Grauerholz, the late William Burroughs, the late Norman Mailer, and the late Norris Mailer. And of course the late Harold Conrad and his wife, the late gorgeous Mya Lynn.

Also to: Martha Thomases and the late John Tebbel, the late Tom Baker, Lisa Robinson, the late Richard Robinson, Dean Zimmerman (Lisa's sister), the late Marty Thau, the late Leee Black Childers, the late Bob "Rocking" Rudnik, the late Cyrinda Foxe, Bebe Buell, the late John Mauceri, Larry Kerson, the late Mel Blake, Jonathan Marder, Chris Stein and Debbie Harry, the late Clem Burke, the late Amos Poe, the late Philippe Marcade, the late Alan Vega, the late Arturo Vega, the late Joey Ramone, the late Dee Dee Ramone, the late Tommy Ramone, the late Johnny Ramone, and (the living) Linda Ramone. Also special thanks to Norma and Herb Rabinowitz, Daniel Rey, Geoffrey Shields, Jenny Shields, the late Dave Voght, Phil Caivano, the late Nicky Caivano, Dave Wyndorf, Ed Stasium, and the late Glen Buxton.

And the late Lori Klein, Susan Arrons, Henry Noble, Esther Fortunoff, and Tina White.

Also to Susan (Daisy) Hulme, a.k.a. Mrs. McKnucklehead, Dawn Manners, Neal Colgrass, Rebecca Vasquez, and my collaborator on *Resident Punk*, Crispin Kott, as well as his father, Gary Kott, who helped me to stop drinking.

Extra Special Thanks to Lee and Mandy Cowls for providing a home away from home, as well as the late Mrs. Gloria Cowls and Mr. Seth Cowls.

Also to: Bill Brown, Jane Hamilton, Dr. Sharon "Mitch" Mitchell, Tom Byron, Bill and Virginia Kelly, Dave Friedman, the late Nick Tosches, Josh Alan Friedman, Chuck Bernstene, the late Fred Lincoln, Kelly Nichols, Kelly Holland, Ruby Tuesday, Chloe, Dr. Annie Sprinkle, Roger Young, Ron Jeremy, the late Ron LaBrecque, Joan LaBrecque, Pat Livingston, Vickie Livingston, Nancy Livingston, the late Bruce Ellavsky, Pam Ellavsky, Ginger Lynn, the late Bill Margold, Eric Edwards, the late Gordon McNeil, Lucie Vonder Haar, the late Gloria Leonard, the late Georgina Spelvin, the late Marilyn Chambers, Roy Karch, the late Chuck Traynor, the late Linda Lovelace, Henri Pachard, Carol DiRenzy, the late Sharon Holmes, Dawn Schiller, Tricia Devereaux, the late Russ Hampshire, Ray Pistol, Treasure Brown, Paul Fishbein, Steve Hirsch, Steve Orenstein, Patrick Collins, the late Chris Cox, the late Cass Paley, Tom Lange, Bob Souza, the late Glen Souza, Roy Karch, Kevin Beechum, Tommy Sinopoli, Eric Danville, Joel Steinberg, Wayne Clark, Lenny Camp, Johnnie Keyes, Rebekah Poston, Rob Black, Lizzy Borden, Tommy Byron, John Stagliano, Ted Paramour, Phil Vannatter, Rhonda Jo Petty, Jeanna Fine, Nancy Pera, Veronica Vera, Candida Royalle, Tom Zupko, Nina Hartley, Josh Alan Friedman, Al Goldstein, Al Ruddy, Ed Sharp, Al Bonanni, Tera Patrick, Evan Seinfeld, Seth Warshavsky, Jonathan Silverstein, Adam Glasser, Paul Dinin, Tempest Storm, Kitten Natividad, Bunny Yeager, Bob Rich, Edna Buchanan, Ed Horning, Dr. Carleton Riddick, Mike Mauger, Paul Thomas, Jerry Butler, Seka, Traci Lords, the late Robert "DiB" DiBernardo, Sammy "The Bull" Gravano, the late Louis "Butchie" Peraino, the late Joe "The Whale" Peraino, the late Anthony Peraino Sr., the late Gerard Damiano, the late Harry Reems, the late Marc Stevens, the late Bobby Hollander, the late Teddy Gaswirth, the late Teddy Snyder, Bobby Genova, Marcella Cohen-Auerbach, Marc Carriere, the late Brad Carriere, Roscoe Jefferson, C. J. Laing, Sue Nero, Bud Lee, Michael Cirigliano, Michael London, Dave Hadley, Bill Amerson, Laurie Holmes, Jill Kelly, Leroy Griffith, Jim South, Daniel Metcalf, Dian Hanson, Christy Canyon, Jamie Gillis, Serena, Annette Haven, Rob and Rachel Rotten, Bobby Elkins, Bana Witt, Humphrey Knipfe, Suze Randall, John Waters, Roger Ebert, Russ Meyer, Ann Perry, the late Doris Wishman, the late Hugh Hefner, Vulture, Carol Connors, the late Nora Ephron, the late Sammy Davis Jr., Mark Prosperi, Fred Biersdorf, Phil Smith, Jim Mitchell, the late Artie Mitchell, Jack Boulware, Bob Chin, Laurie Smith, Bob Vosse, Bunny Bleu, Heather Hunter, Joe Sarno, the late Larry Flynt, Steve Rudnick, Pam Ellavsky, Vickie Livingston, Fred Schwartz, Tom Blake, Vannessa Del Rio, Tiffany Clark, the late Larry Levenson, the late Mickey Zaffarano, Patrice Trudeau, Larry Parrish, Bruce

Kramer, Tony Bill, Kathy Jean, Dick Phinney, Bruce Mouw, Don Fernando, Richard Pacheco, Joel Sussman, Sheri St. Clair, Reb Sawitz, Marty Bernback, Tracy McCourt, the late John Holmes, Vickie Livingston, Mike McGrady, the late Eddie Nash, Jeanna Nash, David Lind, the late Pete Hamill, Michael Alago, Mr. Marcus, Nadine Strossen, Jim Powers, Lorene Smith, the late Don Gilbert, Judge Richard S. Seward, Patti Harrison, Paul Hetrick, John J. Waltzer, David Clark, the late Nadia Childes, Kaylynn, La Tonya Underwood, Ralph L. Morgan, Alvine Nunes, Jennifer Ouellette, Alan B. Andrews, the late Jimmy "The Weasel" Fratianno, Ed De Roo, Chi Chi Larue, Max Hardcore, Willie the Cameraman, Sean Michaels, Andrew Blake, Paul Camacho, Tina and Dom at A'Dello Winery, Ryan Adiie, Matt Mulhall, and Amy and Tony Cadaver.

And last, but not least, Ruby Gottesman and Ginger Coyote. As well as Dino DiStefano and Mary Beschen for their spectacular vision and craftmanship.

Of course, Kelly Capaldi, you thought I was gonna forget about you? Talk about your lack of fucking faith! Geeezz-willikers!

I would also thank my former transcribers and copy editors: Vanessa Weiman, Nora Greening, Natalie Butler, Skylaire Alfvegren, Angela Devotti, Heather Richardson, Pauline F. Holly, the Amazing Ed Webb, Jeff Guziak and Adam Rehmeier, and C. Marlo. Feinberg and all the other generous fans who've transcribed bits over the years.

Also with all my love, thank you to the late SHANNON McNAMARA for spending five glorious months with me. Miss you.

Also Atheena Viscousi, and my big sister Patrice Adcroft.

Also to Doris and Dick Goodwin for their loving support, Fred Zollo, and Bill Brown for letting us take over his house in Carol Gables and listening to me whine. Also to Jane Hamilton for all her support and hiring me to write the Marilyn Chambers comeback movie, *Still Insatiable*.

Also to Tim Connelly, Charlotte Lesher, Cass Paley, Mary Ann Walters, Steve Walters, Dr. Sharon Mitchell, Steven Lampert—our computer expert, our MailBoxes Etc. Man; W.T. "Doc" Maloney, Steve Mass, Dr.

Steven York, Dr. Robert Marantz and his late wife Joan, Joanne Sorenson, Eric Rasmussen, Chloe, Kelly Holland, Nica Ray, Eric Danville, Ruby Tuesday, Tom Greening, Cynthia Lee Berryhill, Meredith Meyer, Amy Elkins, and Tony Vick and his lovely wife Nancy. Also to someone very special, who I was with the night before he died—my thanks to the late Eliot Cohen. I still miss him every day (even though it was impossible to get him off the phone). Also my thanks to Iris Berry, Julia and Simon, Linda Mars, and to Richard Hyland—a.k.a. "Johnny Joyce"—the man in black. And to Margaret and the late Wayne Kramer. Also to Mark "Fuckface" Groubert, may he find happiness, wherever he is.

I'd also like to thank my family, the late Mrs. Ellen McNeil, my late Aunt Margaret Clossick, my late Aunt Mary Wilson, my late cousin Gayle Wilson, Paul Wilson, my late Uncle Bill Clossick, my brother, Craig McNeil, and his lovely wife, Amy, their two kids, Moira and Sean, and their grandkids Forrest and Andie Mac. Also my sister, Lauren Backman, her husband, the late Ken Backman, and their two daughters, Ainsley and Ashleigh Backman. And to my cousins Lynda and Wayne MacNeil, and Rope Burns Russell. Also to my real mom, Mrs. Diane Brown, who gave me my first job (she's still cleaning up the mess).

Also to my extended family, The McCains: my thanks go to Mark McCain and his lovely wife, Caro, and to Ann and Chris Evans, and to Laura McCain-Jensen, and to the late Peter McCain and his lovely wife, Joyce McCain, and their two sons, Luke and John. Also to the late Marion "Billie" McCain—and especially to Harrison H. McCain for his kind words to me in Chicago.

Also my thanks to my agents, editors, directors, publishers, producers, lawyers, and accountants: Max Edwards, Susan Lee Cohen, Ann L. Clark, Rick Chillott, Glenn Yeffeth, Morgan Entrekin, Amy Hundley, Ed Seaman, Leyla Turkkham, Michael Randall and his wife, Fenton Lawless, Angela Ching-Kaplan, the late Bill Brown, Mary Harron, Fran Pelzman, Floyd Mutrux, Graydon Carter, Ash Carter, Callie Angell, curator of the Warhol archives at the Met, the late Seymour Stein, and the late Linda Stein, as well as Mandy Stein. Also John Gillies, Michael Hogan, Ed Dwyer, the late Bob Guccione Sr., the late Michael Kennedy and his lovely wife, Eleanora Kennedy, as well as Sharon King-Hoag.

Also my thanks to the folks at the St. Mark's Poetry Project; Ed Freedman, Wanda Phipps, Douglas Rothschild, and David Vogen. Also thanks to the folks at Court TV—including Bonnie Dry and Mark Fichandler—and Frederica Broomfield, who did such a wonderful job promoting the television show.

And very much love to the late Judy Conway-Greening, who died at home under the loving care of her daughters, Mary and Nora Greening.

Also my apologies to Stephen King for disrupting your reading with William Burroughs. I only have one defense: Quaaludes. Lots of 'ludes.

And last but not least my undying love and blessings on Kristen Steen, who taught me so much about everything.

To my wife, Alexis Arakelian, I know winter sucks and everything looks bleak, but trust me and Padre Pio—the sun will return! Also how can I not mention that you had the coolest parents on the planet, Kathy and Seth Arakelian, readers, quiet and so serene being in their presence. I miss them almost as much as you do, even though we shared such a short time together. And how could I not mention my coolest sister-in-law in the world, Andra Adams, Alexis's sister! I mean, she drag races on the weekends, really! So how cool is that—a drag racing sister-in-law, it doesn't get any better than that!

I know it's a shit time, so let's just get through it!

Too many people died while writing this book and my only hope is they not be forgotten.

—Legs McNeil

With immense gratitude, my wife, Eve Levine, and my kids, Ian and Marguerite Kott; Claudia and Paul Andreassen; Gary and Karyn Kott; my siblings, Morgan Almquist and Amanda Rueby, and their families; Suzanne McCombs; Mike Katz; Chris Marron; Andi Sumpter and Amy Chase; Jason Malmberg; Nathaniel Kressen and the Greenpoint Writers Group; The Flop House; Randy and Jason Sklar; the Music Nerds chat; Max Edwards and Apple Tree Literary; Glenn Yeffeth, Rick Chillot, Scott Calamar, and all at BenBella Books; community libraries; independent book and record shops; and Legs McNeil, who I've known since I was an impressionable teenager, when he hooked me on that most insidious drug, Earl Grey tea (with a splash of milk).

—Crispin Kott

ABOUT THE AUTHORS

Photo by Tom Hearn

Legs McNeil, the original punk, is the co-author of 2.5-million-copy global bestseller *Please Kill Me: The Uncensored Oral History of Punk* (Grove Atlantic, 1997), a book widely hailed as the punk "Bible." One of the co-founders of the seminal *PUNK* magazine, which gave the movement its name and where he was known as "Legs McNeil: Resident Punk," Legs is a former editor at *SPIN* and editor-in-chief of *Nerve*. He is also the co-author of *The Other Hollywood: The Uncensored Oral History of the Porn Film Industry* (Regan Books, 2005), co-wrote *I Slept with Joey Ramone: A Family Memoir* with Mickey Leigh (Touchstone, 2010), and co-edited *Dear Nobody: The True Story of Mary Rose* (Sourcebooks, 2014).

One of the foremost chroniclers of the punk movement, Legs's writing has long been the go-to for on-the-ground accounts of those heady years of New York and London in the late '70s and early '80s. He has appeared in innumerable documentaries exploring the punk years, on networks as diverse as the History Channel, Epix, and VH1. His journalism has appeared in the likes of *Rolling Stone, SPIN, New York Magazine, VICE, Details, High Times, AirMail, The Atavist, Cultured Mag, The Daily Beast,* and many, many more.

Photo by Eve Levine

Crispin Kott is the co-author of *Rock and Roll Explorer Guide to New York City, Rock and Roll Explorer Guide to San Francisco and the Bay Area* (both Taylor Trade), and *The Little Book of Rock and Roll Wisdom* (Lyons Press). A longtime journalist covering music and beyond, Crispin has been published in *PopMatters, Please Kill Me, Nerve, Legsville, Chronogram, Roll,* and many other online and print media outlets.